John Hunter has undertaken extensive excavations in the Hebrides, Orkney and Shetland and elsewhere. He is Emeritus Professor of Ancient History and Archaeology at the University of Birmingham and Affiliate of the Department of Archaeology, University of Glasgow. As a Royal Commissioner on the Ancient and Historical Monuments of Scotland for eleven years he was involved in its merger into Historic Environment Scotland. In 2012 he was awarded an OBE for services to scholarship.

A Companion
to the Small Isles

EIGG, MUCK, CANNA AND RUM

John Hunter

ORIGIN

First published in 2026 by
Origin, an imprint of
Birlinn Limited
West Newington House
10 Newington Road
Edinburgh
EH9 1QS

www.birlinn.co.uk

ISBN: 978 1 83983 081 5

British Library Cataloguing-in-Publication Data
A catalogue record for this book is available from the
British Library.

Typeset by Lexis Books

Papers used by Birlinn are from well-managed
forests and other responsible sources.

Printed and bound by Ashford Colour Ltd, Gosport

Contents

List of Plates and Maps

Plates

William Bald's 1806 map of Eigg
The roofless church, Kildonan, Eigg
The Lodge, Eigg
The Sheela-na-gig at Kildonan, Eigg
Loch of the Great Women and island dun, Eigg

Chapman's 1809 map of Muck
The burial site at Aird nan Uan, Muck
Captain Swinburne's Pier House, Muck
Sean Bhaile settlement, Muck
The 'fort' at Caisteal an Duin Bhain, Muck

William Bald's 1805 Map of Canna
The Nunnery, Canna
Canna cross from the east
Coroghon Castle, Canna

George Langlands' 1801 map of Rum
Kinloch Castle, Rum
The Protest Rock, Rum
MacLean family farm, Carn nan Dobhran Bhig, Rum
The Bullough mausoleum, Rum
The graveyard at Kilmory, Rum

Maps

Acknowledgements

This book results from the collective efforts of archaeologists, historians, travellers in past times and helpful islanders in present times, but not least the Royal Commission surveyors over the last century. I have merely tried to weave the pieces of evidence together to give a readable account of island life over the last few millennia. In this process I have been aided immeasurably by the staff of Birlinn, notably Andrew Simmons and Laura Davey, the advice of Lesley Ferguson from Historic Environment Scotland and the proofreading support of my wife, Margaret. On the islands Sylvia Beaton has provided me with much additional local guidance and Andrew Beaton has kindly provided photographs that were better than the ones I took.

Introduction

This is a book for anyone planning a visit to the Small Isles, perhaps thinking about visiting the Small Isles, or just curious about those odd names – Eigg, Muck, Canna and Rum. In writing it I have done my best to provide something between a readable historical account and a useful travel companion, in order to satisfy all three interests. The way the book is configured reflects this.

The first chapter is a collective introduction to the four islands and is very much a 'taster'. It places them in a wider context and runs through their general history, their social evolution and the ways their landscapes have changed over time. The process starts with prehistory, followed by early Christianity, the Norse, medieval and later settlement including the Clearances, modern social history and events of note. The chapter also introduces some of the general sources for the subject. I have tried to include mostly those works which are edited and available in modern form, or which can be downloaded without cost from the internet. Works which are specific to individual islands are introduced in the chapters that follow; there is a full list of sources at the end of the book.

The subsequent four chapters focus respectively on the four islands, covering similar themes but in greater detail. These chapters will be of particular use to anyone intending to make a visit, in that they also include a list of sites or places of particular note and a map showing their general locations together with a brief description of each. Each entry in these lists of 'Places to Visit' is flagged in the text through the use of boldface and a cross-reference number. The lists and maps can be used to decide what to visit, according to either personal preference or ease of access during the time available on one of the islands. Each of these four 'island' chapters concludes with a list of related further reading.

A good map is essential. The 'Places to Visit' entries identify each location with an eight-digit Ordnance Survey grid reference. Many of the sites are quite extensive and in these cases the grid reference provides a general central point only. These will work best with the 1:25,000 Ordnance Survey Explorer map series (paper or downloaded), rather than the smaller-scale (and more customary) 1:50,000 Landranger series. Even then finding some of the smaller locations can be difficult, especially if they are hidden among vegetation. The best time of year to locate some of the smaller sites is when the vegetation is low in winter or early spring, which is probably when visits are least likely. Life is sometimes a compromise.

These islands are the product of volcanic eruption and as such are characterised by steep terraces and cliffs which can be dangerous. Not all parts of the islands are accessible – especially true of Rum – and visitors would be advised to keep to tracks where possible and to avoid some of the remoter areas. It is always prudent to seek local advice before setting out and to make sure that someone is aware of your intended route. Carrying a compass as well as a map is to be recommended. If visiting caves it is essential to obtain local knowledge about tides.

Places to Visit

These sections comprise a list of sites that reflect each island's history, archaeology and particular events together with a map showing the approximate location of each entry. These sites represent a sample not the totality, and not all of them are easily accessible. Each is numbered and cross-referenced in the text for the same chapter and is also given an Ordnance Survey grid reference and, where available, its unique National Record of the Historic Environment (NRHE) ID number. These can be followed through on the trove.scot website (www.trove.scot), which is a massive database of archaeological sites, buildings and monuments established by the former Royal Commission on the Ancient and Historical Monuments of Scotland (now merged into Historic Environment Scotland – HES). It provides a much greater level of detail and fuller history of investigation than is presented here and represents the next port of call for anyone looking to delve deeper. The easiest means of access is to search via the relevant NRHE ID number and then under the heading 'Place'.

Like many parts of western Scotland these four islands feature placenames which are a mixture of various cultural elements, mostly Norse and Gaelic, with diverse variations and corruptions. As a result spellings may vary. The NRHE is unforgiving when it comes to spelling variations and wherever possible I have adhered to those used in its database, to make it easier to follow up on the information on the sites presented here.

Archaeological sites and monuments are notoriously difficult to measure with any accuracy, mostly on account of changes in vegetational cover, subjective reference points, a lack of clear definition, tape measures flapping in the wind, or personal difficulty in accessing a particular measuring point. As a result the measurements given here are expressed in general terms and are best taken as a guide only.

John Hunter
February 2026

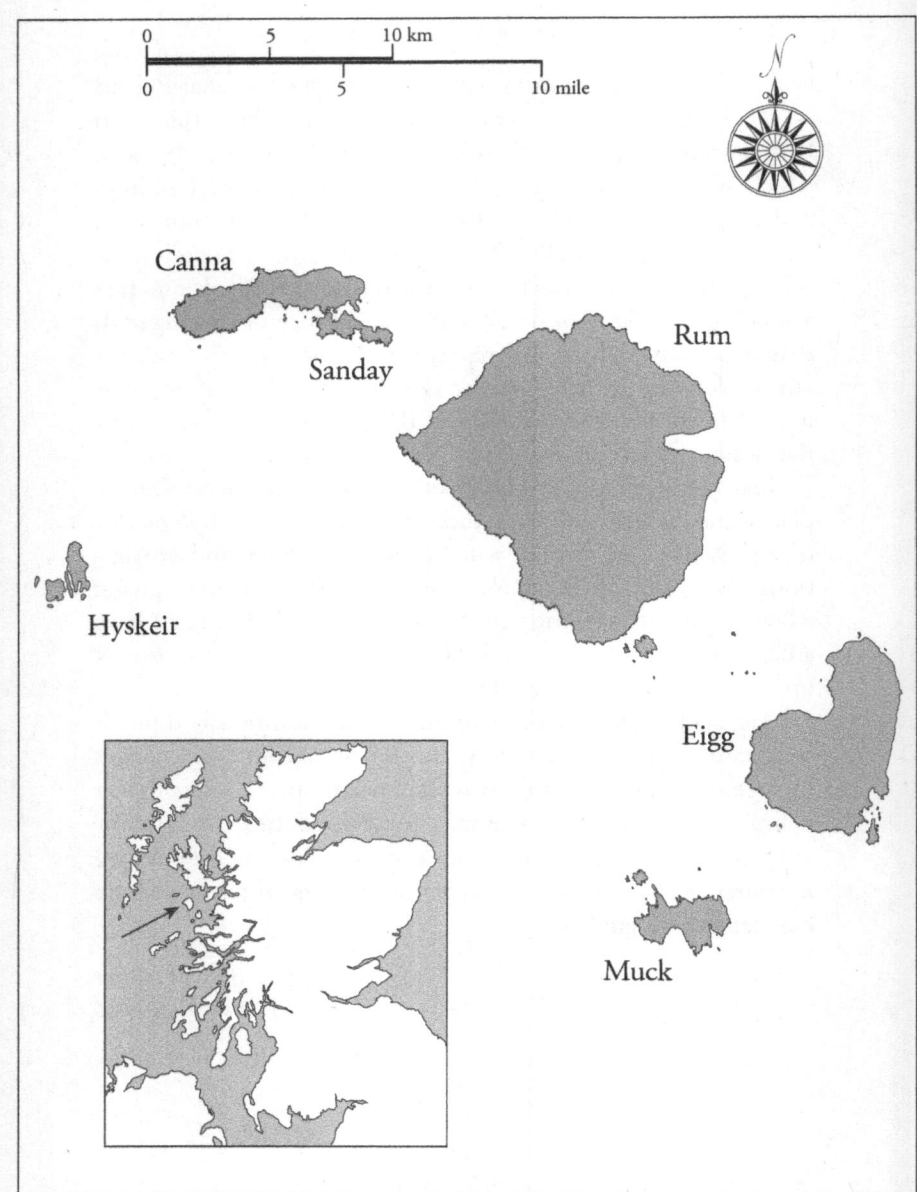

General map of the Small Isles

1 The Small Isles

'Studding the ocean like a necklace'

Introduction

There is little about the Small Isles that can be described as ordinary. Their very names (Eigg, Muck, Canna and Rum) have often been the source of amusement, less so perhaps to their former owners, or lairds, whose titles were traditionally represented by their island name; thus the owner of Muck would be greeted embarrassingly as 'Muck'. One Laird of Rum even tried changing the spelling to 'Rhum', giving it a quasi-Gaelic flavour as opposed to an alcoholic one. The spelling found its way onto a small number of maps before being slapped down by the combined weight of the Ordnance Survey and the Post Office.

Because of these unusual names many people have heard of the islands, but few know exactly where they are. They lie among the Inner Hebrides, cradled between Skye to the north, the Scottish mainland of Argyll to the east and the islands of Coll and Tiree to the south. In a wider geographical setting they lie on latitude N 57°, slightly north of Moscow to the east and the northern part of the Gulf of Alaska to the west, sufficiently far north to be limited in terms of how the land can be used, what can be grown or exploited and what methods of animal husbandry used. Much of Scotland is colder and harsher, however, as the Small Isles enjoy the undeniable benefits of the warmer Gulf Stream.

To their west, the Outer Hebrides – Barra, the Uists, Harris and Lewis – lie too far north or north-west to provide shelter from the westerly Atlantic storms, and although the Small Isles lie only a few nautical miles off the Scottish mainland the seas are often unkind. History is littered with reports of maritime disasters, difficulties of access and communication being lost for weeks on end. There are over fifty wrecks recorded in the waters around the islands. Today, even with modern boats and powerful diesel engines the ferry timetables can often be disrupted. It makes all the more remarkable the efforts and resilience of those who chose to settle there far back in prehistory.

There is a fifth island too, Hyskeir, although this is little more than an uninhabited rock outcrop. It lies further west out to sea, infamous as a graveyard for shipping passing through the Minch until a lighthouse designed by the Stevensons was constructed there in 1904. Before it was automated in the late 1990s it achieved publicity as a result of a one-hole golf course built by the keepers, and through a book written by an assistant keeper, Peter Hill, detailing his experiences. From the top of the light he remembers the islands as 'studding the ocean like a necklace' – the epigraph for this introductory chapter. Seasoned travellers to the Small Isles may remember less romantic times of howling gales, driving rain and ferry crossings reminiscent of theme park rides.

GEOLOGY

The special character of the islands partly derives from their visible volcanic structure, which ranges from the low-lying plateaus of Canna, Eigg and Muck to the precipitous mountains on Rum. Anyone who finds themselves being tossed around Rum in the local ferry service cannot fail to be intimidated by the rocky bleakness of its mountains, which seem to tower almost sheer. Some of them have intriguing Norse names, such as Askival, Trollaval and Hallival, but the Norsemen, who settled just about everywhere else in the area, thought twice about building their homes on Rum. Its shoreline lacked the fertile soils and sandy beaches that were essential for Viking settlement. The other three islands were greener and a safer bet. The peaks on Rum were more likely named as navigation aids for voyages from Ireland or Man around the Scottish west coast to Orkney and beyond.

Rum's inhospitable nature doubtless did much to help it become known as the 'Forbidden Island', although there were more salient cultural factors (see Chapter 5). Geology, however, is a fundamental cause. The island's structure is the result of a series of volcanic eruptions and collapses whereby Lewisian Gneiss and Torridonian Sandstones were pushed up by the movement of magma from deep below the earth's surface and then shaped and reshaped by glaciers over succeeding millennia. This was a geology unfavourable for the development of fertile soils. It generated a landscape of sculpted rock and areas of wet moorland which allowed settlement to prosper only on the few patches of greenery where the rivers ran out to the sea. The widest and flattest of these is at Kinloch on the east coast, which has evolved as the natural and only focal point for Rum's settlement and cultivation in modern times. The rest of the island has an undiminished reputation for hostility. Every archaeological surveyor of my acquaintance who has worked on Rum has found the landscape unforgiving, the terrain exhausting and the midges unbearable.

Although the least attractive and least habitable of the islands, Rum is by far the largest, measuring some 10,000 hectares, considerably more than Eigg the next largest at around 3,000 hectares. Canna follows at around 1,100 hectares with Muck being the smallest at a mere 560 hectares. The three smaller islands are all the result of less dramatic volcanic action, which survives in the form of characteristic volcanic ledges and terraces formed from lava flows. These have weathered over time allowing fertile soil to form, especially on Muck, which seems to have been recognised throughout history as the most fertile. All three islands are greener and lower-lying than Rum and more open and attractive to agriculture.

Exceptionally, Eigg's skyline is characterised by a massive stump of pitchstone, the Sgurr, which can be seen for miles around and results from lava flowing through a deep river valley. When the softer sides of the valley eroded away this curious shape was left standing proud and has all the appearance of a fat human nose pointing into the sky. Being completely anomalous in its environment it inevitably became surrounded by superstition, most notably regarding the seventh-century martyrdom of St Donnan on the island, allegedly at the hands of large warrior women who were drowned in the nearby loch (see Chapter 2). The island has an alternative name, 'Eillan nan Banmore', meaning 'Island of the Great Women', which reflects this event.

Environment

The modern landscape of all four islands is very different to the one that would have been encountered by the first people to reach the islands over 9,000 years ago. Pollen records suggest that these nomadic folk would have been greeted by an environment of scrub woodland thick with species such as willow (*Salix*) and hazel (*Corylus avellana*), particularly in more sheltered parts. Remarkably, the island of Rum, despite limited soil potential on the lower slopes, was given the early superstitious name of 'Riogachd na Forraiste Fiadhaich', meaning 'Kingdom of the Wild Forest'. The nomadic people who first inhabited the islands were obliged to live off the land and move seasonally to take advantage of the ripening of natural foods and the movement of animals for hunting. To them the islands must have provided a hunter-gatherer environment that was worth the effort and risk of getting there in small skin boats or dugouts, one where hazelnuts, berries, fish, shellfish and the eggs of sea fowl were plentiful. They may have been particularly attracted to Rum for its bloodstone – a hard, exotically coloured cryptocrystalline quartz, often with red spatters, which could be knapped into useful tools. Evidence for these early people is frustratingly difficult to pin down, but excavations have shown their presence on Rum and they were no doubt active on the three adjacent islands too.

The same pollen records show these same tree species of willow and hazel to be in decline from around the mid fourth millennium BC, a shift which is now considered to be attributable not entirely to climate change, as originally thought, but to a process of deforestation at the hands of the first permanent settlers. The appearance of grasses, seeds, weeds of cultivation and evidence for soil erosion in the pollen record at this time points in the same direction. From around 3500 BC nomadic movement through the islands in the quest for seasonal subsistence must have given way to permanent farming. The earliest settlers were arriving, clearing the land and setting about raising crops and animals, and were overwintering for the first time.

The deforestation necessary for farming may have had unintended consequences in the way it affected the local soil hydrology. Together with greater exposure of the land to rainfall, particularly in periods of climatic cooling, deforestation provided the right conditions for the formation of peat. Seen in many other places across Scotland, the unwitting exhaustion of soils through over-cultivation also played a part. This was a long-term effect, but is visible in the archaeological record. Areas of settlement on higher ground became denuded and populations were forced to move to lower slopes, leaving their field boundaries, houses and enclosures to become enveloped under blanket peat over the centuries that followed. In the Small Isles this probably started before the end of the later Bronze Age, sometime in the late second millennium BC, from when remains can still be seen in the partial exposure of early walling and hut foundations, such as those on the western side of Canna. Destruction of woodland seems to have been almost total, but in the absence of much natural timber on the islands peat was a valuable fuel. It could be cut, dried, stored and burned for heat and cooking. Rum was particularly well endowed and in the late eighteenth century it exported peat as a commercial commodity to neighbours that had little, such as Muck.

Wood was a scarce commodity throughout the Western Isles and mostly arrived in the form of drift timber collected from the shore. It was normally considered too valuable to burn and was used in construction. In his tour of the Hebrides Dr Samuel Johnson mislaid his oak walking stick on Skye and assumed it had been stolen. 'It is not to be expected', he commented sarcastically, 'that any man in Mull, who has got it, will part with it. Consider, sir, the value of such a piece of timber here.'

ARCHAEOLOGY, SURVEYS AND SOURCES

Knowledge of the islands' early history depends largely on the vagaries of archaeological discoveries, landscape interpretation, secondary sources and anecdote. For prehistory, before written records began, surviving archaeological remains provide the only pointers to what may have been happening, how subsistence economies worked and where people built their homes and reared their families. Archaeology is not always forthcoming in these respects; it has to rely on what has survived and gives only a general rather than detailed picture of the past. In islands such as these, where cultivable land was at a premium, shelters and houses were built adjacent to the best land in the most preferred locations. The same locations were used for habitation over and over again, each successive population tending to destroy the evidence of the one that went before. It is not difficult to pin down where some prehistoric settlements might have been, but there is little evidence for their duration. Moreover, structural elements such as turf and timber are poor archaeological survivors.

There has been sporadic archaeological excavation and survey of the Small Isles over the years, starting with the antiquarian activities of the owners of Eigg, the MacPherson family, in the late nineteenth century. Their interest was in burial mounds, although they paid some attention to material that surfaced from ploughing. One family member, Norman MacPherson, a professor of Scots law at Edinburgh University, published a paper in 1878 on the artefacts he had discovered there, and this drew wider attention not just to Eigg but to the other three islands too. It was also later to attract the interest of the lugubriously named Royal Commission on the Ancient and Historical Monuments of Scotland (RCAHMS), whose survey work was carried out on a county-by-county basis by a team of field investigators. It produced a detailed volume on each county in what was known as its 'Inventory' series. Work on the Small Isles volume commenced in 1914 but was disrupted by the war. This would explain the somewhat paltry publication that followed in 1928 as part of a volume in which it was tagged in with the monuments on Skye. Only fifteen Small Isles sites were identified, most being on Canna. This was hardly surprising as the surveyors were only in the islands for a week.

The Second World War may have disrupted any further interest until 1972, when the archaeology arm of the Ordnance Survey mapping department began more systematic field survey before it was shut down under the quango-axing policies of a newly elected government in 1979. The Royal Commission returned to the islands in 1983, then specifically to Canna in 1994 to carry out further survey work, this time in association with aerial photography, then to Eigg and Muck in 2003. The accidental discovery of worked bloodstone on Rum dated to the Mesolithic a year later was the catalyst for a major excavation. This was the first excavation on the islands since the days of the MacPhersons almost one hundred years earlier, and the first to have a scientific basis. Subsequently, professional excavations were conducted on Eigg, and university-led teams from Dundee, Bradford and Birmingham and from the National Museum of Scotland have all been active in the islands in harness with the

Royal Commission, which continued its field survey work on Rum between 2010 and 2012. The National Trust for Scotland, owners of Canna, have also been conducting their own investigations for conservation purposes. Thanks to this growth in archaeological work, aerial photography and field survey there are now well over one thousand archaeological sites documented in the Small Isles by comparison with the fifteen published in 1928. The majority of these are described, many with photographs, on Historic Environment Scotland's database of sites known as trove.scot (www.trove.scot).

From the seventh century onwards archaeology was not the only tool available to those investigating the history of the Small Isles. The early Christian period brought with it literacy and a wealth of annals, chronicles and early histories, many of which contain snippets of useful information about the islands. They continue through into the Middle Ages, though often consist of little more than short observations or mention of particular individuals. By the eighteenth century there are lengthy descriptions, official documents and records of travellers, all of which present a much greater level of detail.

Foremost among these are the often fascinating if boring-sounding 'statistical accounts' that were written for every parish in the country starting in the late eighteenth century. These accounts were the responsibility of the parish minister of the day, who was required to give a general description of his parish and its people under the four main headings of geography and topography, population, agriculture and industry, and other miscellaneous issues. Ministers seem to have had a certain amount of licence as to what this did or did not include. Some chose to do the bare descriptive minimum, while others wrote extensively on, for example, resources, schools, the poor or antiquities and provided a much more vivid historical snapshot. The first (or 'Old') *Statistical Account* for the Small Isles parish was compiled by the Rev. Donald McLean and written in 1794 (OSA 1796). It falls into the latter category, and even details the optimum times for planting and harvesting, animal husbandry, prices of food and labouring costs. McLean was a minister who knew his parish and his parishioners.

The second (or 'New') *Statistical Account* was written in 1836 (NSA 1845), confusingly by another minister with the almost identical name of Rev. Donald MacLean. His *Account* is somewhat shorter and rather cursory. Much of his text is taken up by a personal reminiscence of his visit to the 'Massacre Cave' on Eigg, and by the geologies of the islands, for which he relies heavily on other people's work. His writing gives the impression that he found compiling the *Account* a rather irksome task and that what he writes is often little more than a paraphrase of his predecessor's text. Records indicate that as a minister he was not noted for his efforts, later being dismissed for neglect of duty following allegations of drunkenness, adultery and indecent exposure. His *Account* might justifiably be taken with a pinch of salt.

One of the most objective accounts drawn on here is *The Rev. Dr John Walker's Report on the Hebrides of 1764 and 1771*, which constitutes a major record and analysis of the population demographic at parish and township level and has since been edited and discussed by Margaret McKay (1980). The figures for the Small Isles specifically have been analysed in a small booklet entitled *Lost Ancestors* by Julian Munby (2007). Another 'official' late eighteenth-century document of note comes in the unlikely form of the record of visits to the islands by the British Fisheries Society in 1787 and 1788 (see Campbell 2002), which is remarkably informative about island life.

Of all the available records, the most absorbing are the accounts of the 'tours' undertaken by well-heeled and educated travellers from the Scottish cities and from England. It was fashionable in the later eighteenth and nineteenth centuries for those who could afford it to travel to more distant parts of the country, or even abroad, and the Hebrides became part of a popular itinerary. Travellers' descriptions introduce personal views and observations and make a welcome change from some of the dull legal and official documents that preceded them. Many of the early travellers who undertook these journeys were caught up in a period of enlightenment, interested in matters of scientific curiosity such as flora, fauna, geology, antiquities or local traditions. Some were more interested in recording contemporary people and places. Later, thanks partly to publicity from the travels of Dr Johnson and James Boswell in 1773 (Levi 1984), journeys through the Western Isles seem to have become a tourist 'must do' for those with sufficient means, although Johnson and Boswell themselves never reached the Small Isles on account of bad weather. The Highlands opened up as a new recreational vista which was able to satisfy the various appetites of those who perceived it as a strange and distant world.

Some travellers were rather patronising in their accounts. There was a tendency to comment on the islanders as being primitive in terms of their living conditions and their habits (and especially their hygiene), as though they were museum exhibits from a different culture. For such writers a blackhouse was not something of constructional or even ethnographic interest, but rather a dingy smoke-filled hovel within which people were obliged to live. Many of these sources are useful not simply in presenting a picture of the islands in the eighteenth and nineteenth centuries, but in showing that in many respects little had changed over the previous centuries. The descriptions, particularly those on land use, could just as well have been applied to the Middle Ages or an even earlier era. It was a picture that began to be erased only from the late nineteenth century through developments in transport, technology and social mobility.

Apart from A.O. Anderson's *Early Sources of Scottish History*, first published in 1922, which is a starting point for the early Christian sources, useful works include Donald Monro's *A Description of the Occidental i.e. Western Islands of Scotland* (1549) and Martin Martin's *A Description of the Western Islands of Scotland circa 1695* (both in Withers and Munro 1999), and especially Thomas Pennant's *A Tour in Scotland and Voyage to the Hebrides, 1772* (Pennant 1776). The late eighteenth-century naturalist and traveller Edward Daniel Clarke also recorded some unique descriptions (Otter 1825). Later works of note include Edwin Waugh's *The Limping Pilgrim* (1883) and the geologist Hugh Miller's record of a voyage around the Hebrides undertaken in 1845, *The Cruise of the Betsey* (1862). Both writers spent some time on the islands as opposed to just passing through.

More recent works include Denis Rixson's *The Small Isles* (2001), which is an enviable compilation of historical sources drawn together to create a thematic history of the islands; also his *Hebridean Traveller* (2004), which takes a wider geographical perspective. The present author's own *The Small Isles* (2016) formalised the substantial academic and survey endeavours carried out by the erstwhile Royal Commission on the islands since 1925 into a single volume covering the archaeology of the island chronologically in some depth. Much of the information underpins this book, which is intended as a more practical companion. In some more specialist areas, such as the study of carved crosses in the wider context of the early Christian West, Ian Fisher's comprehensive *Early Medieval Sculpture in the West Highlands and Islands* (2001) is to be recommended, as is Mary Miers' *The Western Seaboard* (2008) for details of historical architectural matters. Peter Hill's reminiscences *Stargazing: Memoirs of a Young Lighthouse Keeper* (2003) will give a flavour of both the weather and the seascape around the islands.

Prehistory

The earliest known site lies on the eastern side of Rum at Kinloch Fields, where bloodstone was worked from Mesolithic times some 9,000 years ago. Excavation has shown the site to have been used seasonally by a transient population, the traces of which survive only as a scatter of material and occupation debris. There is no longer anything to see, but bloodstone pebbles can sometimes be collected off the shore on the south and south-west parts of the island having been washed down from the mountains. These early folk may have considered that bloodstone's rich colouring gave their arrowheads special powers during hunting, or somehow enhanced their scrapers and blades when working wood or skins. Historically it has been surrounded by superstition.

There are a number of prehistoric burial remains in outlying parts of the islands, often quite substantial and located in prominent positions, their visibility making them a target for antiquarians who plundered them under the guise of archaeological investigation. The consequences of such activity are at their most frustrating on Eigg, where the late nineteenth-century owners, the MacPherson family, appear to have dug into anything remotely resembling an ancient burial mound and selectively removed whatever they found interesting. Items they found less interesting seem to have been discarded, as presumably were any human remains that accompanied them. By any definition it was a form of treasure hunting, but it was also the accepted antiquarian culture of the day and was rife in most places during the nineteenth century. On Eigg it did at least yield and safeguard a Viking sword now in the National Museum of Scotland in Edinburgh and a series of prehistoric pottery vessel fragments, allowing us to evidence the various period cultures that existed there.

Most early settlement sites seem to have been spared the interest of antiquarians, presumably because they were unlikely to contain objects of intrinsic value. Eigg probably has the best survivor in the form of a likely Neolithic house outline at Galmisdale dated to around 3000 BC, but judging from pottery types recovered from mounds on Canna there are similarly dated sites there too.

Bronze Age sites abound, especially in the high moorlands on the west side of Canna and the east side of Eigg, where the vestiges of stone hut circle walls, enclosures and boundaries protrude through the blanket peat. The term 'hut' tends to be used for want of a more precise definition, given that it is applied to buildings that addressed a variety of functions. Some may have been domestic, others may have been used for farming or storage purposes. In general they are circular, typically between 7 and 10m in diameter, although some can be more ovaloid. The walls tend to be thick, up to 1m wide, presumably to take the weight of a low roof. They attest to complexes of small farming units dating back to the Bronze Age.

A little later is the souterrain on Canna, an underground passageway leading to a chamber. Sometimes known as 'earth houses', these monuments tend to belong to the Iron Age and are best seen as storage areas for food or other materials as opposed to habitation. More bizarre, and less easy to date – in fact, less easy even to describe – is a remote site on the east-facing cliffs on Eigg known as the 'Oracle Cave'. This is an impressive natural feature with a modified entrance near the top of the cliff at Sron na h-Iolaire. It has the reputation of being not only a ritual site but also the anecdotal eighteenth-century meeting place of a pair of lovers from two warring families in the mould of Shakespeare's *Romeo and Juliet*.

One surprising source of evidence for prehistoric settlement is the humble rabbit. Buried structures tend to be full of voids and soft soils from disturbed settlement activity and make a convenient habitat for burrowing animals. Rabbits have been rife on Canna and Eigg and their activities have tended to create small piles of burrowing upcast or 'scrat' at the entrances to their warrens. This upcast is a valuable source of archaeological material, mostly pottery which has been scraped up and can be diagnostic of particular periods and cultures. Prehistoric pottery from the Neolithic and the Beaker Period (Bronze Age) has been found in scrats beside several earthen mounds and allows the sites to be classified accordingly. Since rabbits have not been introduced on Muck this particular pointer to material culture is absent there, with the result that Muck artificially appears less well endowed in the archaeological record than the other islands.

Not all archaeological sites have been recognised from excavation, survey or even rabbit activity. Some discoveries are due to serendipity and are completely random. A case in point is the Bronze Age metal workshop identified on Eigg, which is one of the few known such sites in Scotland. This was found by complete accident when someone digging a grave to bury the family cat came across bronze-working debris. On Rum bloodstone debitage from fashioning blades and scrapers dating back to hunter-gathering communities came to light during ploughing, not through systematic survey, and ignited a major archaeological investigation.

A number of early monuments stand out in the landscape, and intentionally so. These are the promontory 'forts', so called because they sit on coastal promontories and possess attributes that are perceived as being in some way military, such as defensive ramparts, outer protective walling and fortifications. All utilise existing geological outcrops on or near the shoreline, usually with a natural sheer cliff face and an access point on the landward side. The access point has in most cases been narrowed down by walling and protected by excavated ditches and ramparts. Several appear to have the remnants of small structures inside. They belong to the Iron Age (very broadly 800 BC to AD 100). Some dominate the coastline, most notably at Caisteal an Duin Bhain on Muck, overlooking the harbour; others are less impressive, but all are in prominent positions and are easily visible from the sea. It is possible that the enigmatic 'Oracle Cave' may belong to the same period and genre.

The function of these modified promontories is still open to discussion, but the idea that they were intended for warfare is now losing credibility. They are located in places where coastal outcrops happen to exist rather than those which might have strategic significance for military or defensive purposes. There is some reason to think they were used as refuges in times of danger, but this would have offered little military advantage. A community barricaded inside would risk being starved to death while an invading enemy marauded round about, burning and looting. Moreover, the site at Corragan Mor on Eigg is situated in such a precipitous place that it can barely be accessed even by islanders from the landward side. The Ordnance Survey maps still refer to these sites as 'forts', but it is unlikely that they possessed any military capability. What is significant, however, is that the modelling and enhancement of natural features on this scale can be argued to indicate the presence of an organised community under direct leadership. These 'forts' are visible testimony to power and control and might best be seen as deterrents to any passing boats with malicious intent.

Christian impact

The first documentary sources are the product of early Christian activity, which was the conduit through which literacy began to flow, notably from Iona, which had become one of the hubs for Christian missionary activity in western Scotland. Other centres included Whithorn and the Isle of Man, but all had their roots in the common culture of Celtic Christianity. Often alluded to as 'The Age of Saints', this was the period, from the later sixth century, when monks travelling northwards through the Hebridean waterways may have been a relatively common sight as they sought to find retreats and spread their mission. Some of these monks were individual eremites seeking out isolated places in order to follow a life of austerity and piety; others were cenobitic, groups of monks setting out to establish more permanent communities from where the Christian mission could be preached more widely. The Small Isles were in an awkward position politically, lying in a type of bandit country between feuding Pictish and Dalriadic tribes, but the islands nevertheless had their fair share of ecclesiastical establishments according to the brief references in the historical record. These references were made by monastic scribes and typically occur in various early chronicles, martyrologies and hagiographies (lives of saints), which often mention little more than a place and a name, sometimes a date. From these sources we hear of the monk Beccan who was reputed to have been a poet on Rum, of Columba himself in a place called 'Hinba', argued by some to be on Canna, and of Donnan on Eigg. Donnan achieved greater press having been martyred on the island, where the location of his death, Kildonnan, bears his name. In all four islands the importance of place is very clear. Donnan's mission was continued at Kildonnan by the monk Baithne, and the site developed an enhanced status through into the Middle Ages as an important Christian and ceremonial centre with noble patronage. These references to monks are amplified in the chapters that follow. There will almost certainly have been other active ecclesiastics who escaped the historical record and whose place in history has not therefore survived.

To these few references can be added a number of placenames which stand out as belonging to this era. The most common are those with the 'kil-' element, almost certainly derived from Gaelic 'Cille', meaning chapel or cell. These include 'Keill' on Canna, 'Kiel' on Muck, 'Kildonnan' on Eigg and 'Kilmory' on Rum. The names tend to be in areas associated with long-standing Christian burial. 'Papadil', the name of a small township located in one of the more remote areas of Rum, is a Norse word meaning valley or glen of the 'papa' or priests, suggesting there may have been an established religious community there known to the Norsemen in the ninth or tenth centuries. By contrast the name 'Sgorr nam Ban-naomha', attached to a site located on an almost inaccessible terrace on Canna, has the meaning 'Cliff of the Holy Women' and relates to a series of structural remains characteristic of a monastic arrangement of early Celtic type. The likelihood of it being a nunnery makes it all the more intriguing. To these can be added a small number of reputedly 'holy' wells and springs, such as St Columba's well on Eigg, to which are attached numerous anecdotes and tales.

Evidence for early Christian activity is more tangibly provided by the presence of sculptured stone found on all four islands. These survivors are likely to be just a small proportion of those originally created, having lasted by chance through the havoc wreaked by Vikings and the later disruption brought about by the sixteenth-century Reformation and the nineteenth-century Clearances. Two of the surviving carvings show that cultural influences other than Christianity were also at play: the figural, animal and secular depictions on the standing cross at Keill on Canna and on one of the Eigg crosses. Neither would be out of place in the ninth or tenth century, and both testify to a persisting level of Christian worship in the area despite the Viking savagery recorded earlier on Iona. Raiding undoubtedly occurred in monastic outposts other than Iona, given that monasteries were poorly defended and the pickings were good, although no raids as such are recorded for the Small Isles. These raids nevertheless prefigured a more organised Norse settlement in the Hebrides, one which either absorbed Christianity or provided it with a degree of patronage which may be reflected in the survival of the Canna cross. Whatever pre-Viking structure of control or ownership may have existed at the time was probably simply absorbed under a new ruling Norse elite, such that to most islanders there was little change. It hardly mattered to them whether the person to whom they owed rent (and probably never saw) was Gaelic, Norse or Scottish.

There is a currently a total of around twenty-six carved stones on the islands that relate to this broad early Christian period and these are described in the respective chapters below. Sixteen are from Canna, six from Eigg and two each from Muck and Rum. Most are fragmentary. With one exception all were recovered from or near to known graveyard sites. The exception is the simple inscribed cross shaft at Bagh na h-Uamha on Rum. This was found on the shore lying in the sand at low tide in front of a cave. Given its weight, it is unlikely to have been washed very far from its original location. Apart from the fine standing cross with complex incised decoration at Keill on Canna, few of the examples are likely to be in situ. Many feature much simpler early incised crosses or more complex cross heads but all are either fragmented or moved from their original positions. Those that survive are probably only a fraction of those originally held on the islands. We know, for example, that at Keill on Canna in the early nineteenth century many gravestones and memorials were robbed and used in the walling for containing the flocks of sheep that would soon populate the island. We are told, too, that the islanders secretly took some of the best pieces of carved stone and buried them to keep them safe.

Norse impact

From Norse times onwards our understanding of human life throughout the Scottish islands becomes clearer. Norse control of the islands was probably achieved during the ninth century, their landscapes being populated by dispersed farms which practised a mixed economy, namely one that combined the husbandry of a few animals and the growing of crops on a small scale. During the summer months the animals would be moved from the intensively cultivated lower land adjacent to dwellings and up to higher pastures, in order to take advantage of the summer grazing. It was probably these traditions that broadly underpinned island life in the subsequent centuries, providing testimony to Norse influence in a more enduring way than the few physical objects that survive. Life followed a cycle of island tradition – farming, fowling, fishing and animal husbandry – that had been established over the centuries and took into account what was possible and practicable given the quality of a landscape set in a raw climate dominated by wind and rain. The pattern of how things were done and when they were done had been long established, probably back in late prehistory, and represented a strict survival routine that was not open to divergence other than by technological innovation. By around AD 1200 the concept of dispersed farmsteads was being replaced by small nucleated settlements or groups of dwellings later known as townships, or 'tunships', where life relied more heavily on community involvement. It is difficult to pin down exactly when, or why, this occurred.

It was not until the later eighteenth century that technology finally reared its head within this system, in the use, for example, of different types of plough, threshing machines or even tile drainage pipes instead of lazy bed furrows. Before that time, for a man to vary the methods used by his father, his father before him and his father before that would have been to risk the very survival of life on the island. It is fairly safe to assume that until then farming practices were of long standing and had been determined purely on environmental grounds. The deep suspicion with which islanders treated the arrival of the potato itself – a food source which was later to stave off starvation and save lives – typifies their unfaltering trust in tradition and their reluctance to absorb new ideas.

Unfortunately, because the farming cycle was so prescriptive, it was easily derailed by poor weather, bad harvests or disease. Family life cannot have been easy by any stretch of the imagination; it often entailed spending the whole summer preparing for winter to the exclusion of everything else. The Franciscan priest Cornelius Ward who travelled to Canna around 1625 was upset to find that his preaching had little effect on the islanders. 'They were', he said, 'intent on the crops, not their salvation, and, as it was autumn, they paid more attention to the harvest than to their souls.'

The same long-standing traditions also saw the embedding and persistence of Norse placenames, which are common but far from exclusive in the Small Isles. Numerous Gaelic names together with those which contained elements of both cultures reflect a general admixture of Irish, Gaelic and Norse. Many names have changed or become corrupted over time, not least by a trend towards re-Gaelicisation. Moreover, the names that have come through to us today were recorded by the Ordnance Survey in the nineteenth century. At that time the Ordnance Survey was a quasi-military body and placenames for mapping purposes were collected by foot soldiers of unknown educational background who were sent out into the field to gather information from local inhabitants. These were recorded in 'name books' and later found their way onto map sheets. The spellings of the names, or even the names themselves, depended very much on who gave the information and how the words were ultimately written down. In some instances the names had only ever been used orally. Moreover, the collecting of names occurred well after the Clearances in the first half of the nineteenth century, when many of the folk who were familiar with traditional names had left or been driven out. Placename study is not an exact science, as is well illustrated by the comments of the Rev. Donald McLean in the first *Statistical Account*, in which he noted that 'there are names of places, which the present inhabitants do not fully understand, that seem to be derived from a language or languages to them unknown; but supposed to be Danish'.

To make matters even more interesting (and confusing) he pointed out that each island had two sets of names, one for use when on land and one for use when at sea. Superstition dictated that it was bad luck to use the wrong one. The reason for this is unclear, although it seems to have been part of a more major fear of the sea's supernatural powers. These names also included seemingly arbitrary points at sea which could be triangulated from landmarks on the shore – for example, to mark where fishing might be particularly good. Inadvertent use of the wrong name could cause a fishing venture to be abandoned for fear of drowning. The first *Statistical Account* lists the sea names that were known: Eigg was referred to as 'Eillan nan Banmore' (Island of the Great Women), Rum was called 'Riogachd na Forraiste Fiadhaich' (Kingdom of the Wild Forest), Canna was called 'An t'Eilean Tarsainn' (The Island Lying Across) and Muck was known as 'Tirr Chrainne' (Pig Island). All appear to be Gaelic-derived without Norse antecedents.

The surviving names of undeniable Norse origin tend to be those which refer to topographical features such as headlands, valleys or slopes, or to a few habitative elements relating to farms or dwellings. The fact that the names were applied in a Norse tongue does not indicate anything more than a Norse influence that may have been dominant; it does not necessarily imply that the land was flooded by Norse people. All that was needed to maintain control was the establishment of selective settlements for a few leading Norse families. By the time of the erection of the Canna cross with its mixture of iconographies the days of hostility from the open seas were well past. The islands were now evolving to be populated by folk with more diverse cultural backgrounds whose ethnic differences diminished as time passed and intermarriage took place.

It is interesting that so few of the Norse placenames on the islands have a prefix derived from a Norse personal name. This would support the view that the Norse population was in the minority even if its political influence was dominant, which would also explain why the tangible survival of Norse remains is remarkably low. The main artefacts discovered are from Eigg and consist of a sword and two wooden stem posts from a clinker-built vessel scientifically dated to around the tenth century. The Norse were first to introduce clinker-built boats of this type, which were faster than the skin boats or dugouts that had hitherto been used around the islands, as well as being considerably more sophisticated in construction and seaworthiness.

Boats were an important component of island life. Our modern perception of islands is one of remoteness, for the simple reason that they lie outside a vehicular road network. In earlier times they were not considered remote because they were part of a seaways infrastructure which facilitated travel, communication and subsistence. Island life was not just better suited to maritime communication than it is today, it relied upon it, movement from one island to the next being frequent and routine. The sea provided a thoroughfare, not an obstacle, especially in the summer months.

Understanding the nature and unpredictability of the sea and its tides would have been second nature to islanders. Fish was, after all, a staple part of their diet. The fact that one of their most fruitful places for catching seals was among the dangerous currents far out at Hyskeir says much for their boatmanship and tenacity. By contrast, roads or pathways seem to have been relatively neglected. Scotland was a country upon which, according to the ever-cynical Johnson, 'perhaps no wheel has ever rolled'. He may have been correct; islands looked outward to the sea, not inward to the land.

Given the importance of sea travel for the islanders, evidence for early harbours and jetties is surprisingly difficult to find. Many landing places may have relied on natural rock outcrops, possibly modified with additional material at sheltered points around the coast. Not far away from the findspot of the wooden boat stems on Eigg there is a rock formation traditionally referred to as a landing place. It is unclear the extent to which this has been modified or even canalised, but some opinion sees it as a deliberately fashioned feature of the Viking Age.

With such a tradition of Norse influence it is surprising that only one likely Norse dwelling has been identified in the Small Isles, on Muck, but is unexcavated and hence unproven. There will doubtless be others whose remains lie under successive generations of later buildings and have yet to be found. That said, we have a very poor archaeological return for a group of islands relatively rich in Norse placenames and lying on the edge of the main Norse shipping lanes along the west coast of Scotland. It again supports the view that the islands were more Norse-influenced than Norse-populated.

Norse influence was more keenly reflected in the Norse-derived system of landholding that was used during this period in much of the Highlands and Islands and which continued until the eighteenth century. This was a land-division system based on units known as 'ouncelands' and its subdivision 'pennylands' which was widely deployed and which survives, for example, on Eigg in the name 'Five Pennies'. Ouncelands represented units of land quality rather than land area, Rum being valued at one ounceland, the same as the much smaller Muck. Eigg was by far the most valuable in this respect, at five ouncelands, with Canna at two and a half. This goes some way to explaining why of the four islands Eigg was seen as so important.

Ouncelands not only formed the basis of a rental or taxation system but may also have covered a wider allocation of rights and privileges for various resources such as harvesting of seaweed, fowling or hunting. These may sound like trivial perks but were important subsistence factors during times of the year when food was short. The shoreline could provide rich pickings of shellfish or fish from traps. Cliffs were traditionally good sources of seafowl and their eggs, despite the inherent dangers in collection. Travelling through the islands in 1845, geologist Hugh Miller noted that the people of Eigg had once been 'bold cragsmen' but that they no longer 'peril life and limb for the mere sake of a meal, save when they cannot help it'. He ascribed this to the introduction of the potato, which made fowling redundant other than for recreation.

Medieval and post-medieval landscapes

The documented history of the Middle Ages and beyond is one of clans and warlords and is confusing at the best of times. To the layperson it seems littered with a bewildering vocabulary of titles such as factors, tacksmen, baillies and proprietors, and a plethora of unpronounceable names in a context of alliances, dynasties, treaties and clan disputes within a constantly changing political landscape.

The picture is both vague and complex. Around the twelfth century the Small Isles, together with parts of Argyll and the

Western Isles, but with the exception of Skye, became part of lands governed by the Lordship of the Isles and thus embroiled in the political disturbances that accompanied it. This lordship was ostensibly still under Norwegian sovereignty but later morphed into a Norse–Gaelic overlordship founded by the House of Somerled, taking the form of what might justifiably be referred to as a rogue state. Although Somerled was killed in 1164 and Norwegian sovereignty effectively ended at the Battle of Largs in 1263, the lordship continued independently, albeit with some difficulty, until 1493, when it finally succumbed at the hands of James IV, King of Scotland.

During the earlier part of this lordship, surviving documentation suggests that Eigg and Rum were both significant parts of the estate and continued to be important to various claimants, including the Earldom of Orkney but more significantly the Kingdom of Man, where the rivalry of different factions culminated in control being vested through the MacRuari branch of Somerled's dynasty. The two islands were central to a powerful domain and may have been useful bargaining chips between rivals in the continuing power struggles between different factions, Eigg in particular, given its traditional religious status and its central geographical position.

Contrastingly, Canna and Muck seem to have been under ecclesiastical ownership. Muck was almost certainly under the control of the Bishop of the Isles, based on Iona from around the seventh century, and later under that of the Bishop of Man and Sodor (the Western Isles). Canna is alluded to in a papal bull of 1203, which suggests that it too belonged to the Church. This is hardly conclusive evidence, but the fact that the two pairs of islands tend to be referred to separately in documents suggests that they were under different controlling influences, even although both nominally bowed to Norse sovereignty until Largs in 1263.

The lordship was powerful in the region into the fourteenth century and controlled the areas now known as the Uists, Barra,

Rum, Eigg and parts of the western seaboard of Argyll, but not Canna and Muck. Its lands passed through marriage to the Clanranalds, who held them through to the nineteenth century. It seems that the Clanranald branch of the family may also have viewed Eigg as a place of political advantage in view of its religious importance and the status that would be acquired through patronage of it. Rum was a different matter altogether, its only merit being its deer and its hunting potential. Hunting would satisfy the sporting interests of society's upper echelons and was a popular pursuit depicted on the carved crosses on both Canna and Eigg. It is not inconceivable that Rum was used as some kind of sporting estate for the leading families and their chieftain. If its early name of 'Kingdom of the Wild Forests' is anything to go by, it would have provided a natural habitat in which deer could thrive and become quarry for those who enjoyed hunting them.

Hunting is certainly attested on Rum in the form of deer traps, or 'tynchells'. These consisted of pairs of walling or scree lines built in a simple funnel shape running for distances up into the mountains. Deer were driven into the wide mouth of the funnel by dogs and chased down into the narrow part where they became trapped in a small enclosure and were slaughtered. Building these and organising the hunt itself would have required a level of manpower and authority unlikely to have been provided by Rum on its own.

By the fifteenth and sixteenth centuries uncertainty and division were increasing throughout the Western Isles. The Reformation saw Church estates appropriated by secular powers, both Canna and Muck being taken into lay ownership. Canna became part of the Kingdom of Argyll but was leased out to the Clanranald family, while Muck passed through the hands of several families before ending up under the MacLeans of Coll. Rum also passed to the MacLeans of Coll at some point in the fifteenth or sixteenth century. Being no longer part of a larger estate its value as a hunting reserve may have diminished and the deforestation required for alternative land use may have reduced the wooded habitat necessary for deer. Eigg was the only one of the islands to be under consistent ownership throughout, remaining the property of the Clanranalds until early in the nineteenth century.

During this period of clan division, and to some extent because of it, a major catastrophe took place on Eigg, probably in 1577. This is usually referred to as the 'Cave Massacre' and relates to a long-standing feud between the islanders and the MacLeods from Harris, details of which are discussed in Chapter 2. In brief, it is said that the islanders all took refuge in a cave at the south of the island to avoid retribution for an incident in which they had murdered some of the MacLeods. Their hiding place was spotted and the MacLeods lit a fire at the entrance to the cave, suffocating all those inside with the smoke. Questions remain as to how many islanders perished and the effect the massacre had on the community thereafter. Accounts of the event vary and details of the incident no doubt became embellished over time.

This was not the only serious incident to have occurred. Barely a decade later the four islands were recorded as having been attacked by Lachlan MacLean of Duart, allegedly in harness with Spanish soldiers from a wrecked Spanish galleon at Tobermory on Mull. This was a revenge attack provoked by the Clanranalds' participation in acts of desecration on Iona. All four islands were 'wrecked and spoiled', according to a late sixteenth-century account. Families that survived the burning of their homes were put to the sword. Again, there are questions regarding numbers and the effects of the attack.

While the Small Isles played some part in the political dynamics of the time, they were rarely pivotal. Certain islands may have held specific advantages, such as fertile soils, deer hunting or prestige bestowed by their Christian status, but they were not geographically strategic and the historical references to them are often tangential to some more newsworthy event. The folk who lived on these islands had little, if anything, to do with the wrangles and feuding that went on over their heads. They just got on with trying to work, pay their rents and subsist on whatever was left. Political events impacted upon them only when their owners were in dispute and they became a soft target for the aggressor. The Highlands were fiercely clan-based, each clan closing ranks behind its clan leader in times of adversity, notably against the Scottish and English Crowns, culminating in the 1745 uprising and the massive clan defeat at Culloden a year later. The islanders' involvement in disputes was usually as unfortunate pawns in a larger tribal game in which they had little interest other than that of duty.

DEMOGRAPHICS AND TOWNSHIPS

We have some details of the inhabitants of the Small Isles shortly after the time of the uprising thanks to a survey of the population commissioned in the 1760s. It was undertaken by Neill McNeill, a catechist living on Eigg, as part of a report on the wider Hebrides commissioned by the Church and the government. This was carried out under the auspices of the Rev. Dr John Walker, a distinguished academic who described McNeill as 'a sensible and careful man'. The survey's value lies in the fact that it provides a detailed snapshot of the population before the Clearances changed the face of the landscape and its society irrevocably. It gives a total population figure of 1,159 (Canna 253, Eigg 459, Rum 304 and Muck 143), significantly lower than the 1821 peak of 1,620 some half a century later. To put it in perspective, the current population of the four islands is fewer than 200 souls. Using rounded figures there are currently roughly 100 people on Eigg, 40 on Rum, 30 on Muck and 20 on Canna.

Walker's 1764 *Report on the Hebrides* also lists the full name of each individual, their age, family relationships and family units, and sometimes the names of the townships they lived in. It provides a remarkable demographic data set. Moreover, the census was also designed to capture the changing balance between Protestant and Catholic which had been an issue of concern since the Reformation. The parish of the Small Isles, consisting of Muck, Eigg, Canna and Rum, had been established in 1740. Formerly a Catholic stronghold, it now contained a mixture of the two denominations, the respective ministers both being accommodated on Eigg, as was the parish school. Each family's religion was ascribed accordingly in the survey and McNeill was not one for mincing his words: 'The Island of Eigg', he wrote, 'is for the most part inhabited by papists.' This emphatic distinction between Protestant and Catholic was of long standing within the islands, as was the acrimony; there was even a time on Eigg when the Catholic priest was reduced to celebrating mass in one of the caves known as 'Uamh na Chrabhaidh' (Cave of Devotion) at the south of the island. The common burial ground on the island still shows Protestant and Catholic burials located at opposite ends.

The two tables below provide a more detailed breakdown of the population which generally reflects the land quality of the respective islands, Eigg having the largest figures. It is interesting to note, however, that while there is a fairly equal gender balance in Canna, Rum and Muck, on Eigg this is roughly skewed 60/40 in favour of females (Table 1). There is no apparent reason for this unless it can be ascribed to the capture and deportation of men after the uprising and the heavy defeat of the clans at Culloden. It is otherwise curious that this should be so pronounced on only one island. Table 1 also lists the number of families on each island. This might theoretically equate with the number of dwellings, although some dwellings may have been shared. The number of families also allows a crude estimation of the number of persons per household, roughly five on the basis of these figures, Canna perhaps slightly larger. Most were simple family units consisting of parents and children but some were multigenerational, a small number even containing servants. One of the largest, at Kildonnan on Eigg, consisted of ten people: thirty-year-old Alexander McEachen, his wife, their five children

Table 1. Population breakdown of the Small Isles in 1764,
by island, gender and family units. Figures derived from
Walker's *Report on the Hebrides*.

Island	Families	Males	Females	Totals	Est. per household
Canna	44	124	129	253	5.75
Rum	57	147	157	304	5.33
Eigg	88	183	276	459	5.21
Muck	28	72	71	143	5.10
Total	217	526	633	1159	Average 5.34

Table 2. Population breakdown of the Small Isles in 1764, by
island and age (in twenty-year bands). Figures derived from
Walker's *Report on the Hebrides*.

Island	0–19	20–39	40–59	60–80	Over 80	Total
Canna	125 (49%)	67 (26%)	47 (19%)	13 (5%)	1	253
Rum	149 (49%)	86 (28%)	41 (13%)	23 (8%)	5 (2%)	304
Eigg	187 (41%)	154 (34%)	73 (16%)	42 (9%)	3	459
Muck	69 (48%)	40 (28%)	25 (17%)	8 (6%)	1	143
Total	530	347	186	86	10	1159

(all under the age of ten), his sister, his aged father and a servant.
The age range across the islands (Table 2) also makes for interesting reading. It shows that almost half the total population of
each island was under the age of twenty, with a rapid fall-off
after that age. Less than 20 per cent of the population was aged
between forty and fifty-nine and less than 10 per cent over sixty.
This was a young population by any standards, which might
be argued to suggest peaceful and prosperous times with an
optimistic future. Many modern Scottish islands would welcome
a similar demographic.

Walker's *Report* gives a reasonable idea of how life was structured on the islands in the mid 1700s. The population was grouped into small villages or townships, each household representing a family unit and paying rent or rent in kind. The number of houses in each township varied, some being in single figures, others more substantial. For example, the township of Kilmory on Rum had seventeen families, whereas Papadil on the other side of the island had only three. A typical arrangement was that an island would be leased from the proprietor (owner or laird) by a single tenant (tacksman), who would in turn exact rent from the islanders as subtenants. The levels of rent, or rent in kind, were not necessarily fixed. Each household also enjoyed use of the land for its personal benefit as well as a share of the produce, a general picture of which can be gleaned from McLean's first *Statistical Account*, written a few decades later:

> The terms allow them to have no fixed standard. Many of them have one fourth of the crop they make with the plough, being generally barley and oats, and a third of the crop they make with the spade, and manure with sea-ware, which is principally potatoes, and grazing for two cows with their followers. This must afford them but a scanty subsistence, especially in years of scarcity, when they have a numerous family of weak children; but, with the aid derived from the shore, they are enabled to live.

SHIELINGS, KELP AND THE 'OLD SYSTEM'

An aspect of of the farming tradition that may have been introduced in Norse times and which continued throughout the Middle Ages and into the period of Walker's *Report* was the practice of transhumance. During the summer months the sheep and cattle would be shepherded by individuals from the farm, often the girls, who would stay up in the hills in small temporary structures known as shieling huts, collecting the dairy produce and keeping an eye on the animals. These temporary structures, which were barely the size of a toilet cubicle, were typically beehive-shaped with stone footings and low walls covered with drift timber and turf which was replaced annually. They had to be crawled into. Some were slightly larger with an additional chamber for storage of dairy produce. The shielings tended to be located where there was a readily available supply of stone on the hill land. This could lie adjacent to patches of scree or earlier quarries, or by the stony sites of earlier monuments and buildings from the centuries before settlements moved downslope. Their location, therefore, was not entirely random and many sit on top of earlier archaeological remains.

Summer life in Highland shielings has been the subject of many stories and was a rich part of local life, although perhaps less so in the Small Isles where the distance between the shielings and the townships would require only a relatively short journey. In many parts of the Highlands the girls would stay in the hills during the summer months and food would be brought up for them on a weekly basis when the dairy produce was collected. This was usually performed by lads from the township, the process being supervised by a matronly figure stationed there to prevent any illicit liaisons from taking place. Many did take place and island traditions are rich with stories of the subterfuge and tricks that were employed to distract the chaperone. One of the best descriptions of a group of shieling huts is by Thomas Pennant, writing in 1772. Although made during a visit to shielings on an island near Jura, his description is likely to have been typical of those elsewhere:

These formed a grotesque group; some were oblong, many conic, and so low that entrance is forbidden, without creeping through the little opening, which has no other door than a faggot of birch twigs, placed there occasionally: they are constructed of branches of trees, covered with sods, the furniture a bed of heath, placed on a basket of sod[s], two blankets and a rug; some dairy vessels, and above, certain pendant shelves made of basket work, to hold the cheese, the produce of the summer. In one of these little conic huts, I spied a little infant asleep, under the protection of a faithful dog.

Sometimes referred to as the 'old system', it was a subsistence system that relied on a degree of communal activity in the rearing of stock, ploughing, fishing, harvesting and the use of shielings. The community consumed what it produced and when times were hard it resorted to shellfish. There was a tendency to cling to a conservative regime despite the evolving (albeit distant) world of urbanism, industrialisation and economic change that characterised the eighteenth-century Lowlands. When this world eventually began to impact on the islands the response was to resist rather than to adapt, making the demise of the 'old system' inevitable. This demise occurred slowly but inexorably as the changes crept in, with the general realisation by landowners that larger farms of sheep and cattle were more remunerative than rents from small-scale tenants. The Highlands were particularly suited to pastoralism and a good income was to be had by exporting cattle south by means of the developing rail, road and bridge network that was now linking the Highlands and Lowlands more closely than ever before.

This opening up of a new economic world had several consequences. First, it showed, probably for the first time, that external forces could influence the simple subsistence livelihood of island populations. The production of a subsistence surplus for export left the islands seriously exposed to the ups and downs of an external economy, such as resulted from the national need for the supply of food resources to satisfy the growing populations of the industrial Lowlands or to support the wars with France in the early nineteenth century. Secondly, the move to larger farms was a significant shift away from the ethos of subsistence farming and the communal activities which were fundamental to the traditional social fabric of the islands. Thirdly, increased external demand gave landowners an excuse to push up rents, employ more workers and increase their own profits. They became, or had aspirations to become, a wealthy business class and sought the same trappings of luxury and status they were now seeing among the industrial barons of the Lowland cities and in England. This alienated the old clan-based society even further from its roots. Finally, the opening up of the commercial world and the business aspirations of the proprietors fostered the need for rents in cash rather than in kind or by barter. This was new territory for tenants, who had little experience in marketing their goods. Where the islands had once provided land for communities to work for themselves, that land now became little more than a marketable commodity with business opportunities. With profitability dependent on larger rather than smaller farms, the days of the township were numbered.

This exposure to market forces was nowhere more apparent than in the rise and fall of the kelp industry. The peak population of the Small Isles at the beginning of the nineteenth century was mostly the result of kelp burning, to which Scottish islands found themselves particularly suited. Kelp (seaweed) abounds in the coastal regions and was traditionally gathered and spread over fields to rot as manure. However, because of its alkali (potassium) content for making glass, soap and even explosives it became a significant commodity. It was sent down to England where it fetched a good price. Kelp could be easily harvested and burned down on the shoreline to produce cakes of impure alkali. All it needed was a flat flagged area retained by kerb stones, many of which still survive along the shores of Canna and Sanday. They bear a remarkable similarity to certain types of prehistoric grave and have been misinterpreted accordingly by some archaeologists to their great embarrassment. The kelp-burning process was described in detail by the naturalist Edward Daniel Clarke, who visited the islands in the late eighteenth century:

The usual mode is to cut a portion of kelp annually from the rocks, taking it from the same place only once in three years. After the kelp has been dried, it is placed in a kiln prepared for the purpose, of stones loosely piled together, and burned. After it is consumed, and the fire is to be extinguished, a long pole pointed with iron is plunged into it and it is stirred about; the result of the burning being, by this time, a thick glutinous liquid, which runs from the kelp in burning. As soon as this liquid cools, it hardens and the operation is at an end. It is then shipped off to market.

The high prices paid for kelp products were seized upon eagerly by lairds and islanders alike and gave rise to a period of plenty. Island populations swelled to satisfy demand as more folk came to exploit the new-found wealth. Kelp burning took place on an almost industrial scale, some historians suggesting that this was as close as rural Scotland ever came to the Industrial Revolution. As the price of kelp rose, however, so did the greed of the landowners, who demanded a greater share of the profits. The rents imposed on the islanders increased as a result, so much so that, for many, kelp harvesting was no longer worth the effort. Some looked towards emigration as a way out and took the opportunity to join the growing numbers of émigrés from western Scotland on the uncomfortable voyage to Canada. In compiling the first *Statistical Account* at the end of the eighteenth century, Rev. McLean commented that 'the country was overstocked with people' and that there was simply not enough land to go round. An ancillary problem lay in the custom of designating family land to married offspring, which meant that plots became smaller and smaller and of less subsistence value.

Moreover, the rich pickings to be had from kelp were not to last. After the Anglo-Spanish wars (1796–1808) the international markets opened up and cheaper imports of barilla soda started to be exported to England from Spain. Within a few years Scottish prices were being undercut and the bottom eventually fell out of the kelp market. The 'new' economy fell into recession with inevitable consequences, given that the islands' populations had grown beyond the point at which they could subsist without kelp income. Poverty became rife, the level of hardship being visible on all the islands, where virtually every inch of cultivable land was converted into lazy beds for growing potatoes.

The lairds were no longer in receipt of the income they needed (or wanted) from the kelp and began to look for alternative sources. The introduction of sheep became an attractive proposition, offering a more reliable income stream than trying to elicit rent from islanders who had no money. Another not insignificant factor was that the fields had been deprived of the benefits of kelp spreading for several years to the detriment of the arable soils.

THE CLEARANCES

The census returns of 1821 show a population of 1,620 souls in the four islands – a peak figure in the parish's historical record. Given the available resources and limited employment opportunities, such a population no longer seemed economically viable to many lairds. This affected not just the Small Isles but numerous places throughout rural Scotland where the fashion of sheep farming was seen as a more reliable source of future income for the landowners. The resulting 'Clearances' created social havoc on an unprecedented scale, involving both social migration within Scotland and emigration out of Scotland to the New World. Many townships were 'cleared', the people evicted to make way for the sheep and their houses demolished with much of the stone being taken away. Fortunately, thanks to early estate mapping there is good evidence as to the locations of some of the townships and the houses within them. There are, for example, plans of Rum, Canna, Eigg and Muck drawn in 1801, 1805, 1806 and 1809 respectively which show the townships and in some cases even individual houses before they were demolished, as well as the locations of cultivated fields (see plate section). With the exception of the map of Rum, they were drawn up for the purpose of selling the islands to help pay off the social debts of the Clanranald family and to facilitate 'improvement' of the landscape by creating space for sheep and dividing units of land into crofts. This process superimposed linear land division over the foundations and boundaries of the old townships and drastically reduced the number of people needed to live there. On Canna families were moved wholesale onto the adjacent island of Sanday before being given assisted passage across the Atlantic. In many abandoned townships, such as Harris on Rum or Kiel on Muck, the clusters of grass-grown stone foundations and street lines are still visible.

On Rum the laird arranged for islanders to be given assisted passage on two vessels destined for Nova Scotia, the first in 1826. The second, in 1828, took all but two families, leaving the island to be populated by 8,000 sheep instead. One family was that of a shepherd living out at Papadil, retained to help with the sheep; the other was the MacLean family living at Carn nan Dobhran Bhig (Cairn of the Little Otter) on the south side of Kinloch Bay. The MacLeans were allowed to remain on the island because they held a *duthchas* – an ancient clan right of tenure.

By the time of the 1831 census the total population of all four islands had fallen to barely a thousand. In 1843 around 140 people left Eigg for the New World. These were evicted not through pressure from sheep, but through overpopulation and poor harvests which induced poverty at a level not previously seen. From then onwards the populations continued to slide, only stabilising in the later twentieth century.

Sporting estates and later ownership

By the early nineteenth century Rum was owned by the MacLeans of Coll, while Canna, Eigg and Muck all belonged to the Clanranalds, who were obliged to sell them around the time of the Clearances in 1827. From that point the four islands were taken in different directions by their new owners, details of which are covered in the respective chapters below. One of these directions involved an emphasis on sporting estates.

The creation of Balmoral Castle in Aberdeenshire by Prince Albert in the mid nineteenth century and the development of its estate for hunting purposes set in train a fashion for similar sporting estates among the nobility and more affluent gentry. Eigg was the first to fall into line under the ownership of the MacPhersons in 1827, where land was redesigned for pheasant shooting. The subsequent owner, Lawrence Thompson MacEwen, who bought Eigg from the MacPhersons in 1896, had the idea of turning the island into a deer park. It never succeeded but he left his mark in the form of a substantial lodge where guests could be entertained. The subsequent owners, the Runciman family, rebuilt it to its present form in the early twentieth century, by which time the notion of sporting estates was slowly drifting out of vogue. The island was sold four more times until it was finally purchased in a community buy-out in 1997.

The modification of Eigg and the level of hunting that occurred there was nothing by comparison with activities on Rum, where most of the island had traditionally been used for hunting deer. After the failure of the sheep farming which had necessitated the removal of most of the population, Rum was purchased in 1845 by the Marquess of Salisbury, who during the hunting season resided in Kinloch House, a substantial property at the head of Scresort Bay. In order to develop the estate for hunting and fishing he undertook a number of ambitious plans to improve the infrastructure and increase the population. It was of mixed success, the initiative for which he will be most remembered being the extensive dam he had built across the Kilmory river, which was breached shortly after completion.

Rum was later bought by John Bullough, a Lancastrian industrialist who had invented a mechanised weaving device. He was fond of hunting and was to be found in many of the upper social circles in which hunting was practised. His wealth was perceived as 'new money', however, and by purchasing Rum in 1888 he hoped to be able to elevate his social status as the host of a great hunting estate. Sadly, he died before this could be realised, though not before he had built a series of hunting lodges at various strategic points around the island. At his death his son George Bullough inherited the estate and spent his time there entertaining and hunting. He demolished Kinloch House and built Kinloch Castle, which became a focus for louche entertainment. Thanks to his father's invention he had no need to work and pursued a lavish and arguably degenerate lifestyle, testimony to which is detailed in Chapter 5. His extravagances and tasteless expenditures have left a visible legacy on the island's landscape, characterised by his ostentatious funeral monument positioned for all to see from miles around. After his death Rum was eventually sold to the Nature Conservancy Council (now NatureScot) by his widow.

Both Canna and Muck escaped the fashion of sporting estates, being too small, inadequately stocked with game or busily occupied with agriculture. In terms of ownership Canna sits in sharp contrast to Rum. After two further changes of laird it was eventually purchased in 1938 by John Lorne Campbell, who belonged to a landowning family in Inverneill, Argyll. He was not only a scholar and a conservationist, but also an avid collector of all things Gaelic. Together with his wife Margaret Fay Shaw he amassed a collection of Gaelic music, writings and ballads as well as early sculptured stone fragments and artefacts gathered from around the island. They were all curated in their home, Canna House, which has now been turned into a museum. Campbell generously donated Canna to the National Trust for Scotland in 1981. He died in 1996 and is buried in woodland that he himself planted, his grave being marked by a simple unassuming headstone with a Gaelic inscription.

Muck tells a different story again. The Clanranalds sold the island to Captain Swinburne, a naval man. He had an enviable knowledge of seafaring, was a respected authority on fishing and did much to foster fishing more widely among the islands. Fishing had never been undertaken at much more than a domestic level in the Small Isles. According to the first *Statistical Account*, cod and ling were caught off the coasts of Canna and Muck for the reason that they could be landed at the nearby harbours there. Fishing may have been undertaken communally inasmuch as it required groups of individuals to launch a boat of any size, but it had never been attempted at anything approaching a commercial level. Muck contains some of the few visible remains of Swinburne's efforts on the shoreline, although there are also less obvious remains on other islands, notably Rum, where fish traps are still evident at low tide. In 1896 Swinburne sold the island to Lawrence Thompson MacEwen, who also purchased Eigg. Muck has been owned by the same family ever since. The MacEwen graves lie in a prominent position on the island in a mound which they share with their Bronze Age farming predecessors in a rare demonstration of cultural continuity through time.

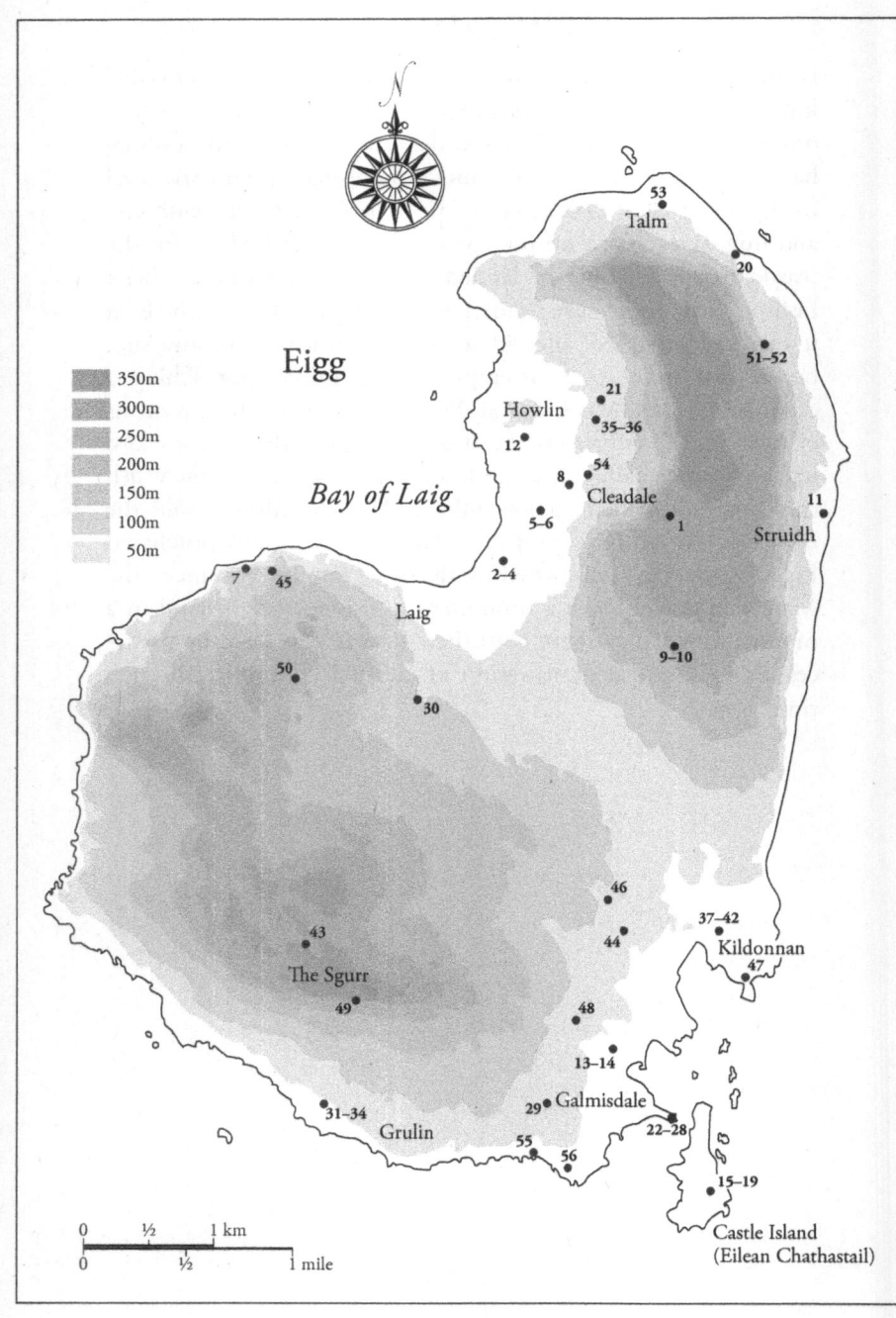

Eigg

Talm 53

20

51–52

21
Howlin 35–36

12

8 54

Cleadale

5–6 1 Struidh 11

Bay of Laig

2–4

7 45

Laig

50

30 9–10

350m
300m
250m
200m
150m
100m
50m

The Sgurr

43 46

37–42

44 Kildonnan

49 47

48

13–14

31–34 29 Galmisdale

Grulin 55 22–28

56

15–19

0   ½   1 km
0   ½   1 mile

Castle Island
(Eilean Chathastail)

2 Eigg

'The islanders of Eigg are an active, middle-sized race, with well-developed heads, acute intellects, and singularly warm feelings'

Introduction

When it comes to past political and ecclesiastical importance, Eigg stands firmly head and shoulders above the other three islands. Over the centuries there evolved a symbiotic relationship between Christian status and noble patronage which brought the island to political prominence. It can be no coincidence that after the creation of the Small Isles parish in 1740 the island became the home of the parish school, the school teacher, the doctor and the two ministers, Protestant and Catholic, who served all four islands. Eigg also housed the largest known population of all four, recording over 546 souls in 1841.

Some of the advantages of the island also lay in its natural character: it was large (around 3,000 hectares) and relatively fertile. It was not so much the quality of the land – although that was generally accepted as being good – as the fact that the landscape was divided naturally into areas of pasture and arable. Martin Martin, writing in the late seventeenth century wrote that 'the whole is indifferent good for pasturage and cultivation', while the first *Statistical Account*, written in 1794, described the island as being 'pretty equally divided as to crop and pasture grounds'.

This division into crop and pasture reflects the underlying geology of Eigg, which results from volcanic lava flowing from Rum and solidifying as a series of escarpments, producing lower and upper terraces. The upper terraces sit at the north-east and south-west of the island, separated by a long geological gully between the two which runs north-west to south-east. The Gaelic word 'Eagg', meaning hollow or groove, for a feature of this kind may have given the island its name. The surfaces of the lower terraces were softer and more easily weathered and provided reasonable arable soils, whereas the higher terraces were harder and better for good pasture. Given that the island practised a mixed farming economy, it had the best of both worlds. As an added bonus it had the benefit of Eilean Chathastail (Castle Island), which lay adjacent to the southern tip of the main island and created a sheltered stretch of water for reasonable harbourage between the two. The first *Statistical Account* refers to this islet as having seasonal occupation for tending cattle during the summer months. The 'Castle' name presumably results from the nature of its cliffs on the seaward side, but there is no evidence for fortifications there. On the main island, the massive outcrop of pitchstone nearly 400m high, the Sgurr, which gives Eigg its distinctive profile and its character, also results from lava flows running through a deep valley, its jutting shape having been formed when the softer sides of the valley eroded away leaving it exposed. The geologist Hugh Miller was fascinated by it, wrote of it copiously in 1845 and also identified the fossilised remains of an ancient pine forest in the grit which underlay it.

Reference to a contour map emphasises the distinction between the upper and lower terraces and by the same token explains why settlement from the Middle Ages onwards has been focused next to the good arable land on the lower slopes, concentrated to the north of the geological gully around the Bay of Laig and to the south in the Galmisdale/Kildonnan area. The lower terraces also continue in a strip around the east of the island and around the south-west, where the soils are less favourable and where settlement has been more limited.

The best maritime access is at the south around Galmisdale. This has probably always been the 'business' end of the island. Robert Thompson, owner of the island in the late nineteenth century, built his lodge nearby in 1896, and the important ecclesiastical site of Kildonnan lies just a short distance away. The modern ferry terminal and commercial premises are now also concentrated there. The whole island is relatively small, about 8km as the crow flies from the pier at the south to the very northern tip; the east-west distance is about 7km. The modern road system runs up the centre of the island only, and along the south-west edge.

An overview of monuments on the island is effectively a reflection of the geology. Apart from the Sgurr, the general lie of the land is not dramatic though it contains some steep cliffs, particularly at the east. Historically, the lower terraces with the better soils have seen the main areas of settlement, notably in Cleadale, Howlin and Laig to the north in a landscape of ruined townships, lazy beds and later regimented crofting boundaries, and in Galmisdale and Kildonnan to the south-east. All lie within a scatter of earlier remains, but Kildonnan is probably the most absorbing in view of its roofless chapel, its tradition of St Donnan, its sculptured stone memorials and its long-standing burial tradition. It represents the Christian heart of the island and a focus of secular patronage through the Middle Ages.

There are also narrow strips of land below the cliffs to the east and north-east at Struidh and Talm respectively. These are more difficult to access but contain patches of rough pasture, shieling huts and enclosures among the rocks. Some of these appear to overlie earlier structures. Struidh is also the location of the so-called 'Oracle Cave', which takes the form of a vast natural feature made even more impressive by human modification. On the higher terraces to the north above Struidh are the remains of prehistoric hut circles and boundaries largely buried under peat.

There is also a relatively fertile area to the south of the Sgurr in a similar strip of secondary land which houses the former townships of Upper Grulin and Lower Grulin.

The coastline of the island is best accessed by the modern harbour next to Kildonnan Bay in the south, the Bay of Laig in the north-west, which is also the site of lines of Pictish burials, and a bay slightly further north, sometimes called the 'Singing Sands'. The rest of the cliffs are not served with pathways, especially at the west across the moorland. There are numerous caves; those at the south, including the so-called 'Massacre Cave', can be accessed with care but the majority of the cliffs are not visitor-friendly.

The history of the island, including its recent chequered ownership, is presented in greater detail in *Eigg: The Story of an Island* (1998), written by the island historian Camille Dressler. This is the most comprehensive account available and covers a full range of historical and social perspectives, including the community 'buy-out'. Another useful modern account is Suzanna Wade Martins' *Eigg – an Island Landscape* (2004 edition), which takes a particular interest in the archaeology and the historic landscape. There is also a broadsheet produced by the former Royal Commission that contains a large-scale map and an outline history (2003). Earlier works include *The Cruise of the Betsey* by the Edinburgh geologist Hugh Miller, who spent some time on Eigg in 1845 (the quotation at the head of this chapter is his), and former owner Norman MacPherson's paper on the history and archaeology of the island, published in 1878. Full references are given in the 'Further Reading' section at the end of the book.

Prehistory

The Mesolithic hunter-gather communities that made their way to Rum can hardly have failed to see the characteristic outline of Eigg as they sailed across from the mainland. It was a natural place to stop en route, where they would have encountered a much less challenging environment for subsistence. Bloodstone on Rum may have been the initial attraction but Eigg would have provided the better food basket. Mesolithic material has yet to be found on any of the four islands other than Rum, but it would be astonishing if those islands' natural food stocks had not been exploited. Temporary shelter would also have been available, particularly in the numerous natural caves and rock crevices that surround the Eigg coast.

By the time of the Neolithic (around 4000 to 2500 BC) there is evidence for early, more permanent settlement in the form of house foundations, probably part of a farming infrastructure, at **Galmisdale** (23) at the south of the island. According to parallels such as Stanydale in Shetland (one of the few places where Neolithic buildings have been excavated), it is likely to date from around 3000 BC.

Neolithic artefacts and burials are better evidenced, although most of the information derives from the enthusiastic spadework of the late nineteenth-century owner Norman MacPherson. His collecting was selective, however, and he was not always specific about findspots. Much of his recording (published in 1878) focuses on ecclesiastical aspects around the ruined church at Kildonnan, particularly the discovery of buried containers and bones, but he also lists items recovered across the chronological spectrum. Some of the objects he collected can be identified with a Neolithic burial, notably a polished stone axe of porcellanite from a former cairn above the Bay of Laig. Other items were accumulated more randomly, although artefacts from one burial excavated by his colleague even included a scale plan and section. This author's own excavation in the Kildonnan area uncovered the vestiges of at least one robbed Neolithic cairn near the current Christian cemetery, suggesting a long-standing tradition of burial in that place. The cairn contained fragments of a Beacharra bowl, usually dated to around 4100 to 3350 BC with a typical distribution in the Clyde area. This gives further credence to the putative chambered cairn nearby, reused by Vikings according to MacPherson, and suggests that Neolithic burial was more widespread on the island than the current landscape indicates. The Clyde-focused Beacharra bowl and the porcellanite axe with a likely Northern Ireland provenance suggest that Eigg was far from being isolated from the wider Neolithic world.

MacPherson's spadework also produced a late Bronze Age socketed axe-head (*c.* 1400 to 800 BC) of a type usually found in Yorkshire, thus further strengthening Eigg's wider geographical connections. This is almost certainly from a burial on the island but is unsourced. Several likely Bronze Age burial cairns have been recognised, however, notably some which are fortunate in having escaped the destruction of modern agriculture, at Eilean Chathastail (**Castle Island**) (**15** and **16**), at **Galmisdale** (**22**) and on the summit of **Druim na Croise** (**12**). These all probably belong to the earlier part of the Bronze Age (*c.* 2500 to 1400 BC). None has stood the test of time (or of human intervention) well. There is another near the **Eigg Lodge** (**13**), damaged through being incorporated into a garden design, and MacPherson records one at Kildonnan which was removed in 1861 to make way for a road. Sadly, his 1878 assertion that there were still many mounds left unexplored no longer holds good.

Burials apart, the remainder of the Bronze Age landscape on Eigg is relatively rich. It includes a plethora of hut circles and boundaries protruding through the moorland in various higher parts of the island. There are more hut circles on Eigg than on any of the other three islands. These tend to lie around the 100 to 200m contours, such as that on Beinn Tighe, at **Cnoc Smeordail** (**9**), and represent individual farmhouses with enclosures and field systems abandoned by their communities during a period defined by climatic change and soil exhaustion. They were probably occupied in the first millennium BC. Other examples are at the **Bay of Laig** (**2**) and at **Sliabh** (**50**), where two have been plundered and, like others, later exploited for their stone. Some hut circles also appear on the lower slopes, suggesting that others may have been ploughed out or destroyed by later farming practices. Survivors include those at **Howlin** (35), at **Sandavore** (48) and at **Struidh** (52) on the remoter east side of the island.

These hut circles provide visible testimony to the Bronze Age community on Eigg and give some idea of the way the landscape may have been divided up and worked between small groups of farming families. A wider understanding of Bronze Age life emerges, however, with the discovery of the remains of a metalworking site at Galmisdale, which was accidentally exposed during the burial of a pet cat in 2001. Such sites are extremely rare in Britain and the discovery was followed up by excavation. This yielded various fragments of clay moulds used for producing socketed axes and knives, as well as crucibles and stone tools. It appears to have been a temporary workshop defined by a crude stone setting, probably established by an itinerant smith who would travel the islands plying his wares during the first millennium BC. It begs fascinating questions as to where the material came from, how he was paid and his status as a craftsperson. The site has now been excavated and covered up.

In later prehistory the most physically obvious monuments on Eigg, the 'forts' or smaller 'duns', belong to the Iron Age, *c.* 800 BC to AD 100. There are probably seven of these on the island, or at least seven that are obvious, each one representing a natural rock promontory modified with either ditches and ramparts or walling, or both. Their practical defensive capabilities are limited, as is their suitability to act as a refuge in times of local aggression. They are probably no more than symbols of power, the additional walling being cosmetic.

All but one are situated on promontory locations, effectively providing viewsheds that encircle the island and which are visible to incomers approaching from any direction. Two on the east and south-eastern approaches reflect the inappropriateness of calling them 'forts'. One, at **Corragan Mor** (11), is almost impossible to access from either sea or land, while the other, at **Rubha na Crannaig** (47), lying on the coast just below the farm at

Kildonnan, is easier to access and seems remarkably vulnerable to approaches from any direction. The most dramatic fort is probably at **Poll Duchaill** (45), which lies on the north-west coast flanked by gullies and an outer wall.

There is a concentration of three forts at the south and south-west which arguably 'protect' or oversee the main area of later activity on the island. Whether this reflects that it was also an important centre in the Iron Age is a matter of speculation. It could simply be that a number of suitable promontories happen to occur in that place. Probably the most splendid originally, but now the saddest, is that at **Galmisdale Point** (28), where only some outer walling survives as an apology to twentieth-century development. Of the other two, one lies nearby just west of **Galmisdale House** (29) and the other is at **Grulin** (31). All three are (or were) significant visual landscape features.

The final example is the great pitchstone ridge, the **Sgurr** (49) itself, although it required little modification other than a single wall, now collapsed, across its neck at the west. This can be traced for about 80m, which, if contemporary, seems far longer than necessary to inhibit access. The surfaces are barren, exposed and make little sense as a refuge; there are no internal features.

A more obvious refuge lies nearby in the adjacent upland loch known as **Loch nam Ban Mora** (43), or 'Loch of the Great Women' (see below). In the loch, about 50m from the shore, is a small islet which has been modified artificially with a pitchstone wall. Some similar small forts or 'duns' have shallow under-water trackways leading to them, but there is no sign of one here, although folklore claims that there are underwater stepping stones set so far apart that only the legendary large warrior women with their great strides could use them. According to one seventeenth-century account, the fort was only large enough to contain 'a certain number of men and women with their bairns'. Given that the loch sits in a remote position in the higher moorland terraces, one wonders where they must have been living in order to use it.

Much the same could be said of the remarkable modified cave site on the eastern cliffs amid the scree on the terrace at **Struidh** (51), sometimes known as the 'Oracle Cave'. The character of the site fits awkwardly into any chronology but sits best in the Iron Age in view of its general fort-like appearance, which consists of an artificial platform surmounted by a circular walled enclosure which may once have supported a building. The inside of the enclosure leads down into a boulder cave about 7m long from which small chambers open off. Some of their sides have been formalised using coarse walling. Deposits of midden material including animal bone fragments and shells across the cave floor suggest that it was used over a lengthy period. What is perhaps even more remarkable is that its existence is given a natural focus by a pair of near-vertical basalt columns which rise up to the top of the cliffs behind it and are enhanced by the walling. This is a natural landmark deliberately emphasised by modification and intended to be seen from afar as an expression of the importance and power of someone able to organise its enhancement. Its temple-like qualities have been considered by some to designate it as a special place, possibly with ceremonial or religious connotations.

The location, or somewhere near it, also appears to have been that of a lover's tryst. Camille Dressler recounts how in the seventeenth century, at a time when the MacLeods, sworn enemies of the MacDonalds of Clanranald who owned Eigg, were escaping from the clutches of the Scottish Crown, one of the MacLeods took refuge in the uninhabited Struidh on Eigg. He kept himself alive living off shellfish and hiding in the caves and shieling huts. In the summer he was noticed by a girl who had come up to the shielings with her father's cattle; they became friendly as the days went by and she continued to visit him in secret even when the shieling times were over. When her father eventually found out he threatened to kill her lover because he was a MacLeod, but he eventually relented and the two were married. The list of names in Rev. Walker's *Report on the Hebrides* of 1764 shows a small number of MacLeods living on the island among all the MacDonalds. Given the amount of MacDonald blood spilled at the hands of the MacLeods, and their mutual hatred, it would be interesting to know how well the new couple became integrated into the Eigg community.

Christian impact

Eigg would appear to have been a prize example of missionary activities emanating from Iona and elsewhere in the sixth and seventh centuries, in the later Middle Ages becoming an important Christian centre under secular patronage. Much of this status derives from the unfortunate demise of Donnan, a missionary from Ireland who was martyred there in AD 617 along with fifty-two monks. His martyrdom seems not in doubt, but its nature varies according to source and anecdote. A distillation of sources indicates a common version thus: an invading group of Picts acting under orders from their leader arrived on the island to murder him and his monks for using their territory without permission. It is debatable as to whose territory it was at the time, although it was claimed by the Pictish queen of Moidart to be the place where she grazed her sheep. Eigg was in no man's land between Pictland and Dalriada, and Donnan's death may have been intended to make a political point.

The Pictish factor here may be no coincidence, given that a series of likely Pictish burial cairns lie on the north coast of the island at the **Bay of Laig** (3). There are at least fifteen of them located on the storm beach in two groups. The better-preserved ones lie in a line at the south-west, the other group in a slight arc about 40m to the north-east. This type of burial is rare in the west of Scotland but is well attested in the Pictish heartland in the north-east, where radiocarbon dates have placed them within the middle of the first millennium AD. This makes them likely to be broadly contemporary with Donnan himself and gives some strength to the argument that Eigg was established Pictish territory at the time.

There are other, more embellished accounts of the martydom, several of them belonging to early Irish annals, in which Donnan and his monks are said to have been at prayer in his chapel at Kildonnan when the invaders arrived to execute them. Donnan begged that they be allowed to finish their prayers before being put to death and this request was granted. The most trustworthy account derives from the early seventeenth-century Irish *Martyrology of Donegal*:

> Donnan of Eigg, abbot. Eigg is the name of an island in which he was after he left Ireland. And sea-robbers came one time to the island, while he was celebrating mass; he begged them not to kill him till he had concluded the mass; and they gave him this favour. And afterwards he was beheaded, and 52 of his monks along with him. And all their names are in a certain old book of the books of Ireland.

Some sources identify the invaders not as 'sea robbers' but as warrior women of great size (the Picts were a matrilineal society) who slaughtered Donnan and the monks and heaped up the bodies in a pile. Shortly afterwards a light appeared over the bodies and a strange seductive noise was heard. The women became entranced and followed the light as it moved away from the chapel into the moorland. It led them up to the Sgurr and then into the loch where they all drowned, hence the name 'Loch nam Ban Mora', meaning ' Loch of the Great Women'.

There can be little doubt that the martyrdom occurred in the area of Kildonnan ('Cille' meaning church or chapel). This location contains (from north to south) a roofless church of the early sixteenth century, the modern Catholic burial ground, an open space where excavations in 2012 identified Neolithic burial cairns and Iron Age material, the modern non-Catholic burial ground and finally, at the south, the older, densely packed post-medieval burial ground. In the nineteenth century an ornamental Viking sword was found slightly to the east of the open space (see below). The modern farm of Kildonnan lies slightly further to the south again and had the status of being one of the main farms on the island. It stands just above the coastal promontory 'fort' at Rubha na Crannaig. All in all, the area reeks of historical importance.

Keyhole excavation at **Kildonnan** (37) in 2012 at various points in and around the burial ground at the south indicated that a ditched and palisaded enclosure had been partly incorporated into the modern rectangular graveyard walling. This circular enclosure has all the hallmarks of a Celtic monastic unit including the enclosure itself, the *vallum monasterium,* which separated the world of God on the inside from the outer secular world. A central oratory or chapel may have lain in the centre. The site is now completely covered by post-medieval graves. A good analogy for what it may have looked like in Donnan's time, however, lies on Canna (Chapter 4, site 36), where a similar site lies completely exposed at the base of the cliffs. The same excavations at Kildonnan also identified the remains of a medieval stone building below the roofless church and on roughly the same alignment, suggesting that the church had a much earlier footprint. It would be reasonable to assume that the whole Kildonnan area has been used for Christian worship with little break since Donnan's time. The roofless church was almost certainly the church alluded to by Donald Monro in his *Description of the Occidental i.e. Western Islands of Scotland* of 1549 (Withers and Munro 1999) and also referred to as 'the old popish chapel' in the first *Statistical Account.*

Although it is not clear exactly where on Eigg Donnan was buried, several sources point to a common location slightly to the north of the roofless church. Martin Martin was taken to his supposed burial place there in the late seventeenth century, and two centuries later the spade-happy Norman MacPherson who owned the island, aware of the story, dug up 'a stone basin' in roughly the same place. The basin contained a small number of fragments of human bone but the nature and whereabouts of both are no longer known. The first-edition Ordnance Survey map of 1877 identifies a 'stone cist' there and the first *Statistical Account* describes how a 'sepulchral urn' containing bones but no skull was ploughed out in the vicinity.

If the number of fifty-two slain monks is to be believed, it reflects a quite considerable monastic community and not one that could necessarily be accommodated at Kildonnan alone. While it is possible that the adjacent coastal promontory at Rubha na Crannaig was utilised for this, none of the internal structural remains there have been dated. The *Annals of Ulster* record the later death on Eigg of the monk Eogan around AD 725, which would suggest that Donnan's community may not have been permanently obliterated by his demise. Eogan was described as 'princeps', which would indicate headship of a sizeable foundation, possibly one with a patronage that survived the political traumas of the Middle Ages. The name 'princeps' would also indicate the superiority of the Roman as opposed to the Celtic Church in the Small Isles at that time.

During the earlier part of this period, however, there may have been an associated monastic outpost some distance away across difficult moorland north of the Sgurr, hidden at the top of the valley known as **Gleann Charadail (30)**. It consists of as many as ten small stone-built structures of various sizes, possibly more, scavenged out of the scree, some with double cells and indications of associated pens. It looks more like a dispersed village than a set of isolated shielings and has the benefit of a watercourse running through it. Several of these beehive-like structures would not be out of place among the cells of an early Celtic monastery used for accommodation by monks. Confusingly, the landscape that follows the stream to the north-west all the way down Gleann Charadail contains numerous small huts and features, making it difficult to distinguish one group from another. Sadly, none of them are datable. While this particular group of ten structures bears some physical similarity to shieling huts, they are, unlike most shielings, grouped together and are not particularly well sited for transhumance purposes. That said, there is no reason why, as a suitable source of stone, even if not ideally placed, they might not have been reused as shielings later. Moreover, apart from being difficult to reach they are also difficult to find, and it is hard to believe that their concealed location was anything other than deliberate. If indeed they did provide a monastic function, from location alone they must have belonged to a type of remote asceticism for personal contemplation and prayer quite distinct from the cenobitic mission activities of Donnan. Perhaps this hidden community was the post-Donnan solution to maintaining a Christian presence in the turbulent times that followed.

The roofless church at **Kildonnan** (38) was probably built by the Clanranalds in the middle part of the sixteenth century, replacing the earlier version identified from excavation. It now lacks both an east gable end and a roof. There is a tomb recess inside the north wall which bears the Clanranald coat of arms and a date of 1641. More unusually, there is a bizarre sculptured head resting on a pillow set into the inside of the west wall. It seems unlikely to be in its original position and has a pagan feel to it. Opinion differs as to what it represents, possibly a mother goddess symbol, or a rare depiction of a 'sheela-na-gig' figure. The latter were images with explicit sexual features occasionally found in churches and considered to be located for moralising purposes. The majority are found in Ireland but there are a handful of examples in Scotland, including some on Iona. They have a vague date range within the Middle Ages.

Inside the church there are lines of grave markers, originally including some which show incised crosses or decorative elements probably dating from the seventh to ninth centuries. These are now in the more secure environment of the porch of the modern **Catholic church** (5) to the north-west of the island.

A further example was discovered in the southern graveyard in 2012 and added to the collection. All show simple grooved or pecked crosses, although one is unusual in having been created on a triangular slab. Another has been re-erected in the roofless church. This is taller than the others, but is less than 1m high and shows an equal-armed cross with square terminals and a square centre set within a circular margin.

The most significant pieces, however, are unquestionably the two fragments of an ornate cross-slab made from reddish sandstone, now also housed in the porch of the Catholic church. The upper fragmant has an incised circular cross-head with interlace on one face together with the Latin lettering 'IHU XPI' (referring to Jesus Christ), while the lower fragment has a panel of key patterning on the same face. The back of the slab is quite different and shows on the upper fragment what appears to be a hunting scene with a bearded horseman and various animals, probably a dog, a bear and a bird, all with Pictish affinities. An incised cross has been squeezed into the scene and may have been added later. The scene is matched on the same face of the lower fragment with elements of more animals. Interestingly, while the cross-head face of the slab was designed to be set in the ground and viewed vertically and is slightly tapered at the bottom for that purpose, the hunting scene is depicted running along the length of the slab. One interpretation is that it was originally a rectangular slab with Pictish-type decoration and was later reused in a Christian context by tapering, carving a complex cross on the blank face, squeezing a simple incised cross within the hunting scene on the other and reorientating to place upright in the ground. The hunting scene could be from as early as the sixth or seventh century, the cross from as late as the ninth or tenth century.

One final later sculpture of note is the prominent cross displayed outside in the churchyard at **Kildonnan** (39) depicting animals and plants. This elaborate piece probably reflects the wealth of the Clanranalds and belongs to the fourteenth or fifteenth century. It takes a dominant position on the landscape but the base is modern and its position may not be original. Placenames on the island containing the element 'Crois' suggest that there may have been other standing crosses – Crois Moraig near Grulin, Druim na Croise near Cleardale and Crois Mhor near Kildonnan itself. According to Miller, the last of these was said to have been marked by 'a rude cross' which had been part of a chain of crosses visible from the sea. This is reminiscent of the concept of stations of the cross, or may simply have been a delineation of the monastic boundaries. Either way, such crosses further attest to the rich tradition of Christianity on the island and to its importance.

Another aspect of this tradition is reflected in at least three holy wells on the island. One, **Tobar Challuim Chille** (54) (St Columba's Well), lies to the north near Cleadale, and another, Tobar na Bean Naoimh (Well of the Saints), near the Sgurr. Martin Martin writing in the late seventeenth century may have confused the former with one he identified in the area around Five Pennies, which is since unlocated. It was said to be beneficial for those who lived on the island but detrimental to those who came from elsewhere to benefit from its powers. The latter well also lies near the cross-named Druim na Croise, which would give the site added Christian emphasis. Martin also alludes to a well referred to as St Katherine's Well on the south coast, thought to be near Grulin, which he claimed was held 'in great esteem' by the islanders and known to be good for curing diseases. He recorded an element of ritual there which involved people drinking the water and dancing round it 'sunways' annually on 15 April.

The continued strength of the Roman Church on Eigg is worth pursuing. The island was fervently Catholic up to the Reformation and did its best to remain fervently Catholic thereafter, despite the best efforts of the established Church to convert the islanders. Even by the time of Walker's *Report* in 1764 there is a clear intention to distinguish between 'Protestant' and 'papist' islanders, the latter being implicitly stigmatised. After the Reformation Catholic worship continued, in private rather than in secret, and not always in the most convenient places. In the sixteenth century the visiting priest was obliged to conduct mass in a cave on the south side of the island. Known afterwards as **Uamh Chrabhaichd (55)** (Cave of Devotion), it has a cavernous interior and a rock formation that provided a natural altar. Later worship took place in designated houses, the hard earth flooring obliging worshipers to bring their own peats to kneel on. Eventually Cleadale House became used as both a church and a presbytery, until the present **Catholic church (6)** was constructed in 1910, dedicated to St Donnan.

In Scotland the Reformation took place in 1560. The Protestant minister for the Small Isles was initially based on Rum for reasons that are unclear, possibly because Rum was the least Catholic of all four islands and was therefore considered an easier living. In the mid eighteenth century the residence transferred to Eigg, where a magnificent **Manse (44)** was to be built, completed in 1790. It was a huge building but cold and draughty and is now sadly derelict. It had a substantial walled garden and a glebe barn which has now been converted into a field centre and hostel. Worship took place in the schoolroom until the current **Protestant church (46)** was built by the MacPhersons in 1862. This new church is a simple rectangular building with lancet windows and bears biblical quotations on the interior panelling written in both Gaelic and English.

Norse impact

Despite the Norse ransacking of Iona at least twice in the early part of the ninth century, there is no documentary evidence to show that Eigg, despite its attested Christian importance, was ever attacked. In the twelfth century, as part of the Small Isles group together with the Western Isles and parts of Argyll, Eigg came under Norse control by virtue of being part of the Lordship of the Isles under Norse sovereignty. Norse authority, however, seems to have been little more than nominal and the lordship effectively became independent. Any residual semblance of Norse overlordship was terminated by the Scots at the Battle of Largs in 1263. By that time, Norse influence had become imprinted on Eigg, not in terms of a physical archaeological heritage, of which there is only a tantalising glimpse, but by virtue of placenames and the organisation of landholding.

Most of the surviving archaeological remains from this period were recovered during the MacPherson ownership, but their findspots and context were not always recorded. MacPherson himself excavated two Viking graves in 1875 which, from his descriptions, would appear to have been secondary burials set within existing prehistoric burial cairns, both located at Kildonnan, south of the ecclesiastical area (see above). One cairn contained corroded fragments of a sword with a wooden scabbard to which was attached a small fragment of leather, a whetstone and a bronze brooch shaped like a thistle. The other, smaller cairn produced an iron sword, beads of jet and amber, a bronze brooch and a hone which MacPherson described as being 'much worn with use', with a perforation for hanging from the belt.

MacPherson's most exciting object, however, also from the Kildonnan area, was a silvered-bronze sword hilt that was recovered in 1830 during the levelling of a 'hillock'. The hilt itself, thought to be of the ninth century, is decorated with silver plates showing great attention to detail and is now housed in the National Museum of Scotland, Edinburgh. The field where it was reputedly found was recorded as 'Dail Sithean' (Field of the Tumulus) and it seems likely that the 'hillock' was a burial mound. According to MacPherson, the findspot was located by 'a blind old man of very retentive memory', which leaves some doubt as to the integrity of the whole story.

A ninth-century date for this presumed warrior grave gives some credence to the possibility of contemporary hostilities, but it also suggests that if this and other Viking burials were taking place on Eigg at the time, then the Norse occupation of the island was becoming consolidated. Although the island lacks anything in the way of archaeological evidence for a Norse domestic population in this period, such as foundations for longhouses or Norse artefacts, there seems to be a possibility that Eigg was used for boat building. This arises from the discovery of two boat stems – parts of a wooden boat keel made of oak, each about 2m in length – which MacPherson described as belonging 'not to a canoe but to a boat built of planks'. These were discovered during the draining of a moss in the area around the **Bay of Laig** (4) and were parts of the clinker-built vessels used by the Norse of the time, the stems appearing to be in the process of being fashioned to take the longitudinal strakes that constituted the hull. The practice of keeping the timbers wet was to make them more malleable for later working and is well attested in Scandinavia. Moreover, the find location of the moss was at the head of a former lake which, according to tradition, had been used by Viking ships and was known locally as 'Sron na laimhrig', or 'the landing point.'

While there are a number of Norse placenames on Eigg, it is far from blanket coverage. Dressler suggests that approximately two thirds of Eigg placenames contain Norse elements, proportionally fewer than on Canna. Many other names are of Gaelic origin, or are corruptions. All of them are extraordinarily difficult to interpret as a result of factors outlined in Chapter 1. Some Norse examples have suffixes which are topographical, such as '-dale' or '-dail' (valley or glen), or coastal, such as '-ness' (headland) or '-aig' = 'vik' (bay). Other names may relate to farming landscapes, such as 'Tobhta Dhughail' (Norse 'topt', homestead or field). The absence of both personal and settlement names of Norse origin, whilst frustrating, may also be indicative of an island population which remained substantially Gaelic and Gaelic-speaking. Norse superiority may have been vested in little more than the taking of the main farms and lands by an elite few, whereby taxes and dues would have been exacted in much the same way as before. The existing population simply carried on.

The Norse exploitation of Eigg manifests itself in the way the island was divided up into landholdings using the Norse 'ouncelands' system. Ouncelands and their subdivision into 'pennylands' was the Norse method of land assessment which took into account land quality as opposed to land area. Eigg seems to have been highly esteemed, being valued at five ouncelands, by comparison with Rum, which was valued at only one ounceland, despite occupying over three times the land mass. This was due partly to the quality of Eigg's farmland, but also to the status the island afforded. Denis Rixson's research into how the land might have been divided, published in 2001, suggests that the farm boundaries shown on early nineteenth-century maps can be projected back in time to identify the physical shape of each of the five ouncelands that constituted the landholdings. Interestingly, four of the five ounceland areas have names that contain Norse components (Grulin, Galmisdale, Cleadale and Houlin), the other, Kildonnan, the main farm on the island, being Gaelic. It is unclear when this landholding division took place. It may have been as early as the ninth century and involved a simple transference of power over a pre-existing system. Unfortunately, there is no evidence as to what any pre-existing system might have been.

Medieval and post-medieval landscapes

By around AD 1200 the dispersed farmsteads of Norse and pre-Norse times were beginning to morph into small nucleated settlements which might arguably equate with the ounceland division of landholdings. This usually involved a main tenant and a series of subtenants, with rent or dues payable to the proprietor or owner of the island or to their representative. In the sixteenth century these dues might also have required the subtenants, those who worked the land, to provide a fighting force, according to the Clanranalds' military intentions. These small settlements or 'townships' effectively became self-sufficient units relying partly on communal activity. This was the system that survived through into the mid nineteenth century and was mostly static, in that the same domestic sites and structural footprints were used throughout. Island life may have seemed uncomfortably tedious, but the tedium was broken on a number of occasions which were of sufficient import to have appeared in historical accounts.

The most famous incident is undoubtedly one that occurred around 1577, when the entire population of Eigg, argued to have been in the order of four hundred people, was massacred in a cave on the south coast of the island. It stemmed from a clan feud between the owners of Eigg, the MacDonalds of Clanranald, and the MacLeods from Harris. The story goes that a group of MacLeod sailors were passing Eigg and were cast ashore on Eilean Chathastail (Castle Island), where they molested some local women who were working there, presumably at the shielings, and stole some cattle. Word reached the Eigg folk while this was ongoing, a boat was immediately dispatched and the intruders captured and put to death. This in turn prompted the MacLeods to send a large force out from Harris and mount a substantial retaliation. When the MacLeod fleet was seen on the horizon, the entire population of Eigg is said to have hidden in a cave on the south of the island, at **Uamh Fhraing (56)**, now known as the 'Massacre Cave'. The cave has a narrow entrance disguised by a waterfall but opens out internally into a large cavern. After three days of searching, the MacLeods were about to leave frustrated but saw an Eigg scout who had been dispatched to see if the coast was clear. The cave was spotted, some sources recording that the scout's footprints were seen in fresh spring snow. The MacLeods lit a fire of heather and thatch at the entrance and filled the cave with smoke. According to accounts, the entire population of the island, men, women and children, were suffocated. The bodies were left there to rot.

There is little doubt that the event took place, but the extent and nature of the massacre may have become embellished over time. The cave became a popular destination for curious travellers, including Sir Walter Scott, who had no qualms about souvenir hunting among the bones during a visit in 1814, when he acquired, according to Hugh Miller, 'a grinning skull'. The ghoulish description in the first *Statistical Account*, which recorded the bones as being 'still fresh and some of the skulls entire, and teeth in their sockets', was unhelpful in discouraging visitors, as was Hugh Miller's lengthy description of his own visit, in which he observed the bones as being 'of a brownish, earthy hue, here and there tinged with green' and the floor of the cave as resembling a charnel house.

The surviving human remains were eventually collected by the minister, exasperated by all this macabre attention, and buried somewhere in the churchyard at Kildonnan. Massacre tourism has lessened but not stopped completely. Occasionally bones in the cave missed by the minister are found by curious holidaymakers and require forensic attention by an equally exasperated Police Scotland.

It is questionable as to whether the entirety of the island population was choked to death in the cave. It seems odd that folk from townships in the north part of Eigg, where there are also caves, would have travelled at a moment's notice to the other end of the island to seek refuge. It is also hard to believe that total depopulation occurred and that the island required a complete repopulation for which there is no other record. The first *Statistical Account* refers to only forty skulls being found, although many may have been purloined by earlier souvenir hunters. It also refers to a boat full of islanders escaping to the mainland. While there is every reason to believe that some form of massacre occurred, it is unlikely to have been wholesale and may have become confused with other attacks on Eigg which occurred shortly after.

Barely a decade later, in 1588, Eigg was in trouble again. Lachlan MacLean of Duart, who was in dispute with the

Clanranalds for allegedly desecrating Iona, attacked Eigg and the other three islands in the group on the basis of their Clanranald affinities. Interestingly, the attack force is said to have included Spanish sailors from the Armada vessel the *San Juan de Sicilia*, stranded at Tobermory on Mull. They were used as mercenaries in exchange for being provided with food. According to sources, the houses on all four islands were burnt to the ground and the inhabitants, including women and infants, put to the sword. Taken at face value, Eigg would seem to have been completely decimated twice in the space of eleven years.

More was to come. According to sources, around a century later a group of sailors from Eigg berthed at Skye and had a brawl at the inn in Armadale with a group of soldiers from a naval frigate, the *Dartmouth*, also berthed there. During the fracas one of the *Dartmouth*'s soldiers was killed, and their commander, a Major Ferguson, ordered the ship to be taken to Eigg for revenge, allowing his sailors to run riot on the island, burning and plundering as they went. They captured a particular young woman and took her back to the ship, where she was defiled by the men before having her hair cut off and being sent home.

Finally, in 1746, a year after the Jacobite uprising in which the Clanranalds had played a prominent role, the Small Isles received further unwanted attention, this time from royalist forces taking a heavy-handed approach to Clanranald properties. This was on the pretext of rounding up any residual Jacobite rebels and confiscating arms under the terms of the so-called Disarming Act. In the summer of that year a naval ship, the *Furnace*, arrived under the command of a Captain Ferguson, noted for his brutality. He demanded the islanders hand over all their arms on pain of having their houses burned, their cattle killed and the menfolk taken prisoner. In a curious set of circumstances, Captain Ferguson came across a document listing the names of men from the island who had been supportive of the Jacobite cause. As a result thirty-eight men were taken aboard the *Furnace*, many leaving families behind, and transported first to London and then to Jamaica. Those who survived fever on the voyage spent the rest of their lives working as slaves on the plantations. Back on Eigg their houses were burned down and their cattle killed. This probably intensified clanship bonds rather than weakening them, Jacobite support remaining strong in the islands despite the defeat at Culloden. It is traditionally held that a supply of weapons was hidden on Eigg in case they were ever needed for another rebellion.

DEMOGRAPHICS AND TOWNSHIPS

The first reliable set of population figures appears two decades after the 1745 uprising in Walker's 1764 *Report on the Hebrides*. This provides a snapshot of Eigg in listing the population of 459 souls under the (then) nine township names of 'Gallmisdel' (Galmisdale), 'Gruline' (Grulin), 'Laig' (Laig), 'Claidill' (Cleadale), 'Toland' (Toilain), 'Five Penies' (Five Pennies), 'Sandmor' (Sandavore), 'Sandbeg' (Sandaveg) and 'Killdonan' (Kildonnan). These townships were fiscally responsible to a tacksman and each contained a number of households each of which possessed a degree of independence. Townships and their associated dwellings could vary in nature and size over time, dynamically reflecting need and population change.

About forty years later an 1806 map by William Bald commissioned by the Clanranalds shows eight townships, each with defined boundaries (see plate section). This map also has the benefit of depicting individual clusters of houses as well as cultivatable land and field systems. By then, however, Grulin had been divided into Upper Grulin and Lower Grulin, Five Pennies and Cleadale no longer appeared exclusive and were joined together, and settlement in the Kildonnan township appeared to have shifted to Braigh (Brae) slightly to the north-east. Some of these changes of pattern were the consequence of population pressure, while others more ominously reflect the emergence of larger sheep farms, requiring movement of people and the removal of buildings for the construction of stone walls for the sheep. The first *Statistical Account* indicates a population of around 400, which increases to around 500 by the time of the 1801 census and then drops to 442 by the 1811 census.

The individual buildings in the townships were generally stone-faced on the inside and outside with an infill between the two. This can be seen best in places such as **Five Pennies** (21), Brae and **Grulin** (33 and 34), where the stone house foundations still survive after desertion and robbing and represent the final phase of settlement before desertion in the eighteenth and nineteenth centuries. If there were any Norse and medieval predecessors they lie in the shadows beneath, their building elements used, reused, robbed out or destroyed over the centuries. Early dating of buildings is virtually impossible, and there is no reference to granting of land until the late fifteenth century. This was at **Howlin** (36), where the farmhouse that currently stands on the site probably dates from 1770. It is reputed to have been the first house on the island to have used glass in the windows and lime mortar in the walls.

Bald's 1806 map also shows part of the island's infrastructure in depicting the manse, a meeting house and a mill on the stream near **Kildonnan** (40). The mill was constructed in the early nineteenth century, presumably to provide additional revenue for the Clanranalds by controlling the island's milling. Also at **Kildonnan** (42) is the nineteenth-century farmhouse, the location of what was probably the most important island farmstead over the centuries, together with a horse gin and a bank barn (where the barn is built into the hillside and the upper floor accessed from the higher ground at the back). Both are still standing and relate to the earlier township at Kildonnan before the settlement moved north-eastwards to Brae as shown on Bald's map.

SHIELINGS, KELP AND THE 'OLD SYSTEM'

All the townships had shielings, estimates suggesting that there were more than one hundred shieling huts on the island, located anywhere where there was a reasonable supply of building stone on the upper slopes. Most are single-celled but several are double-celled, internal through-access being made via a 'creep'. It is difficult to give absolute numbers on account of collapse, the decay of the turf used in their construction and, in many cases, challenges in identifying them among the scree and rocks. Without doubt a number were sited to exploit existing stone supplies from earlier monuments, such as those in the north-east part of the island at **Cnoc Smeordail** (10) and **Fhaing Ruadh** (20). Many of them occur in groups, as seen at **Eilean Chathastail (Castle Island)** (17), **Talm** (53) and **Allt Bidein An Tighearna** (1). Some are more widespread, such as at **Grulin** (32). Shielings were temporary structures, and purely functional. They were rebuilt annually with stone and turf, the turf providing insulation for storing dairy produce. Their use seems to have been a Norse-based tradition which continued well into the nineteenth century.

Throughout the later eighteenth century the model of the townships and their associated shielings known as 'the old system' became increasingly vulnerable to changes wrought by a number of interrelated factors, not least of which was the boom and subsequent bust of the kelping industry. The boom resulted in an increased, saturated population which found itself largely devoid of work when the kelp market collapsed in the earlier nineteenth century, at which point levels of poverty rose significantly. It is easy to underestimate the impact of kelping, largely because the tangible remains in the landscape are so few. They survive only as rectangular stone settings near the shore, often enclosing a low grassy mound. Examples of these lie at **Kildonnan** (41), at **Clach Alasdair** (7) west of Laig, at Fhaing Ruadh beyond Struidh and on **Eilean Chathastail (Castle Island)** (18 and 19), one at the north and one at the south.

One unrealised aspect of subsistence in the 'old system' was the exploitation of the island's rich fishing stocks. The islanders had traditionally never considered fishing other than on a domestic level and the Clanranalds showed little interest. The island's fishing habits were limited to small boats and shore-based fish traps. These fish traps were usually loosely built lines of walling across the mouths of small bays and inlets. At high water the fish would swim over the walling into the bay, sometimes attracted by bait, some being trapped when the tide ebbed and the water level lowered. A good example can be seen at low tide in the harbour area by **Galmisdale** (24). There are also remains near Kildonnan and at the nearby Poll nam Partan (Bay of Crabs) slightly to the west, but these are harder to make out.

In the 1780s the British Fisheries Society, having surveyed the fishing stocks and potential in the area, suggested the construction of a fishing village at Galmisdale, but it was an initiative that fell flat for lack of both funding and enthusiasm. Another reason was the lack of suitable harbourage, as noted in the first *Statistical Account*, which pointed out that the island had only 'a tolerable harbour for a few vessels' lying opposite Castle Island. It suggested that, if 'properly planned', the harbour could become a hub for herring busses sailing between the fishing grounds in the north and the markets to the south.

There are now three piers in the harbour area around **Galmisdale** (25–27). The earliest pier (undated) survives at the south-west as little more than a length of boulders piled up to form a crude jetty some 20m long with a slipway cleared through the adjacent rocks. Further to the south a rock outcrop was modified to create an additional longer pier, which is still visible on the part of the island that juts out into the sea south-west of the modern ferry terminal. The Clanranalds finally decided to build a more effective pier that would facilitate larger vessels at both low and high water. This was completed in the 1790s in the same bay but further to the north. Its purpose was not to improve the fishing potential but to optimise the export of kelp, which was becoming more and more remunerative. It can still be seen as a substantial curved construction, almost 50m long, nearly 5m wide and standing 3m proud. It also features on Bald's map of 1806. A rubble pier was added about 50m from its western side in 1877. This curved towards the Clanranald pier, effectively producing a small sheltered harbour between the two with a narrow entrance suited only to small craft. Despite all these attempts, commercial fishing was never realised: ingrained tradition was too strong. The island was left with its few small boats, fish traps and shellfish from the shore.

THE CLEARANCES

The late eighteenth century was not a happy time for the islanders. The first *Statistical Account* paints a miserable picture of the island, noting that the crops were insufficient to feed the population, cattle prices were at the mercy of mainland dealers, rents were high and there was insufficient land for each family, a problem exacerbated by the custom of allocating family farmland to newly wed offspring. The situation was bad enough for 176 islanders to emigrate to Canada between 1788 and 1790. Many had sold their cattle to pay for the fare.

The commissioning of Bald's map was to review the communal township system and organise it into individual crofts. The idea was that this could create smallholdings that would allow a degree of self-sufficiency from more seasonal work and alleviate the growing poverty and emigration caused by overpopulation and the collapse of the kelp harvesting. This innovation is reflected most vividly in the landscape at **Cleadale (8)**, where the west-facing hillside was divided into strips by straight lines of stone walling which ran roughshod over the earlier straggling outlines of townships and enclosures. Intact elements of the old Five Pennies township survive only outside the lines of new walling and show a seemingly ad hoc evolution of enclosures and arable cultivation.

It turned out to be an ineffective solution. The first edition of the Ordnance Survey map, based on survey of 1877, shows the extent to which the island community had disintegrated. The map indicates that, right across the island, large numbers of dwellings were unroofed – in other words, were uninhabited. At Five Pennies, for example, six of the seven dwellings were unroofed, fourteen were unroofed at Lower Grulin and nineteen out of twenty at Upper Grulin. Galmisdale seemed better served with fifteen roofed buildings, but they lasted only until the end of the century, when they were demolished to make way for the owner's new lodge. The island's population reached a peak of 546 in 1841, by which point poverty was rife. Even the faithful potato turned against the islanders in succumbing to blight in the 1840s, although its effect on Eigg was less severe than elsewhere. Fifty years later the population had sunk to 233 – less than half its 1841 peak – thanks to the emigration (voluntary or assisted by the Clanranalds) and eviction necessary to fill the island with sheep. Enforced eviction took place at both Grulin townships in the 1850s, and by the end of the nineteenth century the population concentrations had shrivelled to the three areas around Five Pennies, Cleadale and Galmisdale. There is an account by Miller of a visit to a sick old lady in the mid nineteenth century. He had a slightly patronising view of the islanders (as illustrated by the quotation that forms the epigraph to this chapter), but even he was appalled by the level of poverty in her house:

> It was hardly larger than the cabin of the Betsey and a thousand times less comfortable. The walls and roof formed of damp grass-grown turf with a few layers of unconnected stones in the basement tier, seemed to constitute one continuous hillock, sloping upwards from foundation to ridge. The low chinky door opened direct into the one wretched apartment of the hovel, which we

found lighted chiefly by holes in the roof ... Within a foot of the bed-ridden woman's head there was a hole in the turf wall, which was, we saw, usually stuffed with a bundle of rags, but which lay open as we entered, and which furnished a downward peep of the sea and shore, and the rocky Eilan Chasteil ... The little hole in the wall had formed the poor creature's only communication with the face of the external world for ten weary years ... I learned that not during the ten years in which she had been bed-ridden had she received a single farthing from the proprietor, nor, indeed, had any of the poor of the island, and that the parish had no session-funds. I saw her husband a few days after – an old worn-out man, with famine written legibly in his hollow cheek and eye, and on the shrivelled frame, that seemed lost in his tattered dress. They had no means of living, he said.

Sporting estates and later ownership

During this time of poverty the island was owned by the MacPherson family, initially by Hugh MacPherson, who purchased it in 1827. He was a professor at Aberdeen University as well as a practising doctor who moved in elevated social circles. The family money appears to have come from connections in India. MacPherson bought the island from the Clanranalds, who at that time were settling their debts. He may have done the island a favour, in that his ownership effectively put a stop to any further streams of emigration organised by the Clanranalds. But that seems to be the only favour he did it. Despite owning Eigg for twenty-seven years he never once paid it a visit and seemed reluctant to support the islanders during the potato blight. The plight of the bedridden elderly woman described by Miller dates to his watch. He also sold off the two settlements at Grulin to a sheep farmer from the Lowlands and evicted the people who lived there as part of the deal. Miller's description of the harbour at the time of his visit in 1845 indicates neglect as well as poverty: 'a deserted boat harbour, formed of loosely piled stone, at the upper extremity of a sandy bay; and a roofless dwelling beside it, with two ruinous gables rising over the broken walls. The entire scene suggested the idea of a land which man had done for ever.'

MacPherson died in 1854, a year after the Grulins were cleared, and was succeeded by Norman, one of his thirteen children. A professor at Glasgow University, Norman had spent many summers on the island with his sister Isabella, latterly converting a pair of structures at Galmisdale into a house called the 'Crow's Nest', which became their primary residence and was subsequently modified and enlarged to provide a gentle-manly residence for hunting guests. He was an avid collector of antiquities and spent much of his time digging holes in ancient monuments. To his credit he donated many of the items he discovered to the Edinburgh Museum of Science and Art (later to become the National Museum of Scotland) and published a paper on his findings in 1878 in the *Proceedings* of the Society of Antiquaries of Scotland, of which he was a fellow. He was also aware of the potential of the island for shooting, and together with his sister organised the redesign of the landscape around the main house through clearing and planting in order to encourage pheasants.

MacPherson's activities were but a timid step into the world of hunting estates by comparison with the projects of the next owner, Lawrence Thompson MacEwen, who for reasons unclear to this author preferred to call himself Robert Thompson. He purchased the island in 1896, having previously made his fortune as a journalist-turned-arms-dealer. His interests were in hunting, and his intention was to turn the whole of Eigg into a deer park. This would have required deporting all his Eigg tenants to Muck, which he had purchased at the same time from the Clanranalds, possibly for that very reason. When that initiative failed he allegedly had his tenants moved to a part of the island where they were out of sight and subsequently rebuilt the Crow's Nest into a more stylish lodge. In 1913 the island was sold again, this time to Sir William Peterson, a shipping magnate, who built a much larger and more prominent timber-framed lodge nearby, known as the 'White Lodge', and turned the former Crow's Nest into tennis courts. The new lodge lasted until 1925 when it burned down, ironically the year he died.

The island was subsequently sold to Walter Runciman, a cabinet minister in the Westminster government and a member of another shipping family. He constructed yet a further new **Eigg Lodge (14)** in the flattened area of the tennis courts, this one in the Arts and Crafts style of the Lutyens tradition. It was of cavity-wall brick construction with harling. With modification, this is the building that survives today surrounded by designed gardens of exotic flora. It is a remarkable building in a remarkable setting, but it has a colonial feel to it and is somewhat anachronistic on an island of small stone-built cottages. The design of the garden necessitated the destruction of several prehistoric monuments. It became a second home for the Runcimans and their guests rather than a major focus for hunting, although it did contain a gun room. From then on the island's days as a sporting estate rapidly faded. The Runcimans sold the island in 1966 and it changed hands a further four times in the following three decades, not always smoothly, until it was finally purchased by the islanders themselves in 1997 in a community buy-out.

Places to Visit: Eigg

Allt Bidein An Tighearna

1. Shieling huts. NRHE ID 352662. Grid ref: NM 4831 8831.
There are numerous shieling huts on the slopes above Cleadale.
These two are better preserved than many and are accessible, the
larger being sub-circular, some 1.5 × 2m.

Bay of Laig

2. Hut circle. NRHE ID 22167. Grid ref: NM 4582 8742.
The boulder foundations of this hut circle have a diameter of
about 8m with various other features in the vicinity, notably a
stone boundary which can be tracked for around 150m. Other
lengths of walling may be connected to it, suggesting Bronze
Age land divisions.

*3. Pictish burials. NRHE ID 22145. Grid ref: NM 4670 8790
(centre).*
There are at least fifteen Pictish burials set in lines in two main
groups about 40m apart, recognisable as roughly square collapsed
mounds, each no larger than 5 × 5m. The northerly group is in a
slight arc. Some have kerb stones surviving and a small number
also have earth-fast corners. All have been heavily robbed.

*4. Boat prows. NRHE ID 22163. Grid ref: NM 4720 8780
(centre).*
This is the general location of the bog recovery of two oak
stem/keel fragments argued to belong to boat-building activity
in Norse times. The bay immediately to the north-west is said

to have once been an inland lake, which tradition holds to have also been used as a harbour.

Catholic church

5. Early Christian crosses. Grid ref: NM 4741 8853.

A number of early crosses from the roofless church at Kildonnan (site 38) are held for safekeeping in the church. Most show simple grooved or pecked crosses ascribed to the seventh to ninth centuries. In addition there is a highly ornamented slab which appears to depict a (pagan) hunting scene on one face and an interlaced Christian cross on the other.

6. Church and presbytery. NRHE ID 106200. Grid ref: NM 4741 8853.

This church was built in 1910 to provide a formal and permanent place of Catholic worship on the island. The dedication is to St Donnan. Mass had previously been held at Cleadale House and other places including Uamh Chrabhaichd (Cave of Devotion). The presbytery was built a few years after the church.

Clach Alasdair

7. Kelp kiln. NRHE ID 236659. Grid ref: NM 4535 8826.

As in this instance, these monuments tend to survive only as rectangular stone settings on the shoreline, often enclosing a low grassy mound. This example measures about 3 × 2m and is positioned on a promontory, presumably in view of the proximity of kelp.

Cleadale

8. Township settlement and improvement. NRHE ID 106157. Grid ref: NM 4790 8900 (centre).

This area, roughly 1,300m (E/W) × 700m (N/S) shows how the higgledy-piggledy buildings of the evolved Cleadale township were overlaid by the nineteenth-century crofting improvement scheme on the west-facing slopes. The straight, parallel lines of stone walling of the new land divisions can be seen running down the hillside, superimposed over earlier settlement foundations and land divisions.

Cnoc Smeordail

9. Hut circles. NRHE ID 236660. Grid ref: NM 4825 8767.
These three circular structures probably date to the first millennium BC and represent individual farmhouses with enclosures and field systems. There are at least three quite large huts ranging from 7.5 to 10m in diameter with walls up to 1m wide sheltered by rock outcrops. Possible field boundaries lie in the vicinity.

10. Shieling huts. NRHE ID 352702. Grid ref: NM 4823 8755.
There are probably the foundations of at least five shieling huts here, together with other features. The huts are typically small, sub-circular and barely more than 2 × 2m or 3 × 2m in size. Prehistoric hut circles and boundary walls in the vicinity provided an easy source of building material.

Corragan Mor

11. Fort. NRHE ID 240681. Grid ref: NM 4946 8875.
This Iron Age fort uses a natural outcrop which has been enhanced with stone walling around the base. Some facing stones still survive. Its position makes it highly visible from the sea but awkward to access from either the sea or the land.

Druim na Croise

12. Bronze Age burial cairn. NRHE ID 22166. Grid ref: NM 4740 8936.
Like many other Bronze Age burial cairns this takes a dominant position, here on a ridge overlooking the sea. It now consists of a low, turf-covered mound with a diameter of around 12m and

with depressions from presumed robbing. The 'cross' placename suggests that the location was also used to erect one of the early crosses on the island.

Eigg Lodge

13. Bronze Age burial cairn. NRHE ID 22188. Grid ref: NM 4797 8408.
This is a poorly surviving example which has been incorporated into a landscaping scheme for the lodge grounds. It has an estimated diameter of about 8m and some kerb stones are still visible.

14. Lodge. NRHE ID 106067. Grid ref: NM 4789 8421.
The current building on the site is the last of several former lairds' residences to have existed in the immediate vicinity since around 1827. It is a slightly modified version of the house built in 1927 by the Runciman family to an Arts and Crafts design by Newcastle architects Mauchlen and Weightman. The original flat roof was later replaced by the present pitched one.

Eilean Chathastail (Castle Island)

15. Bronze Age burial cairn. NRHE ID 22176. Grid ref: NM 4874 8380.
This takes a dominant position on the western tip of the islet and is one of the largest on Eigg, measuring roughly 8m in diameter and standing to a height of over 1m. There are some kerb stones visible but robbing is also apparent.

16. Bronze Age burial cairn. NRHE ID 22176. Grid ref: NM 4880 8381.
This takes a high position on the eastern tip of the islet and has a diameter of around 6m, although some of the cairn may have collapsed on the seaward side. There is also evidence of robbing.

17. Shieling huts. NRHE ID 22178. Grid ref: NM 4871 8319.
There are probably about a dozen foundation remains of shieling huts located in the central part of the islet surviving only as turf-covered stone foundations, typically sub-circular and measuring about 3 × 2m. There are also small enclosures and pens, suggesting this was a well-frequented transhumance site.

18. Kelp kiln. NRHE ID 305903. Grid ref: NM 4875 8381.
There are two obvious kelp kilns on the islet. This one at the north is rectangular and measures roughly 5 × 1m with some stony banking visible. There are also local elements of walling and stones that suggest the proximity of other activities.

19. Kelp kiln. NRHE ID 305953. Grid ref: NM 4879 8290.
This sits at the southern tip of the islet and measures roughly 4 × 2m, defined by a low banking of stones. The kiln locations on the islet (one at the north and one at the south) may indicate where kelp was most conveniently harvested and dragged ashore.

Fhaing Ruadh

20. Shieling huts. NRHE ID 301146. Grid ref: NM 4872 9089.
There are at least seven huts in this general area, with sub-circular foundations typically measuring 2 to 3m. One is slightly larger and appears to have two compartments. There are turf-covered mounds and other features in the vicinity from which building stone may have been quarried.

Five Pennies

21. Township settlement. NRHE ID 118020. Grid ref: NM 4785 8975 (centre).
The visible footings of at least twenty rectangular buildings constructed of turf and stone lie in a disorganised manner across a large area approximately 100 × 100m. In association are pens, enclosures and a corn drier. The settlement belongs to the eighteenth and early nineteenth centuries but may have late-medieval

origins. An equally disorganised field system can be traced to the north.

Galmisdale

22. Bronze Age burial cairns. *NRHE ID 22189. Grid ref: NM 4833 8385 (centre).*
These two burial cairns are located together in a dominant position overlooking Galmisdale Bay. The larger lies at the north with a diameter of around 8m and a surviving height of over 1m. The one at the south is slightly smaller. Both show evidence of having been disturbed, although both still have some kerb stones in situ.

23. Neolithic house. *NRHE ID 149414. Grid ref: NM 4777 8346.*
This oval building is arguably the earliest building in the Small Isles. It measures about 8 × 4.5m with thick walls boulder-faced on both the inside and the outside. The entrance is at the end and is flanked by characteristic large upright stones. The closest parallels are on Shetland, dated to around 3000 BC.

24. Fish traps. *NRHE ID 240683. Grid ref: NM 4837 8400.*
There are the remains of one or possibly two traps in Galmisdale Bay. The most obvious lies at the south-west of the bay and is L-shaped and sizeable, measuring about 60 × 50m with an open end facing north-west. Its construction appears to be of loose stones. Located to the north-east is some evidence of underwater lines of stone, but not surviving in any particular shape.

25. Pier and slipway. *NRHE ID 301173. Grid ref: NM 4841 8387.*
The earliest pier is probably represented by this surviving rectangular patch of boulders which juts out for a mere 20m before turning into a crude slipway. The slipway runs for approximately 50m parallel to the current ferry road.

26. Pier. *NRHE ID 301045. Grid ref: NM 4851 5838.*
This originally consisted of rocks piled up to form a crude jetty at
the south-west of the bay to the south of the current ferry road.
It may originally have extended to more than 100m, utilising
a natural line of rock outcrop. Now concrete-clad, it stands to
barely half that length.

27. Clanranald pier. *NRHE ID 106132. Grid ref: NM 4832
8414.*
This well-built pier almost 5m wide was constructed around
1790. It sits at the north-east of the bay and curves westwards
for about 50m. A slightly later, less formal pier was constructed
to the west creating a harbour area between the two measuring
approximately 50 × 50m.

28. Fort. *NRHE ID 22171. Grid ref: NM 4846 8380.*
This rather battered example at Galmisdale Point once held a
dominant position overlooking the bay but has been extensively
destroyed, having hosted a tea room and a car park and having
been bisected by a road. The internal area was probably about
30 × 25m. Some outer walling survives on the southern face.

Galmisdale House

29. Fort. *NRHE ID 269299. Grid ref: NM 4703 8391.*
This small example, perhaps better defined as a 'dun', sits on a
hillock just west of Galmisdale House and about 300m from
the coast. A 2m-wide stone wall with some facing stones evident
partly surrounds it. The stone foundations in the interior appear
to have been added later.

Gleann Charadail

30. Shieling huts or ?monastic cells. *NRHE ID 22160. Grid ref:
NM 4511 8571 (centre).*
There are two groups of hut foundations in the higher reaches
of Gleann Charadail, at least five in each, with mounds and

banking in association. Most have small sub-circular part-corbelled cells, several being double-celled connected via a 'creep'. The remote location, the availability of running water and the 'beehive' huts have given rise to the interpretation of a monastic community.

Grulin

31. Fort. NRHE ID 255793. Grid ref: NM 4544 8417.
This promontory takes a precipitous coastal position but offers little in the way of protection on the landward side, where the flatter ground later contained the congested settlement of the Upper Grulin township. The internal area is barely 20m across and any features have been robbed out for house building together with most of the outer walling, a few stones of which still survive in situ.

32. Shieling huts. NRHE ID 352060. Grid ref: NM 4485 8532.
There are a number of huts spread out in the shelter of the Sgurr above Grulin. Six of these are relatively well preserved, several of them being figure-of-eight in plan with narrow access between cells. The larger cells are sub-circular, typically 3 × 2m with walling standing over 1m high in places.

33. Upper Grulin township settlement. NRHE ID 22191. Grid ref: NM 4550 8420 (centre).
The clifftop township of Upper Grulin survives in the form of the foundations of at least forty individual buildings spread across an area of several hundred metres. These include domestic dwellings, barns, huts and enclosures representing a cluster of around a dozen domestic units. Some of the stone walls are turf-filled. There are also corn-drying facilities and localised lazy beds.

34. Lower Grulin township settlement. NRHE ID 22170. Grid ref: NM 4465 8505 (centre).
The township of Lower Grulin is similar to site **33** above. It lies

about 1 km to the north-west but is roughly half the size and more linear in arrangement. There are about fifteen buildings in the main concentration at Lower Grulin, but with others scattered on the higher slopes. Some of the structures have a rubble infill in the stone-faced walling, suggesting a later phase of construction.

Howlin

35. Hut circles. NRHE ID 22210. Grid ref: NM 4775 9005.
These two hut circles probably represent the replacement of one by another in the first millennium BC. The earlier is substantial with a diameter of around 13m and a wall thickness of *c.* 2m. The later one is smaller with a diameter of about 8m. This had been built against the north-east side of the former and utilised some of its walling.

36. Farmhouse. NRHE ID 147832. Grid ref: NM 4791 8956.
This was built in 1770 and is said to be the first house on the island to have used mortar and glass windows. It may have been used to accommodate both livestock and a family subsequently. The first *Statistical Account* describes it as being the only house on the island to have a walled garden and an orchard. It was re-roofed from thatch to slate in the late nineteenth century.

Kildonnan

37. Monastic enclosure. NRHE ID 22152. Grid ref: NM 4890 8525.
Keyhole excavation in 2012 suggested that this enclosed burial ground was located over an earlier circular ditched and palisaded enclosure which was the *vallum monasterium* of an early Christian centre. There may have been an oratory or chapel in the centre. The current walling follows the curved original enclosure at the north-west corner.

38. Roofless church. *NRHE ID 22152. Grid ref: NM 4885 8536.*
The church is probably of the sixteenth century and contains a tomb recess and the Clanranald coat of arms inside the north wall. The interior contains grave memorials which may be secondary, including several fragments of early crosses which have been moved to the Catholic church for safekeeping. There is also a bizarre, crudely sculptured head on the west wall which may be a 'sheela-na-gig' figure. Excavations in 2012 showed that an earlier stone building stood on the same site.

39. Standing cross. *NRHE ID 108566. Grid ref: NM 4888 8533.*
This fourteenth- or fifteenth-century broken cross depicting animals and plants is positioned in a dominant part of the landscape and probably replaces an earlier version deliberately sited on high ground indicating the ecclesiastical centre. It suggests wealthy patronage, presumably the Clanranalds at that time. The cross was reset in concrete in the 1930s.

40. Mill. *NRHE ID 106075. Grid ref: NM 4878 8519.*
This mid nineteenth century mill has now been converted into a holiday home but still contains some of the original machinery and its suspended wheel. It was fed by a lade which can still be traced for around 600m.

41. Kelp kiln. *NRHE ID 301169. Grid ref: NM 4904 8485.*
This sits on the west side of the bay below Kildonnan and takes the form of lines of large stones defining a rectangular area some 3.5 × 0.75m.

42. Kildonnan Farm. *NRHE ID 108857. Grid ref: NM 4900 8504.*
This was probably the site of the main farm on Eigg throughout much of the island's history. It sits within easy reach of the harbour, the ecclesiastical centre and a sheltered bay. The current farmhouse is from the nineteenth century. It has contemporary outbuildings and a bank barn nearby.

Loch nam Ban Mora

43. Dun or ?crannog. NRHE ID 22148. Grid ref: NM 4553 8723.

Opinions differ as to whether this is a dun (small defensive site) or a crannog (habitation site). Barely more than 15 × 10m in area, it consists of a natural rock outcrop in the loch which has been modified with an outer walling, now largely collapsed but in places standing to around 1m in height. The loch features in the story of the great warrior women who were lured here after the martyrdom of Donnan.

Manse

44. Eigg Manse. NRHE ID 81906. Grid ref: NM 4822 8519.

This was completed in 1790 and extended a century later. Its pretentious size, walled garden and position reflected a desire to boost Protestantism within traditional Catholic areas and to capitalise on Eigg's being the most important island within the Small Isles parish. Its windswept location and dampness caused it to fall out of use.

Poll Duchaill

45. Fort. NRHE ID 202968. Grid ref: NM 4543 8816.

This is probably the most dramatic fort on the island, flanked by natural gullies and protected by an outer wall of which some facing stones still survive. A natural ditch has been modified to present a more formidable landward access with an extremely narrow entrance. The interior covers an area of some 50 × 50m in which can be seen the outlines of several structural remains. These are thought to be contemporary with the fort itself.

Protestant church

46. Church. NRHE ID 108866. Grid ref: NM 4809 8551.

This small rectangular church was constructed in 1862 as a

dedicated location for services that had previously taken place in the schoolhouse. Built of local stone, it has corner buttresses, a slate roof and lancet windows. The internal walls feature inscriptions in both Gaelic and English.

Rubha na Crannaig

47. Fort. NRHE ID 22177. Grid ref: NM 4914 8476.
This relatively low-lying promontory embraces an internal area of about 35 × 25m surrounded by remains of collapsed walling. Inside there is a series of divisions made with earthen banks of unknown date. The suggestion that the fort was later reused for monastic purposes is realistic given its proximity to the ecclesiastical centre at Kildonnan.

Sandavore

48. Hut circle. NRHE ID 352457. Grid ref: NM 4749 8498.
This is a relatively large example located on a terrace north-west of Sandavore. It measures about 10m in diameter and the walls are over 1m thick, with some facing stones still evident in the perimeter. Some traces of banking and field systems lie in association.

Sgurr

49. Fort. NRHE ID 22190. Grid ref: NM 4612 8474.
This great jutting knob of pitchstone with its peak almost on the 400m contour can be seen for miles around but makes an impracticable fortress or place of refuge. There is no evidence of internal workings. The single access point at the west is protected by walling, but this runs for about 80m and seems unnecessarily long. In good weather it can be reached by a defined footpath from the pier and there is a moderately easy trek up to its base at the west with some scrambling required thereafter.

Sliabh, Beinn Tighe

50. Hut circles. NRHE ID 297986. Grid ref: NM 4499 8762.
The two hut circles here are located about 25m apart in an area of other features including shieling huts, which may have robbed much of their stone. One hut circle is about 5m in overall diameter, the other slightly less. The larger of the two has been partly incorporated into a shieling hut.

Struidh

51. Oracle cave. NRHE ID 255803. Grid ref: NM 4929 8989.
This consists of a terraced platform surmounted by circular walling leading into a large chambered cave measuring about 7 × 4m. Inside are lengths of walling that formalise the cave's space together with evidence of occupation debris. The entrance to the cave is flanked by a face of upward-thrusting geological bands that create an impressive façade visible from a distance. The function and date are uncertain, but opinion suggests it to be a ceremonial site, probably from the Iron Age. Access is difficult by any route and is probably best approached from the south. Local advice is recommended.

52. Hut circle. NRHE ID 301136. Grid ref: NM 4947 9020.
This turf-covered feature is difficult to interpret but would appear to be circular with a diameter of about 6m including the collapsed perimeter walling. Some external facing stones are visible.

Talm

53. Shieling huts. NRHE ID 300634 and ID 300635. Grid ref: NM 4760 9080 (centre).
There are probably in the order of twenty huts here in two clusters about 300m apart, together with associated enclosures and pens in what would appear to be temporary summer units in one of the remoter parts of the island. The structures vary in size

according to function, the majority being small and sub-circular, around 2 × 2.5m. The western group also contains a corn kiln.

Tobar Challuim Chille

54. St Columba's Well. NRHE ID 22142. Grid ref: NM 4778 8886.

This is more of a spring than a well and is not easy to find without local assistance. It lies in Cleadale, west of the road and about 30m south-west of site 3, and is surrounded by a loose stone setting about 1m square.

Uamh Chrabhaichd

55. Cave of Devotion. NRHE ID 288495. Grid ref: NM 4723 8344.

After the Reformation mass was held in houses, including Cleadale House, and also in this cave, which became known as the 'Cave of Devotion'. It can be accessed from the shore and has a cavernous interior as well as a natural rock ledge that served well as an altar. Access is possible via a recognisable but steep footpath from the house at Craigard (NM 47861 83678), but visitors should seek local advice regarding the times of incoming tides.

Uamh Fhraing

56. Massacre Cave. NRHE ID 22183. Grid ref: NM 4749 8347.

This is the scene of the alleged massacre of 1577. It has a narrow entrance hidden by a waterfall but opens out into a large cavern. The islanders took refuge here to avoid an act of vengeance by the MacLeods of Harris. Their hiding place was discovered and the MacLeods lit a fire outside the entrance and suffocated all those inside. Opinion is divided as to how many people perished. The site later became a tourist attraction before the bones were removed. Access is possible via a recognisable but steep footpath from the house at Craigard (NM 47861 83678), but visitors should seek local advice regarding the times of incoming tides.

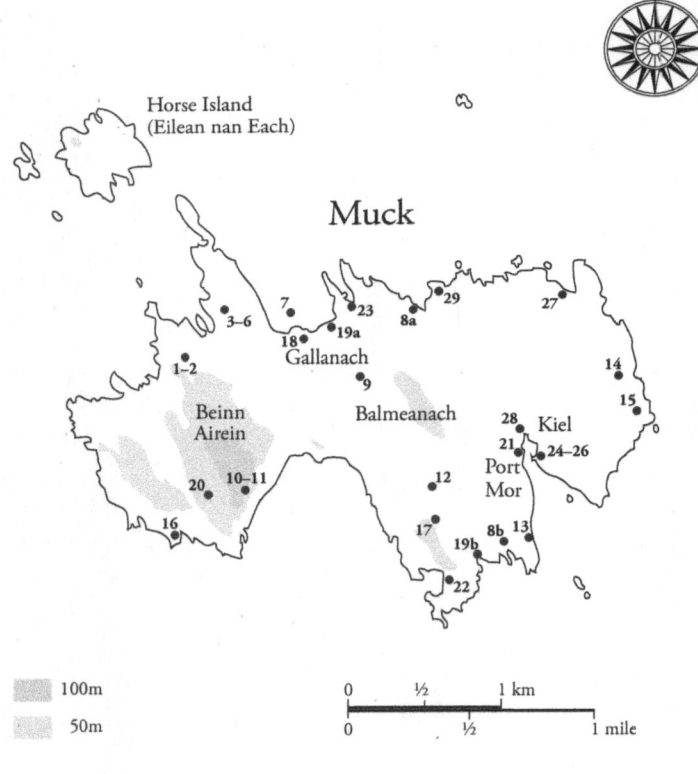

3   Muck

'Upon the whole it is a beautiful little island'

Introduction

Apart from its name, which in many quarters has been seen as perennially amusing, Muck has escaped much in the way of historical comment over the years. This is mostly due to the fact that, unlike Rum and Eigg, it was not a part of the great Clanranald estate which dominated the politics of the Hebrides in the Middle Ages, although it later briefly came under Clanranald control. It belonged to the Church, part of the property of Iona, and documents appear to associate it with Canna. The two were often referred to together and quite separately from Rum and Eigg in view of their ecclesiastical connections. The island may also have been too small (around 560 hectares) to have merited much comment. Rather like some form of poor relation, it tended to be bundled in with the larger islands by travellers for descriptive purposes. Even the Rev. John Walker thought it unworthy of a separate entry in his detailed *Report on the Hebrides* of 1764.

By comparison with the physical profiles of the other three islands, Rum and Eigg in particular, Muck lacked the topographical charisma needed to draw the early visitor ashore for a new experience. The whole island is low-lying, the highest point, Beinn Airein, being a mere 137m tall, whereas Askivall on Rum reaches a height of 780m. There is little in the way of dramatic cliffs, no great knob of pitchstone jutting into the sky as on Eigg, and a coastline, with one notable exception, devoid of forts or any other visible work of earlier generations worth getting excited about. Any well-heeled traveller on a 'must see' tour of the Western Isles in the eighteenth and nineteenth centuries would have been unlikely to give Muck a second glance. The same appears true for the geologists of the day. The second *Statistical Account*, written in 1836, which waxes lyrical and at length over the geological formations of Eigg, Rum and Canna, makes no mention whatsoever of the geology of Muck, despite the fact that they all belong to a common volcanic formation.

This omission was a fundamental oversight in that the island's wealth lay in its geology, which features as a series of low terraces, much more gentle than those on Canna or Eigg, but also resulting from the lava outflows from Rum. The combination of the soft surface rock and blown sand has created a naturally occurring fertile soil which has given the island an envious reputation for farming. While the various travellers' casual descriptions rarely comment on the island, it is the island's excellence for agriculture that is persistently flagged up in the more formal accounts and records. The first *Statistical Account*, written in 1794, emphasises how large the cattle grew 'owing to the fineness of the grass' and that the island had seven ploughs. Some measure of its fertility can be gauged from the fact that neighbouring Eigg, which was over three times the size, had eight ploughs. Some forty years later the second *Account* describes Muck as 'a low fertile island, well adapted for the rearing of black cattle, and for the cultivation of green and corn crops. With the exception of a little hill in the north end, whose summit is covered with heath, it is all green. The grass is of the finest description. Upon the whole it is a beautiful little island.'

Muck has a small annex to it. In much the same way as Eigg has Castle Island lying immediately to the south, Muck has Eilean nan Each (Horse Island) lying off to the north-west. This small island, ostensibly for horses which could be taken across to the main island at certain low tides, was, according to Samuel Johnson in his 1773 *Journey to the Western Isles*, only large enough to pasture three sheep. Conversely, the first *Statistical Account*, written a couple of decades later, emphatically points out that there were no sheep at all on Muck but that the islet could be accessed across a 'foul, rocky narrow channel, which frequently ebbs dry'. Dr Johnson of course never went to Muck owing to bad weather but speaks quite authoritatively in describing the main island as being 'two English miles long, and three-quarters of a mile broad'. His knowledge stems from a single dinner conversation with the Laird of Muck and his wife whilst on Skye. The laird, according to Boswell's narrative, appeared to be more interested in explaining away his unfortunate title of 'Laird of Muck' than in discussing the nuances of life in the Small Isles. It will not have escaped the notice of the sharp-witted and astute Dr Johnson that the laird's wife will have been referred to as 'Lady Muck', although he was too discreet to have commented on it. The laird's insistence on using the name 'Monk Island' instead has some anecdotal credence, in that the island was formerly under Church ownership and may even have once housed a monk, but other sources are more convincing. According to the first *Account*, the name stems from the Gaelic 'Eiltran nan Muchd' (Island of Swine), the island also featuring in Monro's 1549 *Description* as 'Swynes Ile' and in a later source of 1793 as 'Insula Porcorum' (Pig Island).

The reason for this name is not clear. The island is not shaped like a pig, nor like any other animal for that matter. If it was used for keeping pigs, perhaps as part of a larger Church estate, which would make some sense, then it seems rather a waste of good fertile land. One possibility is that the name stems from the Gaelic 'mucmhara', meaning 'sea pig' or whale, given that there are often sightings of whales around the islands. This might also explain the alternative name 'Tirr Chrainne' (Pig Island), which for superstitious reasons was only ever used from out at sea. In any event, the laird's efforts to change the name to 'Monk Island' were short-lived, although this name appears in the second *Statistical Account* and on the 1801 map of Argyllshire by George Langlands, thereby affording the laird's wishes a modicum of immortality.

Despite the undoubted benefits of its soil, Muck was severely constrained in terms of natural fuel resources. There was nothing on the island to exploit other than dried seaweed and animal dung. Peat, the staple fuel of most islands in the Hebrides, did not form in Muck and had to be imported from elsewhere. The following description by the Rev. Donald McLean in the first *Statistical Account* flags up not only Muck's dependency on natural peat as a fuel but also the vulnerability of the islanders:

> Formerly they were provided in peats by Rum and Ardnamurchan; of late their supplies were solely from Rum, with much personal toil and danger. From Eigg they import boat loads of heath, when their peats become scarce. In winter 1790 and 1791 there was a general scarcity of firing throughout this parish, which Isle of Muck most severely felt. They were reduced to the necessity of burning different kinds of furniture, such as beds, dressers, stools, barrels; and also house timber, divots, tangles, straw, etc. to dress their victuals.

This importation of fuel would have been at a cost, or by exchange arrangement, although towards the end of the eighteenth century the lairds of Rum and Muck were from the same MacLean family and the peats were given freely. In return Muck's surplus corn was given to Rum. The arrangement also provided grass for the Muck horses.

The richness of the soil also has implications for the survival of archaeological sites and monuments. Almost the entire land surface of the island has been ploughed or planted repeatedly. Marginal areas may have survived unspoiled until the late eighteenth or early nineteenth century, but population pressures eventually squeezed the ubiquitous lazy beds into every available square metre of land and even parts of the moorland at the west. Apart from some areas of hill ground and a few patches of coastal margin that escaped ground disturbance, there is little visual evidence of early settlement. Persistent ploughing has spread out the humps and bumps that often characterise the locations of earlier field monuments. Moreover, Muck has no rabbits, which can play a significant role in pinpointing buried features. Rabbits prefer to excavate their burrows in the softer subsoils and cavities of buried structures and have a tendency to kick up to the ground surface pottery sherds as they burrow. This is most evident on Canna, where the rabbits have been used not only to identify sites but also to give some idea of dating on the basis of diagnostic pottery types. Given these various circumstances, Muck's historic landscape is probably the most difficult of the four islands to untangle.

The assumption must be that the island was always a popular place to settle simply because the soils were so rich; the various census returns show it to have been fairly consistently populated in post-medieval times, with typically between 140 and 190 souls until around 1821. Walker's *Report* of 1764 records a population of 143 divided among three probable townships – Gallanach, Balmeanach and Kiel – the number then growing gradually before a sudden leap to 321 in the 1821 census, partly as a result of the popularity of kelp harvesting. In the census of ten years later the figure had plummeted to less than half that, thanks to the collapse of the kelp market, the Clearances and assisted emigration.

This period of population growth not only increased small-scale agriculture in the margins, but also created an opportunity for Muck's owner to review how the land might be better organised to cater for the growing population. The intention was to divide the island up into crofts in much the same way as was tried on Eigg. Consequently, a plan of landscape division was drawn up by J. A. Chapman in 1809 under the instructions of the Clanranalds, who were in control of the island between 1799 and 1814 (see plate section). This divided the island into forty-seven units served by roads or trackways. The initiative was never fully implemented, but where divisions were imposed they rode roughshod, as on Eigg, over the existing structural remains and field systems. Towards the end of the century a new owner implemented another set of changes, this time for the creation of a model farm at Gallanach on the north coast. An improved field system, more rectilinear than previously, was laid across the central and eastern parts of the island providing yet another layer of change in an already complex pattern of evolution. Of the four islands in the group, Muck was the one whose landscape was most affected by such changes.

There is very little written that is specific to Muck, although plenty of the more general works cited at the end of this book contain relevant information according to theme, especially those dealing with the natural environment. The island's website also contains a useful list of these. The main Muck-specific work is that written by the late Lawrence MacEwen, Laird of Muck himself, *The Isle of Muck – a Short Guide*. This was published privately, first in 1977 and then again, substantially revised, in 2002. His personal memories have since been drawn together by Polly Pullar in *A Drop in the Ocean: Lawrence MacEwen and the Isle of Muck* (2019). Full references are given in the 'Further Reading' section at the end of the book.

Prehistory

Despite the intensity of cultivation over the centuries, not to mention the absence of rabbits, there are still traces of prehistoric activity on the island. As argued for Eigg, it would be surprising if folk voyaging to Rum in the Mesolithic in the search for bloodstone failed to take advantage of Muck's riches but, again as on Eigg, there are no traces of them. There are a number of rock shelters, especially on Eilean nan Each (Horse Island) off the north-west coast, that would have provided natural shelter for hunter-gatherer communities and these might merit detailed investigation. Evidence of later settlement, however, is provided by a small number of prehistoric objects, probably from the Neolithic, in the form of fragments from flint working recovered from the ground at Gallanach in the north and Port Mor in the south-east. Flint is the most durable of all archaeological materials and suggests some kind of occupation on the island in the period around 4000 to 2500 BC. Debitage of this sort is unlikely to have moved far from the place where it was knapped or worked.

The Bronze Age is only a little better represented with a series of four possible burial cairns on the coastal edges and a couple of hut circles in the western moorland. None has survived intact. Of the burial cairns there are at least two at **Aird nan Uan** (3), taking a prominent position overlooking Horse Island. One was partly disturbed to create a burial enclosure for the island's owners, the MacEwans, in the 1920s, during which burnt ashes were recorded as being found. There are two possible further cairns further away to the south-east. There is also a questionable site near the apex of **Beinn Airein** (10) near the Ordnance Survey triangulation point. Its stature and its summit location are in its favour as a Bronze Age burial site, but its turf composition would be unusual.

At least two hut circles are represented – a poor return from what may have been a well-populated island in the Bronze Age. Some idea of their original density can be seen on Eigg and Canna, where the moorland landscapes are liberally peppered with hut circles and their associated enclosures and boundaries. Although both hut circles on Muck have been ravaged by land use and extensive robbing, their shapes are still visible. The larger one lies at **Gleann Mhairten** (20) in the west, the other is on the moorland at **Beinn Airein** (11).

Among the remains of Bronze Age Muck, however, pride of place almost certainly goes to the discovery of the upper part of a sword dateable by its design to around 950 to 750 BC. This was found on the east side of the island at Carn Dearg during groundworks undertaken in the 1920s. Part of its interest is that it was old at the time of disposal and had been repaired, presumably by the type of itinerant smith who set up his temporary workshop on neighbouring Eigg (see Chapter 2) and may have visited Muck too. The sword is now held in the National Museum of Scotland, Edinburgh.

Evidence of later prehistoric activity, typically in the form of coastal promontory forts or duns, is limited on Muck. This is because the coastline lacks the austere rock formations that characterise Eigg and Canna and which provide natural outcrops for fortification. There are three contenders, two of which are questionable while the third is more spectacular. This is at **Caisteal an Duin Bhain** (13), situated at the south-east of the island with a commanding position overlooking the harbour area and adjacent to the main focus of post-medieval settlement and the long-established burial ground. Sheer on all sides and covering an area of some 30m in diameter, surmounted by a wall, it has a very dramatic aspect. Unlike many of the other 'forts' among the islands it appears on some early maps as well as on Chapman's 1809 plan for proposed land divisions, where it is referred to as a 'castle' and defined as a circular feature. A late sixteenth-century account describes it as 'rock or craig built by the Master and Superior of the island in times of wars which was betwixt him and certain enemies'. Inside are a number of lazy beds, reflecting the population pressures on land in the early nineteenth century. The mere fact that islanders were obliged to utilise such an awkward place for cultivation, and in such poor quality soil, is testimony to the desperation of the times. The beds appear to be in depressions which may originally have been used for quarrying stone for the earlier walling.

The two putative forts are decidedly less exciting, one of them at **Fang Mhor** (16), further west on the south of the island, and the other near Gallanach at the north, on the east side of

Aird nan Uan (5). At the former the natural promontory shows little in the way of human modification other than a wall which runs down the promontory rather than across it and appears to enclose two small coastal terraces. It makes no sense as part of an original design but may reflect the previous existence of building stone there worth utilising. That said, the place is awkward to access from both land and sea and too distant from likely population centres to provide a refuge in times of danger. There are similar issues with the other site near Gallanach. This is a more prominent stack about 20m across with a steep seaward side and a gully on the landward side. While it would make a natural fort, there is no evidence for it having been modified other than amorphous remnants of walling lines nearby which may have had their origins there.

Christian impact

Muck lay along the transmission route that brought early Christianity from Ireland to Scotland in the sixth and seventh centuries and, like the rest of the Small Isles, it became a focus for Christian worship. Sources attest that both Muck and Canna were the property of Iona, which later became subsumed under the authority of the Bishopric of the Isles. Canna is often named in these records, but Muck less frequently, its omission probably owing to its size and status, which accounts for its absence from some other descriptions. One of the early references is that of Monro, writing in the mid sixteenth century, who refers to it as 'Swynes Ile' and, in the same breath, points out that it belonged to the Bishop of the Isles, perhaps suggesting its function as a pig farm on the episcopal estate, despite the waste of good land that this would have entailed. Monro also notes that the island had a good falcon's nest, which might suggest that the bishop enjoyed hawking there as one of his more secular activities. Muck was clearly well known in this respect: by the time

Martin Martin was writing in 1695 he specifically commented that the hawks there were reputed to be very good.

There is no surviving church on the island. Any traditional place of worship is likely to have centred on the burial ground in the township of **Kiel** (21) at the south-east, not far from the harbour and the focus of modern housing. The name itself stems from Gaelic 'Cille' (church or cell). The burial ground of unknown antiquity is defined by a dilapidated sub-circular drystone wall and lies just to the south of the ruined township, although there are likely unenclosed burials further to the west. Tucked into its south-east part are the remains of a small stone-faced structure, probably a chapel, standing up to 1m in height in places. Configurations such as this, with a chapel or oratory set within a burial enclosure, are characteristic of Celtic monasticism, although in this case both enclosure and structure are likely to be replacements for earlier, even timber versions. It is hard to believe that the name 'Kiel' could have evolved had there never been an early church or chapel here.

Another reason for believing this to be an early site is the presence of two cross fragments of early date discovered among the packed memorials within the enclosure. These have now been moved to the nearby shop for safekeeping, where they are on display. One is about 1m tall and features an arced cross within an incised circle on a tapered stone. There is a slight mark in the centre indicating where a compass point was set to allow the arcs to be drawn evenly. The other is much smaller and shows a simple Latin cross with slightly rounded armpits inside a box. Stylistic dating places them within the seventh to ninth centuries. Other memorials in the enclosure relate to nineteenth-century burials, while some reflect a history of islanders lost at sea and during the war years. Many are simple boulder memorials and are unmarked.

Just as the nature of the Christian footprint on Eigg might be interpreted through 'cross' placenames, much the same can be said of Muck. There are two certain locations, one on the headland at the south-east of the island at a place denoted as 'Ru Cross' on the Chapman plan. This appears slightly further south on the first-edition Ordnance Survey map, as 'Rubh' a' Chroisein' (Headland of the Cross). Despite the slight variation in position on the two maps, the general location is significant. The cross would have taken a prominent position on the high ground on the east flank of the harbour, with the dominating fort of Caisteal an Duin Bhain on the west flank. Anyone approaching, in addition to being somewhat intimidated, would have been in no doubt that Muck housed a significant Christian community. It was also a notoriously difficult harbour to access, and there is some merit in thinking that the cross would also have been positioned to provide symbolic reassurance for those entering or leaving.

The other 'cross' location is at some distance from the burial area on raised ground with the name 'Cnoc na Croise' (Mound of the Cross). This was an important position in that it signified the nucleus of Christian activity in its relationship to the chapel and burial ground. It occupied the nearest high ground, where it could be seen for miles around and took on the same symbolic role as similar crosses on both Eigg and Canna. Sadly, there is no evidence of the exact positions of these two crosses on Muck and even more sadly, no evidence of the crosses themselves. If the surviving Canna cross is anything to go by, they would have been richly decorated by the skilled craftsmen of the day.

The later Reformation appears to have been largely successful on Muck, much more so than, for example, on Eigg. Walker's data from 1764 indicate that the majority of folk on Rum and Muck were Protestant, as opposed to the 'papist' majority on the other two islands. This may reflect the interests of their respective lairds rather than the personal beliefs of the islanders themselves. In a story recounted by Dr Johnson, the Laird of Rum, who was related to the Laird of Muck, was on his way to the kirk to listen to the minister deliver his monthly service when he came across some islanders going to mass instead. He 'converted' them by beating them around the head with a yellow stick (presumably a cane) 'and drove them to the kirk, from which they have never departed'. This, Dr Johnson remarked, was why the Catholics there referred to Protestantism as 'the religion of the Yellow Stick'.

Norse impact

In common with the other three islands Muck bowed to Norse sovereignty at some point in the eighth or ninth century. In fact, it may well have been especially prized in view of its fertility and a coastline which, while not especially rich in the soft sandy bays preferred by the Norse, did at least provide a few landings in the Gallanach area at the north. The island offers little in the way of Norse placenames, a fact sometimes ascribed to its rather unremarkable topography. However, given that the Norse were fond of naming every single slope, crest, gully, coastal protuberance or other landscape feature, this seems unlikely. More probable is that there was a minimal but dominant Norse presence on the island overseeing a more populous Gaelic-speaking native community.

Muck's claim to Norse fame lies at the north of the island, east of Gallanach, at a place called **Toaluinn** (29), where the grass-grown foundations of a structure can still be seen on marginal land near the shore. They are only partially visible as a result of overlying lazy beds, probably from the early nineteenth century when the population was at its peak and cultivable soil at a premium. The location is on a storm beach with good access to fertile soil and fresh water, and adjacent to a natural rock-cut slipway into the sea for boat access. This is the only probable Norse building in the Small Isles, defined as such by its size, design and construction. It differs from the foundations of the eighteenth- and nineteenth-century structures in its length (around 13m, plus an outshot at one end) and its unusually thick walls, typically over 2m wide with boulders defining the inner and outer faces. But the key element in favour of a Norse origin is its bow-sided shape, which is distinctive from the more rectangular design of all the other stone foundations on the islands.

Norse houses are rare in Scotland, but the design and construction of this one have strong parallels in Unst, Shetland, and in the Scandinavian homeland. It evidences early settlement, probably in the ninth century, at a time when the Norse pattern of living was 'imported' from the homeland and transferred into a new environment. Unlike the native dwellings it sits in isolation rather than within a group and may even belong to one of the dominant families brought in to oversee the island. Opinion now suggests that domination was by simple transmission of power rather than by burning and looting – a transfer which also allowed the two early Christian crosses to survive relatively intact.

Medieval and post-medieval landscapes

The historical record is silent about any major events in Muck until the end of the sixteenth century, when in 1588, together with Rum, Canna and Eigg, the island was invaded by MacLean of Duart in redress for the alleged desecration of Iona by the Clanranalds. This seems rather unfair, in that Muck and Canna were under Church ownership at that time and had little to do with the Clanranalds, who owned Rum and Eigg. All four islands were recorded as being burned and looted and their populations destroyed. MacLean's men included a mercenary group of Spaniards whose Armada vessel had grounded and who were bribed to join in. A source for the event written shortly afterwards refers to the four islands as 'Canna, Rum, Eigg and the Isle of Elennole', the last presumably being Muck, given that there is no other island in the vicinity. In a court case starting in 1590 the event is recounted in detail, this time the island appearing more positively as 'Ellen-ne-Muk' in a vivid description of how MacLean of Duart had murdered 'a grit nowmer of wyffis, barnis and puir laborers of the ground'. This incident appears to have been the only one of note. The later, mid eighteenth-century assaults which took place on Eigg in a search for arms and rebels after the 1745 uprising seem not to have been extended to Muck, or if they were they were not deemed noteworthy.

DEMOGRAPHICS, TOWNSHIPS AND THE CLEARANCES

Population figures prior to Walker's *Report* of 1764 are unreliable and it is not possible to see what effect, if any, the 1588 atrocity at the hands of MacLean had on numbers. Walker's population figure of 143 divided into twenty-eight families would have been concentrated in townships crammed within marginal land, in which buildings, pens and enclosures were reused or replaced on similar footprints to avoid straying into valuable agricultural soils. Those footprints were probably created centuries earlier, many being reused, extended or widened as population pressures increased. As part of the expansion more and more land was taken into cultivation and more and more lazy beds spread into every conceivable space.

The presence of twenty-eight families begs the question of how many townships there were and where they were located. One early record appears in a report by Thomas Knox, Bishop of the Isles, in 1626. He was describing the state of his diocese and gives a brief island-by-island account in which he refers to Muck as having 'onlie tua tounes' and belonging to the Laird of Coll. Chapman's plan of 1809 indicates three townships, not two, from east to west as Kiel, Balmeanach and Gallanach. If the location of houses depicted on the plan is to be believed, the population centres of Gallanach and Balmeanach lie very close together, suggesting perhaps that Gallanach had been split into two to produce the three townships evident on Chapman's plan. The buildings are schematic but the plan shows settlement foci of dwellings, yards and enclosures as well as basic land use.

The increase to three townships may reflect the growing

population, which had almost doubled by 1786, mostly as a result of the growth of the kelp industry, despite an initial emigration between 1788 and 1790 in which 236 folk from the Small Isles left for America and the mainland. According to Rev. McLean's first *Statistical Account*, most of these émigrés were from Eigg, the number of the Muck contingent being undefined. He also described how 'the country was overstocked with people'. The Muck population continued to increase, however, with a recorded peak of 321 in the 1821 census, until the emigration of 1828, the same year as the almost wholesale clearance of Rum, when, according to the second *Statistical Account*, half of Muck's population also left. Curiously, despite the enormous impact of kelping on the island, which in part necessitated this emigration after the collapse of the kelp market, there is no surviving physical evidence for kelping (or none that this author could find or that is cited in trove.scot) in the form of platforms or kilns.

Another component of the domestic subsistence economy was that of fishing, although it never seems to have been exploited to its optimum, the islanders seeming to rely on the potato as their insurance against starvation. In the mid sixteenth century Monro commented that the island was 'verey guid for fishing', and in 1773 Boswell mentioned that fish abounded around the coasts. There were possible issues with safe harbourage for boats (see below), but nothing that would deter fishing on a domestic level. Local fishing was probably conducted by means of fish traps, which obviated the need for a boat. These consisted of loosely built low stone walls constructed across a bay, over which the fish swam on an incoming tide; when the tide ebbed out again, some of them became trapped behind the wall and could simply be collected by hand or netted. There is a good example at **Bagh a' Ghallanaich (Coralag)** (7) on the north coast, which consists of an arc of boulders set across a beach between two rock outcrops.

Rev. McLean observed in the first *Account* that the coasts of Muck and Canna were good for catching cod and ling but that there were only about fifteen fishing boats in the whole of the parish. Moreover, at the time he was writing the fish were being exported to the Clyde markets rather than being consumed internally. Any boat containing these catches presumably sailed out of **Port Mor** (24) at the south-east of the island, one of the few inlets on the coastline with reasonable harbourage. A slipway some 40m long cleared through the rocks at the north end of the inlet is still visible at low tide and may be one of the places used. A likely boat naust sits next to the slipway, evidenced by a boat-shaped scoop in the ground above the high tide levels with its open end facing seawards. This represents a type of roofless boat house and has strong Norse antecedents. A boat could be hauled in when not needed and sheltered from adverse weather. The naust here is partially stone-lined for a greater degree of permanence. Also at **Port Mor** (25) is a narrower slipway for smaller boats, which lies a little further seaward to the south-east.

According to the first *Account*, there were 'a few creeks, which afford shelter to small boats, but no safe harbour for vessels. In two of the creeks are piers in an imperfect state.' This may have accounted for any larger-scale fishing to alleviate growing poverty. It is difficult to relate surviving remains with these observations or to date them, but at **Port Chreadhaih** (23) on the north coast there is a quay which also appears on the Chapman plan together with a slipway, and there is a smaller slipway through cleared rocks at **Port nam Maol** (27) at the north-east. The second *Account*, written in 1836, reiterated that there was 'no safe harbour' but that small boats could be secured 'by means of a quay built by the inhabitants'. This is likely to have been the primary version of the more southerly of the two piers visible today at Port Mor, which is now concrete-clad but was originally constructed of boulders.

There seems to have been little interest in seafaring in the wider context; in fact, the first *Account* claimed that none of the islanders enlisted for the navy when the laird required it of them. Walker's criticism of the islanders, that they were 'idle to the last degree' because they had no industry other than agriculture, may contain an element of truth. According to Dr Johnson's account (admittedly second-hand), the laird had to import a tailor and a blacksmith when the need arose as there were so few trades on the island.

Chapman's plan of 1809 shows where the growing population was focused. Two distinctive township boundaries run the full girth of the island, roughly from north to south dividing the island into three. The eastern one is marked as a 'stone dyke' but the western one merely a 'March'. The area of Gallanach township lies to the west, Kiel to the east and Balmeanach in the middle. The two boundaries that divide the three can still be traced intermittently through the fields in the form of eroded stone and turf dykes, sometimes connecting natural features or lengths of walling. The first-edition Ordnance Survey map, surveyed in 1877, shows the line of the **Gallanach/Balmeanach (19a–b)** boundary but not that of the **Balmeanach/Kiel (8a–b)** boundary. The second edition of 1903 shows neither boundary, although their alignments can be partially picked out on the landscape by following field boundaries and walls. As elements of land organisation these boundaries had been wiped out in the space of less than a century.

It is difficult to reconcile the numbers of dwellings on Chapman's plan with the foundation remains visible on the ground today. Anyone walking up from the ferry, past the burial ground, will see what is effectively a ruined townscape on a terrace north-west of Port Mor. The place is called **Sean Bhaile (28)**, which is the settlement name within the township lands of Kiel and the best-preserved vestige of the old township system on the island. Despite the foundations being partially buried, it is still possible to walk up what was once the walled main street and count as many as forty separate structures, far in excess of the small cluster of seven buildings shown by Chapman. His depiction may simply be indicative of a multiple settlement rather than showing absolute numbers of dwellings, or it may be an instance of cartographic licence. The same argument may apply to his depictions of individual buildings in the Balmeanach and Gallanach townships (see below). Otherwise, if Chapman's plan is accurate it is hard to explain where all the islanders were living at the time. According to Walker's figures, the average number of persons per household across the parish as a whole in 1764 was approximately 5.3. While there is no precise population figure available for Muck at the time the plan was surveyed, it can be calculated crudely on the upward population trend as being about 250. Using a household quotient of 5.3 this would entail a stock of around forty-seven buildings by comparison with the twenty-nine shown by Chapman.

It is likely that some structures were built after the Chapman plan had been drawn up. Even casual scrutiny shows the buildings at Sean Bhaile to belong to more than one phase of development, although nothing can be dated with any accuracy. The elements that are visible, however, are unlikely to be any earlier than the mid to late nineteenth century. Somewhere within the ruins will be the dwellings which reflect the population peak of 1821 that brought about the major exodus of 1828. The main street itself appears to be the latest part to have been built, being more formal and planned than the rest, the walls on either side being superimposed on or incorporating earlier buildings, including enclosures underneath. This may represent the enforced clearance of people from the rest of the island to make way for cattle and sheep, with the misguided intention that they should make their living from fishing. The density and overall ad hoc nature of the structures below might be seen as a last-ditch attempt to stave this off and eke out a living that would make it possible to avoid eviction or emigration. For many it proved to be a false hope.

The buildings are a medley of shapes and sizes. A few are over 10m in length, the smallest less than half that, with the majority lying somewhere in between. There seems to have been a standard building technique of constructing the walls with two stone faces, an inner wall-fill of turf and slightly rounded corners. The single doorway is invariably in the centre of one of the long walls. The presence of a small number of kilns and associated barns shows that this was an active environment with intended permanency. At the north end of the complex several of the remains have survived particularly well, notably one of the corn kilns, which is in an almost usable condition. This part of the complex, which is well north of the buildings shown by Chapman, is also absent on the second-edition Ordnance Survey map of 1903, leaving open the possibility that the township was still being built and occupied in the early part of the twentieth century.

There is one building that stands apart from the others, however, namely at **Eilean Dubh (15)** on the eastern side of the island, in the township of Kiel and at some distance from the Sean Bhaile settlement. Small and stone-built, it sits on its own next to a watercourse and below the level of the stream. Its location is well concealed, possibly deliberately, and one interpretation is that it represents an illicit still. It is undated, in fact undatable, but appears to have no farming function. Its position by the stream is clearly significant, and believing it to be a still, while colourful, is as good as any other interpretation.

The **Balmeanach (9)** settlement is less spectacular than that at Keil but is still traceable on the ground. The township consists of a thin strip of land running down the centre of the island, with two clusters of building foundations lying in the north near the western boundary dyke. Both of these clusters are shown on Chapman's plan; one group of three has enclosures, while the other group of seven, which lies slightly further to the north, is tightly packed together and now in woodland. There is little left to see on the ground, at best only grass-grown lengths of foundations which have been extensively robbed out. In places, however, there is some evidence of earlier footings, indicating continuity from earlier structures. Balmeanach was probably abandoned in the mid eighteenth century and is not depicted on the 1877 first-edition Ordnance Survey map.

The remains of the Gallanach settlement have vanished almost completely. Chapman depicts half a dozen buildings and two enclosures astride a burn near the shoreline at the north of the island. Three of them are set around an open area in a U-formation as though belonging to a common unit and now lie buried under the modern Gallanach farm buildings. The others lie slightly to the east within enclosed fields but are not obvious on the present landscape. Chapman also shows a group of six buildings and an enclosure some distance away to the south-east on the edge of the dyke boundary with Balmeanach. These sit adjacent to the Balmeanach dwellings on the other side of the dyke and may represent an original part of Balmeanach before the township was possibly divided. There is now little visible other than some slight field undulations.

SHIELINGS AND THE 'OLD SYSTEM'

The mixed farming economy that was the essence of island living from the Middle Ages onwards was one which relied on the practice of transhumance. This required livestock to be moved up into the shielings to take advantage of the summer vegetation. It is surprising that on an island as small as Muck there are so many shieling huts. These are heavily concentrated on the western moorland, where a typical group of six can be found on the finger of land at **Aird nan Uan (6)**. Further south in the Gleann Mhairten area there are at least thirty huts together with a number of associated features. As this is the main moorland region of the island and constitutes about a quarter of the island's total area, it may well be that it was available to all the townships and not just to the folk of Gallanach in whose township the moorland lies. Shortage of pasture was an issue picked up in the first *Statistical Account*, which pointed out that if the islands were to get better organised and arrange 'a proper plan' then there might be mutual benefit with Rum that would 'render their cattle fitter for market'.

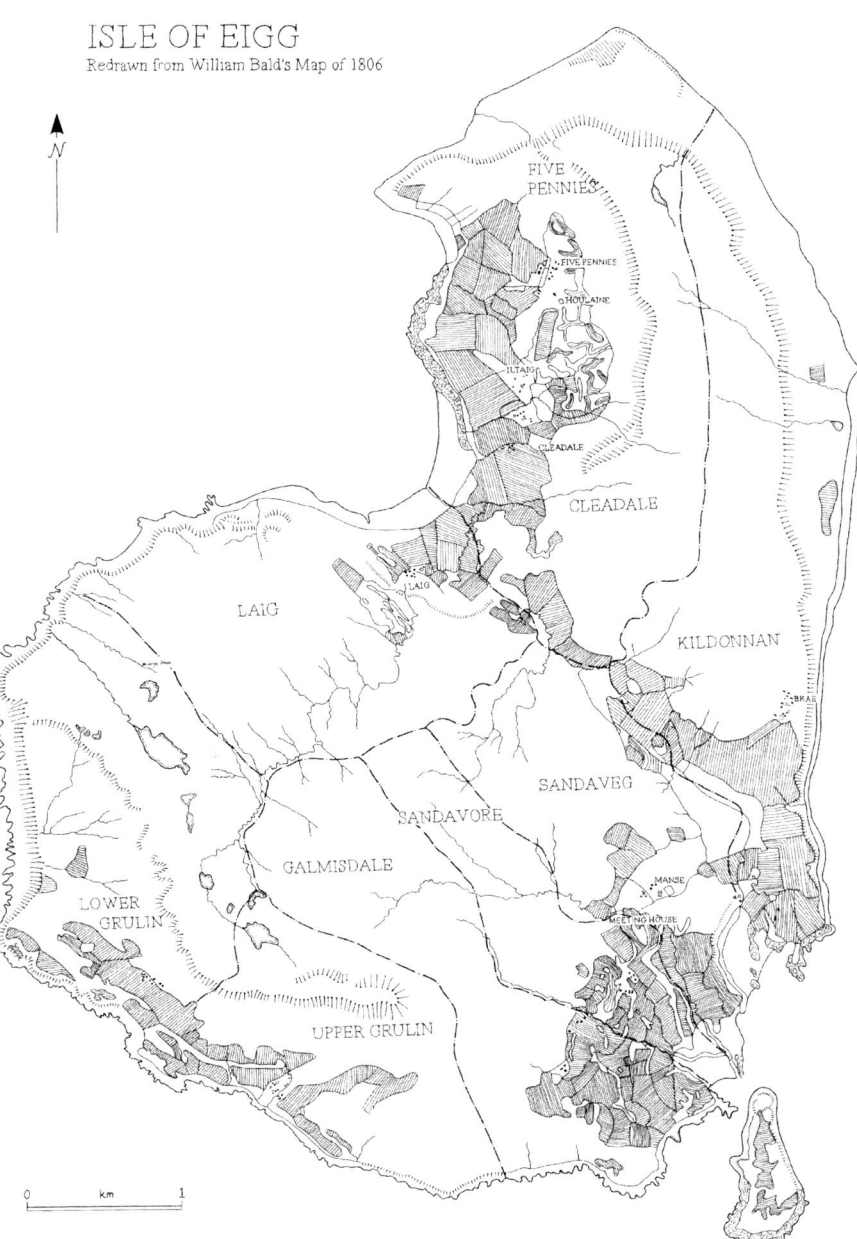

ISLE OF EIGG
Redrawn from William Bald's Map of 1806

N

FIVE PENNIES

FIVE PENNIES

HOULAINE

ILTAIG

CLEADALE

CLEADALE

LAIG

LAIG

KILDONNAN

BRAE

SANDAVEG

SANDAVORE

GALMISDALE

MANSE

MEETING HOUSE

LOWER GRULIN

UPPER GRULIN

0   km   1

William Bald's 1806 map of Eigg (© Courtesy of HES. Traced from the original
while the map was hanging in Eigg lodge and redrawn by Philip Judge)

LEFT The roofless church, Kildonan, Eigg (John Hunter)

LOWER LEFT The Lodge, Eigg (John Hunter)

BELOW The Sheela-na-gig at Kildonan, Eigg (© Crown Copyright: HES)

Loch of the Great Women and island dun, Eigg (John Hunter)

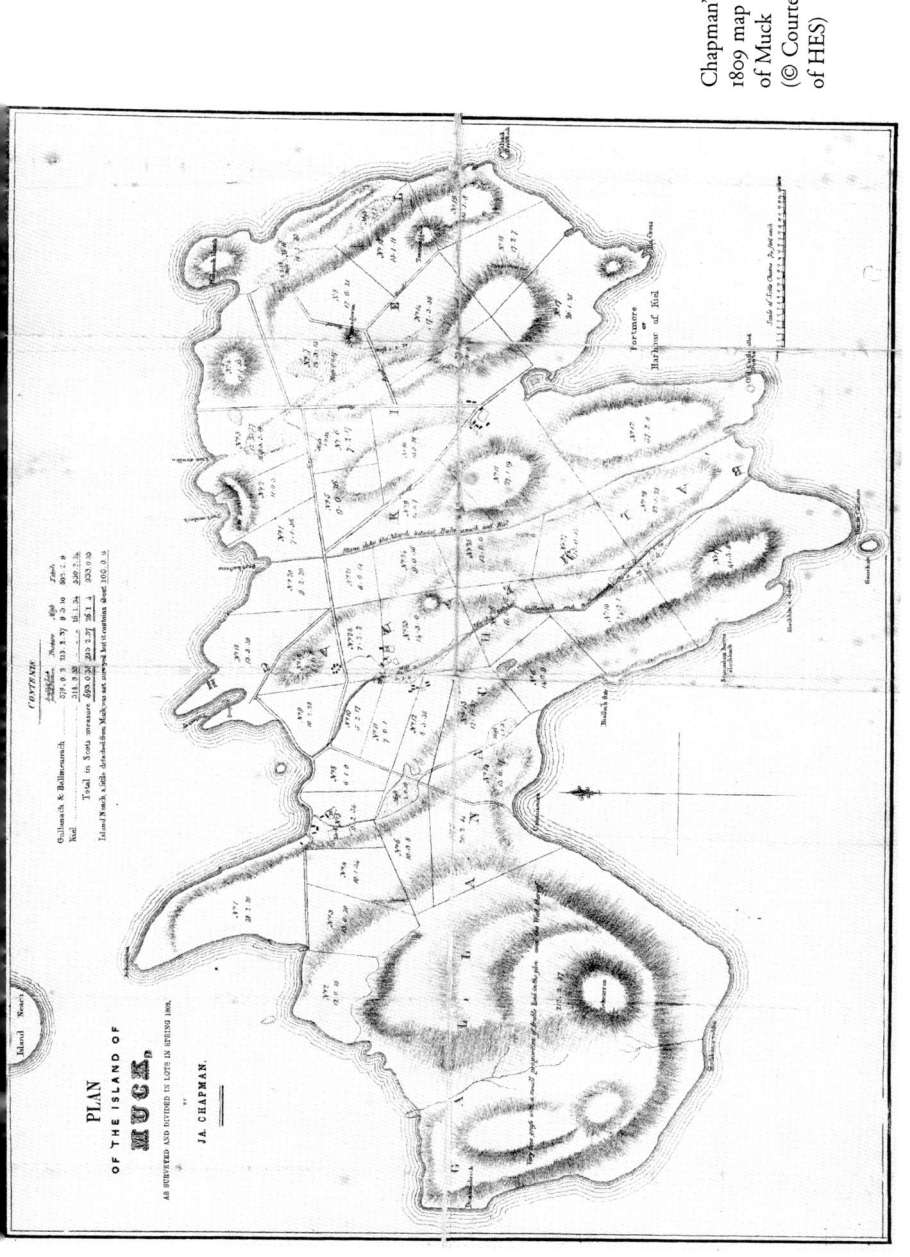

Chapman's 1809 map of Muck (© Courtesy of HES)

The burial site at Aird nan Uan, Muck (John Hunter)

Captain Swinburne's Pier House, Muck (John Hunter)

Sean Bhaile settlement, Muck (John Hunter)

The 'fort' at Caisteal an Duin Bhain, Muck (John Hunter)

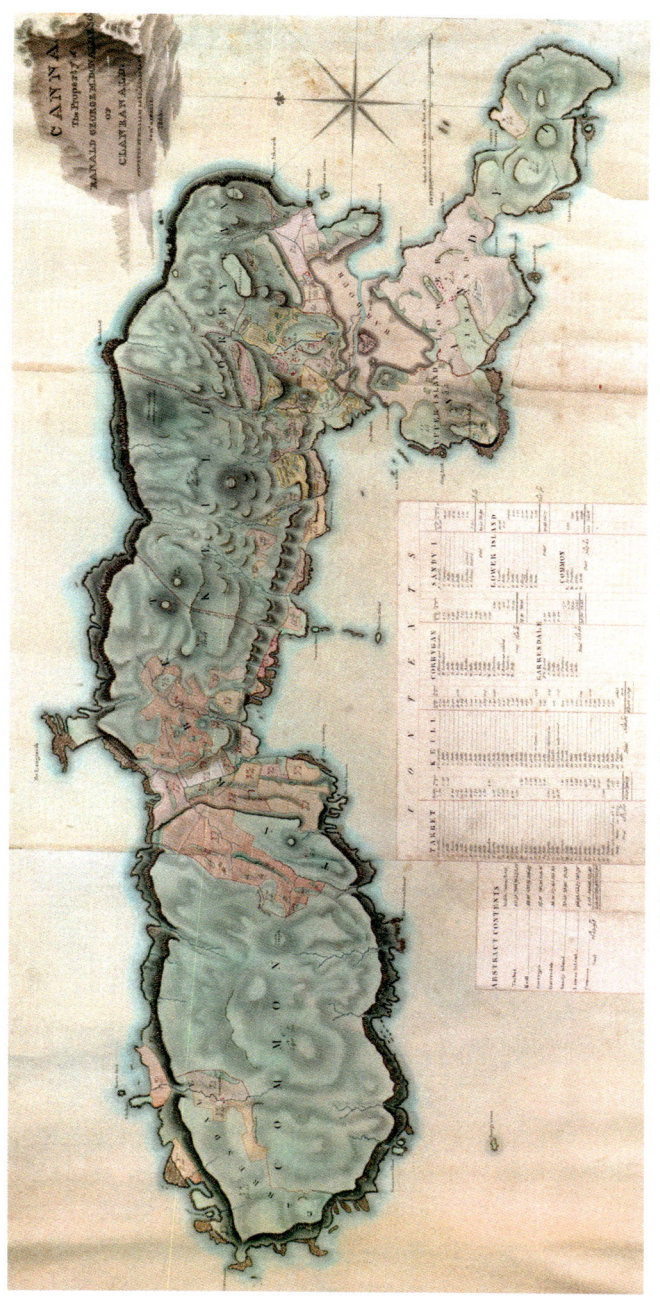

William Bald's 1805 Map of Canna (National Trust for Scotland)
Original map in Canna House.

ABOVE The Nunnery, Canna (© Crown Copyright: HES)

RIGHT Canna cross from the east (© Crown Copyright: HES)

BELOW Coroghon Castle, Canna (© Headland Archaeology Ltd)

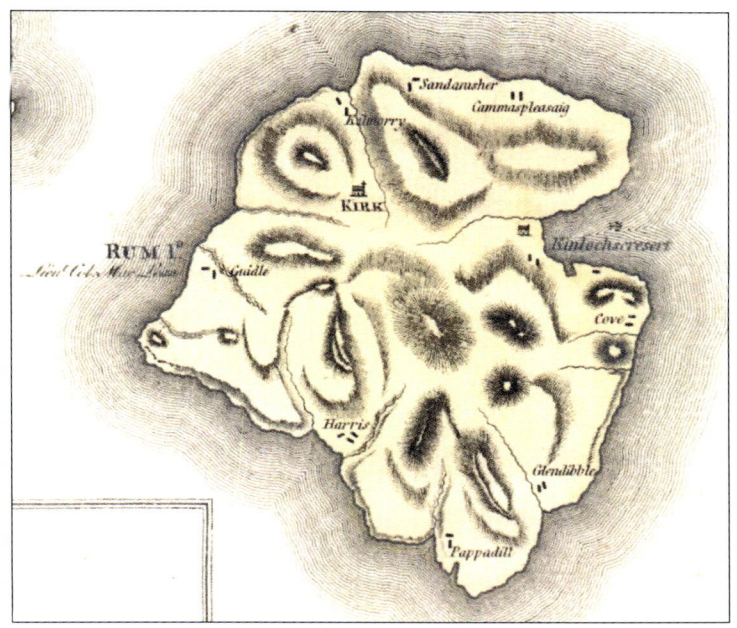

ABOVE George Langlands' 1801 map of Rum.
(Trustees of the National Library of Scotland)

BELOW Kinloch Castle,
Rum (Andrew Beaton)

TOP LEFT The Protest Rock, Rum (Andrew Beaton)

TOP RIGHT MacLean family farm, Carn nan Dobhran Bhig, Rum (John Hunter)

LEFT The Bullough mausoleum, Rum (Andrew Beaton)

BELOW The graveyard at Kilmory, Rum (John Hunter)

The huts in the Gleann Mhairten area are typical of those on the other islands in terms of their construction, consisting of a base of drystone walling and corbelling, some showing evidence of a part-turf superstructure. In most instances only the foundations survive and reflect small structures typically barely more than 2.5m in coarse diameter. Some stand in isolation, others in pairs, with occasional evidence of subdivision for the storage of dairy produce in addition to the temporary accommodation needed for those supervising the stock. Some of them, such as those at **Achadh na Creige** (1) at the north end of the area, appear to be in a more complex, organised local landscape with remains of enclosures, pens, field banks and patches of cultivation, not to mention a rock shelter. There are also remains of a rectangular structure measuring about 5 × 3m, which may or may not be contemporary. They seem more concentrated than those on Eigg and Canna and it is hard to avoid the impression that on Muck this represents not just a seasonal exercise in transhumance but rather an attempt to create a more permanent level of settlement on second-rate land. The circumstance in which this might be relevant would most probably be population pressure, but it might also reflect the need for temporary accommodation or 'camps' for seasonal workers arriving to harvest the kelp. In either case it further indicates the need to cultivate every conceivable patch of land no matter how poor the soil.

There are also some huts on the finger of hill land towards the south of the island, on the east flank of **Fionn-aird** (17) above Leabaidh Dhonnchaidh, as well as a scatter among other patches of higher ground dotted around the island which have escaped agricultural destruction and which show much the same phenomena. There are about eleven huts which sit in groups on a natural terrace on the east face of Fionn-aird, packed around by areas of lazy beds crammed into the spaces between rock outcrops and natural features. The whole landscape is confusing. Some of the huts have been constructed over the remains of others and several seem to sit inside a larger stony enclosure. Some are more rectangular and slightly larger than the typical sub-circular hut. Without archaeological intervention the most obvious interpretation is that the site was originally used for transhumance and consisted of simple shieling huts but was subsequently extended and rebuilt for other purposes. The buildings are nucleated as opposed to being dispersed in the usual shieling way and in this respect, as on Gleann Mhairten, seem to be different from those on the other islands.

Also difficult to explain are a series of field banks on uncultivated land in the south-west part of the island. These may have been used for controlling stock in the higher pastures and would indicate organised activity, possibly in dividing up the common land between the townships. None appear on Chapman's plan and in any event they are earth- as opposed to stone-built. They are virtually impossible to date but are more than likely to relate to cattle rather than the sheep which arrived later. The first *Statistical Account* makes it clear that there were no sheep on the island at the end of the eighteenth century, and the author of the second *Account*, writing in 1836, only mentions that the island was 'well adapted for the rearing of black cattle'. Sheep were introduced in the mid nineteenth century and necessitated more substantial and formal alterations to the landscape in the shape of walling and enclosures. Some of these have survived on Horse Island, where stone walling has been built across narrow coastal gullies either to keep the sheep safely on the island or, more likely, to keep the island's good grass for the horses and force the sheep to graze on the seaweed along the shore. On Canna the abandoned homesteads of evicted islanders were quarried for stone to build sheep dykes and in all probability this occurred on Muck too, but there is no evidence for it and much of the sheep walling will itself have been reused in subsequent improvements.

IMPROVEMENTS

The division of the landscape into plots as defined on the Chapman plan was never fully implemented, but the beginnings of the programme of introducing crofting divisions can be seen in new lengths of walling which match the divisions shown on the plan. Muck was the first of the Small Isles to introduce the crofting system and the plan provides a rare opportunity to see how it was thought out. The divisions were defined by straight lines, presumably using a ruler, and appear to have taken little account of the topography or much in the way of existing divisions, in many cases striding across areas of lazy beds. They also utilised some natural features as terminals. The two township dykes that crossed the island from north to south were overridden in some places, but in others were adapted as boundary lines in their own right.

The intention was to define the crofting units with drystone walling. As well as being labour-intensive the exercise required a vast amount of stone, probably even more than could be supplied from pulling down the empty houses of those who had been evicted. Wall building may have started in the east and south-east of the island, where good examples still survive, but there are other parts of the island where walls are non-existent and where the building work seems never to have started. Abandonment of the programme might be interpreted at Blar na Fionn-aird, west of Port Mor, where a length of wall running up from the harbour area ends suddenly in the middle of nowhere next to a heap of stones, almost as though the workmen had finished for the day but never returned to continue the job.

Every crofting unit was intended to include a small farm dwelling within its curtilage. These are not depicted on Chapman's plan, as his purpose was to present only a schematic division of the landscape, but there is plenty of evidence on the ground to show that many were completed and occupied. Like the surviving field walling they tend to lie in the south-east of the island and usually consist of a dwelling with a yard and a small number of outbuildings, all drystone-built. If, as seems likely, they were built soon after the 1809 plan, their occupation was relatively short-lived. They appear on the first-edition Ordnance Survey six-inch map of 1877 but are mostly unroofed. By the time of the second edition of 1903 only a small number are depicted. The key survivor was the main farm on the island, at Gallanach at the north, later to become the laird's residence. This appears on Chapman's plan and continues to appear on all subsequent Ordnance Survey maps. The presence there of two large late nineteenth-century byres, which are still standing, indicates a heavy reliance on cattle as indicated in both the first and the second *Statistical Account*.

The grass-grown foundations of farming units visible on the ground show that the buildings were relatively well organised into units of domestic dwellings and outbuildings, quite different to the higgledy-piggledy arrangement seen at the earlier foundations at Sean Bhaile. The dwelling component tends to be larger than in earlier examples, and there is a strong element of planning in the manner in which the buildings are set out and constructed. This may be seen clearly in examples at **Cnoc an Fheur Lochain** (14) on the east side of the island, at **Blar na Fionn-aird** (12), west of Port Mor, and on the other side of the island at **Achadh na Creige** (2), to the west of Gallanach.

Later ownership

Although Muck was owned by the MacLeans of Coll during these times, the improvements were handled by the Clanranalds, who took on the MacLeans' debts. In 1854 the island was sold to Captain Thomas Swinburne, who implemented a series of widespread changes. Not only was Swinburne an experienced seafaring man and an acknowledged authority on fishing, but he was also aware of the need for the island to be profitable. In this respect, and like many other lairds, he believed sheep to be the best solution at the time and set about introducing sheep on a large scale. To facilitate this he drained bogs, built or improved roads and constructed stone walls. He realised from the outset that Muck could never be developed commercially unless boats could arrive and depart with a minimum of difficulty. To this end he built Pier House at **Port Mor** (26) to act as a store for boat equipment and salt, together with an adjacent pier. His aim was to improve the fishing not just in Muck but in the whole area of the Small Isles. A very characteristic building with a forestair leading to the upper floor, Pier House was later used as a schoolhouse. A new large pier was constructed just north of an earlier rock pier. It had an adjunct at the head which effectively created a small harbour on the landward side. Swinburne also revamped the road that led north from the pier across the island to Gallanach farm at the north, which was to become the laird's residence. Several of the farm buildings there date to this period and were constructed as a model farm slightly further to the east of the original farm buildings. The improvements at Port Mor, a stone's throw from the settlement at Sean Bhaile and the burial ground, consolidated the importance of the harbour area as a focal point for the island's community. It remains so today with modern housing, the island shop, the community centre and the new roll-on-roll-off ferry terminal.

Swinburne held strong views as to how the local waters could best be exploited for the fishing stocks, particularly the shoals of cod and ling that frequented them. He was conversant with the type of boat best suited to fishing, dismissing the local boats out of hand, and recognised the need to organise the fishing in tandem with defined markets. Like the writers of the two editions of *Statistical Account* many decades earlier, he was well aware of the need for better harbours, although his new pier at Port Mor went some way to address this. He also owned Eilean Shona, an island smaller than Muck lying off the mainland, where he had introduced larger deep-sea vessels. In 1888 he addressed the Napier Commission on the topic of how larger-scale fishing could improve the wealth and security of the crofting community, but Muck was not mentioned in his address, possibly because it had never realised his fishing ambitions.

There are, however, a number of coastal improvements around the island which can be attributed to Swinburne. The quay at **Port Chreadhaih** (23), which appears on the Chapman plan but not on the first-edition Ordnance Survey map, is depicted on the later Ordnance Survey map of 1903 and may have been consolidated during Swinburne's time. It was extended from its original construction and now also has a series of metal mooring rings set into the surface. Also at Port Chreadhaih one of the slipways has been modified using a type of tramway system introduced by Swinburne for hauling up the boats. The track was made of metal runners set on wooden sleepers and can be traced for about 65m at low tide. Elements of it still survive together with a set of bogeys. The fact that this device was necessary must reflect the presence of the type of larger boat that Swinburne recommended. Other traces of his coastline improvements are less obvious but nevertheless reflect his persistence in encouraging maritime interest, even at a local level. These include a narrow slipway cleared through boulders at **Leabaidh Dhonnchaidh** (22) on the west side of Fionn-aird and another at Achadh na Creige to the north. Both relate to individual farmsteads and are presumably late in the sequence. At both these sites the farmsteads have been restored and re-roofed as holiday homes.

In 1896 the island was sold to a new owner, Lawrence Thompson MacEwen, who called himself Robert Thompson. He had been an international journalist who appears to have made his fortune by a sideline in arms dealing. He purchased both Eigg and Muck at the same time, his intention being to turn Eigg into an exclusive hunting estate, for which purpose he proposed to move the entire Eigg population to Muck. The whole initiative fell flat and although he spent time on Eigg enjoying his hunting in a more limited way than he had intended, he made a number of changes on Muck. These included rebuilding the house at **Gallanach** (18) by adding a second storey and a cobbled square, and introducing yet another field system over the one proposed by Chapman. Like Chapman's it was never fully implemented, but elements of it seem to be related to the Chapman system. Vestiges of both are visible on the Ordnance Survey second-edition map in what can best be described as an extremely confusing landscape evolution. MacEwen retained ownership of the whole island, which has remained in the family to the present day. Since the 1920s members of the family have been buried in a mound on the prominent headland at **Aird nan Uan** (4) and remembered in a broken circle of memorial stones containing name plaques. They share the mound with their Bronze Age farming predecessors, in an expression of their common ground and interest.

Places to Visit: Muck

Achadh na Creige

1. Shieling huts. NRHE ID 291760. Grid ref: NM 3990 7969.

This is a complex area of shieling huts, cultivation plots, enclosures, banking, a rectangular structure and a focal rock shelter set in moorland. The area has a complex evolution but appears to have greater degree of permanence than is usual for a shieling site.

2. Nineteenth-century farming unit and slipway. NRHE ID 108861. Grid ref: NM 4008 8009.

This farm unit of three buildings was once part of the new crofting landscape of the early nineteenth century with enclosures and pens. One of the buildings, measuring about 8 × 5m, is complete with modifications and a turf roof, now known as 'Gallanach Cottage'. A kiln barn with kiln stands nearby to the south-east.

Aird nan Uan

3. Bronze Age burial cairns. NRHE ID 22194. Grid ref: NM 4011 8068.

Four probable burial cairns lie in this very prominent position, two on the tip of the headland and two about 80m to the south-east. The largest with a diameter of some 8m and a kerb of boulders has been partly disturbed to create the later MacEwen family burial enclosure on the crest of the hill (site 4).

4. MacEwen family graves. Grid ref: NM 4011 8068.
A broken circle of memorial stones marks what has been the
burial ground of the MacEwen family since the 1920s, incorporated into the earlier Bronze Age burial cairn (site 3). Names of
the family are engraved on metal plaques on the stones.

5. ?Fort. Grid ref: NM 4039 8036.
This prominent stack has a steep seaward side and is defined
on the landward side by a gully, effectively enclosing an area of
some 20m across. Although it shows no modification, it would
be extraordinary if, given its location and size, it had not been
used. Lengths of walling in the vicinity may have been quarried
from it.

6. Shieling huts. NRHE ID 291667. Grid ref: NM 4019 8062.
The remains of six huts are visible on the eastern slope, typically
2 × 2m, five being small but one appearing to have a figure-of-
eight profile. They are isolated from a surrounding landscape
littered with banks of lazy beds.

Bagh a' Ghallanaich (Coralag)

7. Fish trap. NRHE ID 291347. Grid ref: NM 4076 8017.
On the north coast near Gallanach farm, this fish trap can be
seen best when the tide is out. It consists of an arc of stones,
broken in places, stretching across a sandy bay between two
rock outcrops.

Balmeanach/Kiel

*8. Township boundary dyke. NRHE ID 317699. Grid ref: from
8a NM 4110 8039 to 8b NM 4191 7874.*
This boundary dyke of earth and stone once ran down the full
girth of the island but now survives only sporadically as a result
of later landscape divisions. It appears on Chapman's 1809 plan
marked as a 'Stone dyke the March between Balmeanach and
Kiel'.

Balmeanach

9. Township settlement. *NRHE ID 278654. Grid ref: NM 4119 7996.*

Two groups of robbed building foundations can be traced on the ground and are also evident on Chapman's 1809 plan. One group consists of three buildings with large enclosures, while the other group of at least seven buildings sits in woodland slightly further to the north

Beinn Airein

10. ?Bronze Age burial cairn. *NRHE ID 22139. Grid ref: NM 4030 7915.*

The mound here has a diameter of around 6m and seems to be composed mostly of turf to a standing height of about 0.7m. Its size and its classic summit position are convincing for a cairn burial but the turf-based composition would be unusual.

11. Hut circle. *NRHE ID 291887. Grid ref: NM 4032 7938.*

Sitting among other structural remains including shieling huts and a pen, this hut circle is distinctive in its collapse with an estimated diameter of around 7m. Some facing stones and a possible entrance are evidenced among the rubble.

Blar na Fionn-aird

12. Nineteenth-century farming unit. *NRHE ID 278625. Grid ref: NM 4132 7928.*

This farming unit consists of three sub-rectangular buildings set in an L-shape amid a landscape of lazy beds and banking with an adjoining enclosure. The farm building itself, which measures about 8.5 × 4m, is of rubble-faced construction with a doorway in the centre of the long wall protected by a length of baffle walling.

Caisteal an Duin Bhain

13. Fort. NRHE ID 22137. Grid ref: NM 4219 7865.
This represents the modification of an impressive natural promontory sitting conveniently at the harbour entrance. Access is gained through a steep passageway at the north-east and there is a perimeter wall around the top with a diameter of around 30m. Later internal lazy beds may have reused depressions from original quarrying. The thick stone wall that crosses the promontory may relate to later farm units constructed there.

Cnoc an Fheur Lochain

14. Nineteenth-century farming unit. NRHE ID 118008. Grid ref: NM 4257 7982.
The three buildings of this unit sit on a terrace, the largest being the dwelling house, which measures about 9 × 4m and has a fireplace at one end. The byre and the barn form part of an enclosure. There are extensive lazy beds and banking across the whole area.

Eilean Dubh

15. ?Still. NRHE ID 291518. Grid ref: NM 4279 7949.
These footings of a small building measuring about 4 × 2.5m and set in a secluded location sit adjacent to a watercourse. The building bears no relationship to anything agricultural and is (intentionally?) difficult to find. An illicit still is a reasonable conjecture.

Fang Mhor

16. ?Fort. NRHE ID 21858. Grid ref: NM 3963 7891.
This small stack with a natural gully on the landward side shows little in the way of modification other than a length of wall which runs down rather than across the promontory. It makes no sense as part of an original design and there is no evidence

of earlier buildings.

Fionn-aird

17. Shieling huts. NRHE ID 278662. Grid ref: NM 4157 7890 (centre).
Some eleven huts stand on a natural terrace among a confusing landscape of lazy beds and banking extending over a large area. Some are of typical shieling shape and size, but others are larger and more rectangular. Much rebuilding has taken place. It is likely that the site was originally for shielings but has since been developed and extended.

Gallanach

18. Historic modern farm. NRHE ID 108348. Grid ref: NM 4072 8012.
The original farm buildings as portrayed on the Chapman plan of 1809 lay on the shoreline slightly further to the west but are no longer evident. The current farm arrangement, the only farm on the island, was initiated by Captain Swinburne in the nineteenth century as a model farm, as part of his improvement scheme. It was later modified by Robert Thompson, who added an upper floor to the farmhouse and other features including a cobbled square.

Gallanach/Balmeanach

19. Township boundary dyke. NRHE ID 317698. Grid ref: from 19a NM 3929 7966 to 19b NM 4181 7841.
This boundary dyke of earth and stone once ran down the full girth of the island but now survives only sporadically as a result of later landscape divisions. It appears on Chapman's 1809 plan marked as a 'March between Gallanach and Balmeanach'.

Gleann Mhairten

20. Hut circle. *NRHE ID 291856. Grid ref: NM 4007 7906.*
This is one of only two certain hut circles on the island. It has a diameter of some 7m and visible remains of facing stones. There are later huts in the vicinity which presumably utilised its stones. A field bank has now been built directly across it.

Kiel

21. Burial ground. *NRHE ID 22136. Grid ref: NM 4201 7952.*
A sub-circular drystone wall about 30 × 20m defines this burial ground, although there may be earlier burials in the uneven ground further west. Remains of a chapel measuring around 6 × 3m stand in the south-east aspect. The name 'Kiel' (Gaelic 'Cille', meaning chapel) suggests that this was an early focal point for Christian worship. Two early memorials showing simple cross designs, probably from the seventh to ninth centuries, were found here and are now housed for safekeeping in the shop nearby where they can be viewed.

Leabaidh Dhonnchaidh

22. Slipway. *NRHE ID 118031. Grid ref: NM 4182 7857.*
This slipway is represented by a narrow clearance curving through a boulder beach. Visible at low tide it can be traced in a gentle arc for about 40m. It presumably relates to a structure nearby which has since been renovated and re-roofed as a holiday home.

Port Chreadhaih

23. Quay and slipway. *Grid ref: NM 4101 8041 (centre).*
The quay sits in a narrow creek and is depicted on the Chapman plan, being consolidated in the later part of the nineteenth century by Captain Swinburne, who extended it and added a series of metal mooring rings. One of the slipways nearby was modified with a type of tramway system set on wooden sleepers.

Port Mor

24. Slipway and boat naust. *NRHE ID 291504. Grid ref: NM 4223 7943.*

A substantial but rough slipway some 40m long and 5m wide designed for larger boats has been cleared through the rocks at the top of the harbour and probably predates the construction of the first jetty. Adjacent to it is a likely boat naust, represented by a scooped out hollow with its open end facing the sea. A boat could be hauled in and kept safe from adverse weather and seas.

25. Slipway. *NRHE ID 291506. Grid ref: NM 4217 7929.*

This slipway is narrower than the main slipway in the harbour (site 24) and was more appropriate for smaller boats.

26. Pier House and pier. *NRHE ID 292256. Grid ref: NM 4225 7932.*

Pier House was built by Captain Swinburne in the mid nineteenth century for the storage of boat equipment and salt, as part of his plans to improve the local fishing industry. It has a forestair and stands next to his new pier. The original pier in the harbour is the one at the south, which predates the first *Statistical Account*. It was originally boulder-built but is now clad in concrete. Swinburne's new pier has an adjunct at the end which effectively creates a small harbour on the landward side.

Port nam Maol

27. Slipway. *NRHE ID 291403. Grid ref: NM 4248 8044.*

Represented by a line of cleared rocks, this slipway can be tracked for about 35m at low tide and is presumably associated with the ruined farmstead at the head of the bay.

Sean Bhaile

28. Township settlement. NRHE ID 73961. Grid ref: NM 4200 7963.

As the settlement of the Kiel township, these represent by far the largest spread of building foundations on the island, and also the most complex. They cover an area of roughly 200 × 100m and date from the eighteenth to twentieth centuries, if not earlier. Well over forty separate buildings can be identified and there is a 'main street' that runs through the centre. Much of the remaining population of the island was cleared here with the intention that they could earn a living from fishing.

Toaluinn

29. Norse house. NRHE ID 269277. Grid ref: NM 4182 8049.

This is probably the only Norse building known in the Small Isles. In its shape and construction it differs from all other recorded structural remains. It is longer (about 13m with an outshot), has thick, double-faced walling about 2m wide and is bow-sided as opposed to rectangular. The design has strong parallels both in other parts of Norse Scotland and in the Scandinavian homeland.

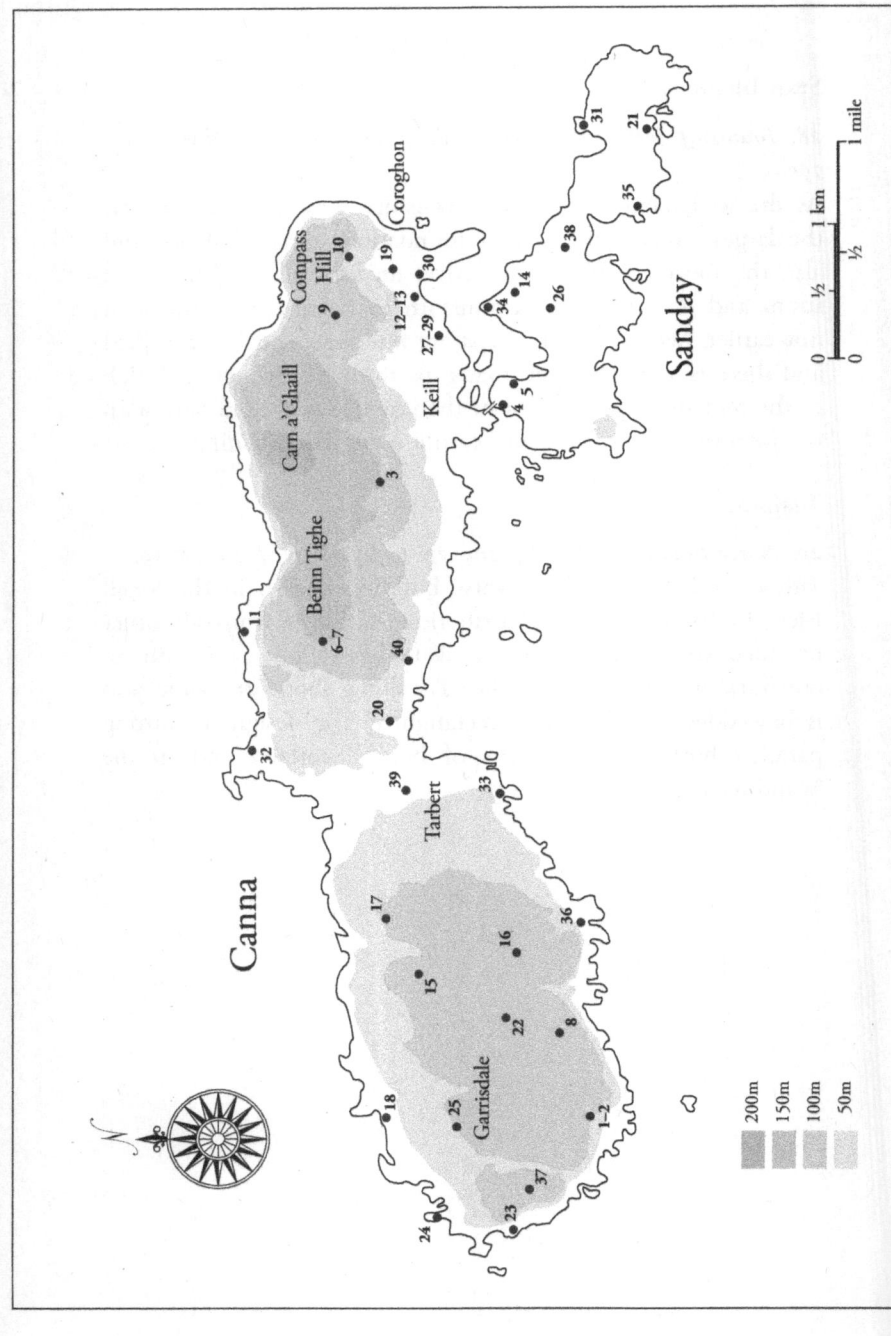

Canna

Compass
Hill

Coroghon

Carn a'Ghaill

Beinn Tighe

Keill

Tarbert

Garrisdale

Sanday

200m
150m
100m
50m

0   ½   1 km
0   ½   1 mile

4 Canna

'Coming to Canna is like coming to the west coast of Norway'

Introduction

Canna, green and terraced, sits at the north-west of the group. Like both Eigg and Muck it has an appendant island, but unlike those of Eigg and Muck this one is easily accessible by foot across the tidal channel that divides it from the main island via an elevated causeway, or across the beach at low tide. The likelihood is that the two islands were once a single entity joined by sand dunes, possibly even in prehistoric times, and were never culturally distinctive. The appendage, Sanday, is much more substantial than either Castle Island (Eigg) or Horse Island (Muck) and plays a more prominent part in the history of its parent island than the other two. Lower-lying than Canna itself with its highest contours reaching barely more than 40m, Sanday gives the impression of having slid down into the sea. The name 'Sanday' almost certainly involves the Norse suffix '-ey', often appearing as '-ay' or 'a', meaning island, the name therefore simply meaning 'Sand Island', which is a self-evident description to anyone wandering its beaches. The name 'Canna', on the other hand, is harder to explain. While the second element probably derives again from '-ey', and therefore covers its island nature, the meaning of the first element has so far eluded placename scholars. Even its superstitious name to be used from the sea,

'An t'Eilean Tarsainn' ('The Island Lying Across'), does little to help. More likely is the suggestion by the last private owner of the island, John Lorne Campbell (of whom much more below), that the name might stem from the Iron Age promontory fort Dun Channa at the west end of the island, the 'Channa' element reflecting a noteworthy person or event of the time. Together Canna and Sanday cover an area of some 1,100 hectares, roughly twice the size of Muck and half the size of Eigg. A substantial part of the southern landscape is fertile, particularly on Sanday, and its greenness stands in sharp contrast to the bleak grey mountains of Rum a short distance away across the Sound.

Canna itself divides topographically into two parts, the east and the west being separated, somewhat like Eigg, by a flat lower valley running across the width of the island and dividing it into two fairly equal halves. The placename 'Tarbert' at the southern end of this divide – a Norse-derived designation for places where boats could be carried across an isthmus – suggest that this might once have been an important place for portage, facilitating a land route across the island from the Sound of Canna north through to the Minch. This central lower valley has also seen the most intensive agriculture throughout the centuries. The western part of the island is barren, its coastline dominated by steep cliffs and volcanic terraces which extend across the northern face of the whole island and which characterise the coastal geology of all the Small Isles. Access to some of these terraces is difficult and the soil is poor, but in the eighteenth and nineteenth centuries, when the population density was at its greatest, every single scrap of usable land was turned into lazy beds and extensively cultivated. Contrastingly, the eastern half of the island consists of the same higher moorland terraces to the north, but with lower fertile terraces to the south opposite Sanday. The northern part also houses the tallest hill on the island, Carn a'Ghaill, which stands at just over 200m, as well as the aptly named Compass Hill, which stands at around 120m at its eastern tip. The latter's curious magnetic properties became an attraction from the seventeenth century onwards, when visitors would make their way to the top to experience the wild swinging of their compass needles. Martin Martin, writing in 1695, noted that his compass needle 'went round with great swiftness, and instead of settling towards the north, as usual, it settled here due east'.

The lower fertile terraces in the central area around Tarbert and in the south-east are the areas where occupation has been most dense. As on Eigg this is a reflection of the geology, whereby the lower volcanic terraces are softer and more easily broken down and provide better soils, whereas the upper terraces are harder and more resilient to natural erosion and soil formation. A fortuitous combination of these lower southern terraces and the profile of Sanday's coastline immediately to the south has created a splendid natural harbour between Sanday and its parent island. This was, as the writer of the second *Statistical Account* pointed out in 1836, 'well sheltered, safe and commodious'. It provided shelter from the prevailing westerlies, was generally acknowledged as being the best harbour in the Small Isles and even in the 1700s was, according to the first *Account*, a focus for commercial trade from the Baltic and its neighbours. There was a saying that if a boat was unable to land on Canna it was unable to land anywhere in Scotland. Even today it continues to provide refuge for travellers, passing yachtsmen and small commercial fishing traffic sheltering from adverse weather.

Canna's fertile lower terraces were praised by many travellers and visitors, one mid seventeenth-century description noting that it was 'fertile, both of corn and milk with abundance of all kinds of sea fishing'. The first *Statistical Account*, written in 1794, records the lower terraces as being good for crops, especially oats, and the higher ground as good for pasture. It also records that Canna and Sanday together had seven ploughs. This gives some idea of its fertility, given that Eigg had eight ploughs despite being twice the size. By the time of the second *Account* the potato had taken over as the major food source, Rev. MacLean alluding to 'great crops of potatoes' and good quality grazing for the rearing of black cattle. Like that of its smaller neighbour Muck, however, Canna's fertility came with a price – it had little natural fuel. The moorlands were too marshy and peats had to be brought in from elsewhere, usually from Rum, and at a cost.

Those same areas of settlement in the south and south-east were probably occupied throughout the preceding centuries, partly to take the best position for optimising land use, and partly to reuse stone building materials from existing dwellings. This is where earlier archaeological evidence is least likely to survive. Elsewhere, on the higher slopes, particularly in the west, survival is better attested and Canna has an enviable resource of Bronze Age settlement in the form of a prehistoric landscape of hut circles and field systems protruding through the boggy moorland, reflecting an active farming community. The moorland also houses an Iron Age souterrain – an underground passageway and chamber – which was probably used for storage. This is unique to the Small Isles and probably belongs to a period of occupation in the first millennium BC that also saw the emergence of important chieftains or warlords who constructed 'forts' on rock promontories around the island. There are at least four of these spread around the coasts of Canna and Sanday.

The moorland also contains many degraded features such as earthen banks, lengths of walling, enclosures, pens, mounds and huts, which can defy interpretation of function or date. A few can be ascribed to early prehistory, and these include burials, as revealed by the activities of rabbits, which tend to select the loose soils around buried stonework for digging and kick out pottery as they make their burrows. Others, especially the small stone foundations of temporary huts, probably belong to shieling practices, whereby cattle were taken to feed on the upper pastures in the summer months, a tradition that had its origins in Norse times.

By the time the Norse arrived Canna was owned, like Muck, by the Church and was subject to Iona. It remained that way until it passed into the hands of the powerful MacDonalds of

Clanranald in the late seventeenth century. As a result of the Church connection Canna and Muck are often mentioned together in early sources, quite distinct from Eigg and Rum. The ecclesiastical connection with Iona is significant and underpins the strong evidence for early Christianity on the island. This is represented not only physically by a series of early carved cross fragments, but also by a tradition that places Canna as 'Hinba', the site of one of St Columba's sixth-century chapels, thought to be located in the current ecclesiastical area of Keill (also known as 'A'Chill') on Canna, where the name itself attests to early Christian activity (Gaelic 'Cille' meaning chapel). This is the place that exhibits a standing cross which contains both Christian and Norse relief decoration. Despite the plethora of Scandinavian placenames on both Canna and Sanday, this cross is the only physical manifestation of a Norse presence on the island.

The current population of Canna and Sanday is about 20, but it takes little more than a casual meander along the island to realise from the vestiges of earlier remains, both structural and agricultural, that the population was previously much larger. Walker's *Report on the Hebrides* of 1764, probably the earliest reliable set of figures and certainly the most detailed, gives a tally of 253 souls. While that figure seems impressive enough, it is significantly lower than the maximum recorded figure of 463 souls in the 1821 census. This resulted largely from the influx of people arriving to harvest the kelp, before the main evictions and emigrations took place to allow for the introduction of sheep. By the time of the 1861 census the population had sunk to 127. There are several kelp-burning sites still visible around the shores of both Canna and Sanday. The increased population of the late eighteenth and early nineteenth centuries led to almost every patch of usable land being brought into cultivation, no matter how awkward to access or how poor the soil. This was even to the extent of lazy beds being cultivated on Canna's narrow volcanic ledges, to the detriment of any archaeological sites which had survived on the island's margins.

Canna was a strongly Catholic island and Walker recorded forty households of 'papists' compared to a mere four that were of Protestants. The average number of persons per household was 5.75, much the same as on the other islands. Unfortunately, Walker does not record the number or location of the townships where the population was centred. The earliest evidence for that comes with an estate map of 1805, which identifies four main settlements on Canna and two on Sanday. The foundation remains of these still survive in places, many of the buildings having been dismantled to construct sheep walling.

Study and understanding of both Canna and Sanday increased immeasurably under its late owner John Lorne Campbell, who purchased the islands in 1938. Together with his wife Margaret Fay Shaw he set about a process of conservation which inhibited any form of development that would be detrimental to the islands' history, landscape or ecology. He also established a vast collection of Gaelic music, ballads and writings in order to preserve local Gaelic traditions, as well as encouraging selected distinguished academics in history, archaeology and linguistics to visit and study the islands at first hand. He generously donated Canna and Sanday to the National Trust for Scotland in 1981.

Campbell's knowledge of the island is encapsulated in his book *Canna: The Story of a Hebridean Island* (2002). All books on the Small Isles cover Canna in one way or another, but Campbell's detailed volume also contains sections on traditions, placenames, trees and flora and fauna, among numerous other aspects. His biography by Ray Perman (2011) provides a fascinating personal dimension to his ownership. The earliest visitor to write about Canna in any depth was Thomas Pennant (1776), but the British Fisheries Society's report of 1788 (incorporated in Campbell's book) also provides valuable information. The carved crosses are illustrated and discussed by Ian Fisher (2001), and the erstwhile Royal Commission has produced a broadsheet on the island which maps and discusses many archaeological remains

(1999). Full references are given in the 'Further Reading' section at the end of the book.

Prehistory

John Lorne Campbell's insistence that any modern development on Canna and Sanday should be minimised, if not prevented altogether, has created an environment in which monument preservation has been high. There nevertheless remains no evidence whatsoever of the Mesolithic communities who collected bloodstone on Rum, a short distance away, ever having taken advantage of Canna's resources. Evidence for the subsequent Neolithic farmers is more plentiful, however, thanks to the activities of rabbits in a number of amorphous turf-covered stony mounds in the area around Tarbert and elsewhere. Their burrowing has thrown up sherds of so-called Unstan Ware pottery, which was common in parts of Scotland in the period from roughly 4000 to 2500 BC, as well as fragments of pottery that can be dated to the Bronze Age. Unstan Ware vessels tend to be shallow and round-bottomed, often with grooved lines below the rim. At Fang Na Fola, west of Tarbert, helpful rabbits have scratted up a type known as Beaker Pottery, which was a characteristic ware from around 2500 to 1800 BC.

Campbell's reluctance to allow change also extended to intrusive archaeology and hence the nature of these sites remains unknown. On a south-facing terrace on **Beinn Tighe (6)**, however, consolidation work by the National Trust for Scotland was able to identify structural remains spread within a dispersed mound roughly 20m in diameter, with associated ard marks indicating cultivation. The material recovered included occupation deposits of Unstan Ware pottery, flint flakes and a bloodstone scraper imported from Rum. The National Trust for Scotland has since carried out small test pitting in order to understand the monument better, and it so far has all the hallmarks of a Neolithic settlement site.

The most common surviving prehistoric sites tend to be the hut circles which appear throughout many parts of the upland landscape on Canna, typically surviving as circular stone foundations, faced inside and out, and with diameters ranging widely between around 4.5 and 11m. They are especially impressive on Canna because they often survive in association with stretches of walling, sometimes hundreds of metres long and sometimes shorter, perhaps representing boundary and field walls respectively. The boundary walling is mostly stone-based using lines of boulders set firmly in the ground and heightened with turf which has since eroded. They point to the existence of a thickly populated Bronze Age farming landscape before adverse conditions forced agriculture on the upper slopes to be abandoned. According to excavated parallels elsewhere, their dates tend to centre on the period from the second half of the second millennium BC to the first millennium BC.

The distribution of hut circles on Canna is almost exclusively at the west, although there are some on the eastern moorland. There are good examples at **Cnoc Loisgte (16)**, about 2km west of Tarbert, and at **Cnoc Rugail (17)**, which lies further north. Both have associated walling which runs down the hillside and joins Allt na Criche Tuatha, the gully which bisects the whole island in what may have been a major Bronze Age land division. It is tempting to think that the longer boundaries were territorial and the shorter ones field systems associated with individual farming units, and there is some support for this hypothesis in the location of the hut circles at **Allt Bhre-Sgorr (1 and 2)** and **Sron Ruail (37)**, on the west side of the same headland, and at **Ceann Creag Airighe (15)**. The problem, of course, is that there is no evidence to show which lengths of boundary were contemporary with the hut circles or with other boundaries, or how they might be dated. Moreover, much of this farming landscape has been submerged beneath the moorland bogs and only sections of it have the courtesy to show themselves to the interested twenty-first-century observer. Post-medieval activity is perhaps partly to blame. Near the late township of Garrisdale at the very north-west, for example, there are hundreds of metres of boundaries but no hut circles, which presumably provided a good source of stone for later building. By contrast the eastern moorland was doubtless as densely populated as the west but has so far produced only a few hut circles, notably at **Beinn Tighe** (7), and little in the way of boundaries.

Burials roughly contemporary with these early farming communities are hard to pin down. The tradition of burials in cairns or mounds was susceptible to later stone robbing for other purposes, although the preference for depositing the dead in remote positions on high ground could be an added safeguard against stone pilfering. Moreover, landscapes tend to be littered with mounds of one type or another resulting from field clearance, collapsed huts and general overgrowth that occurs on abandoned features. This makes distinguishing a Bronze Age burial cairn from a nineteenth-century clearance cairn difficult without invasive excavation. One distinguished early archaeologist, T.C. Lethbridge, excavated what he considered to be a burial cairn containing a funeral pyre on Sanday in the 1920s, only for it to transpire to be a ruined nineteenth-century bothy that had collapsed over its hearth.

It may be partly due to the difficulties in distinguishing a burial cairn from something quite different that only one certain burial can be located on Canna itself, others being found on Sanday. The Canna burial takes the form of a sub-circular mound roughly 14m in diameter at **Creag A' Chairn** (20), in an elevated position overlooking Tarbert. Its dominant position and the survival of large kerb stones around the perimeter tend to define it as a burial mound rather than anything else.

There are several examples on Sanday which are easier to access and can be identified from their positions on the higher ground. Interestingly, they seem to sit in groups of larger and smaller cairns and may represent traditional burial foci used over the centuries. There are six cairns at **Rubha Nam Feannag** (34) on the northern tip of the island jutting out into the harbour. They take a dominant clustered position, away from any agricultural activity to which they might otherwise be related. Another group sits on high ground at **An Doirlinn** (4), overlooking the causeway across to Canna. There are smaller cairns of unknown pedigree in the vicinity.

In the subsequent Iron Age, which roughly covers most of the first millennium BC and dribbles into the early centuries AD, the inhabitants of Canna and Sanday were kind enough to construct monuments that were not only more diagnostic of their time but also more robust. On the downside, however, unlike Neolithic and Bronze Age pottery types, Iron Age pottery was made of a material that is not easy to distinguish from that of much later pottery. In fact, the dark coarse wares found in the Western Isles belonged to potting traditions that ran throughout the Middle Ages into the eighteenth and nineteenth centuries. Consequently, later wares can look little different from those of the Iron Age. Unless there are rims and base fragments to study, even a pottery specialist would be hard pushed to distinguish an Iron Age fragment from one made locally half a millennium later.

Prime among the monuments of the Iron Age are the promontory forts, of which Canna has three and Sanday one. In each case a natural rock promontory has been modified by either walls or ramparts to give it a more impressive air. In common with 'forts' elsewhere in the Small Isles the final result is likely to have been mostly cosmetic. None of them offers much in the way of a fighting platform against invading hordes or a place of refuge for families in times of danger. They are more likely to reflect a leader or warlord showing off his wealth and power and intimidating any intruders. Purpose apart, they signify the presence of a substantial and organised community.

Pride of place goes to the fort at **Dun Channa** (23) at the western tip of Canna, which may (or may not) give some clue as to the name of the island. Sheer on all sides and with a flat, kidney-shaped top enhanced by walling, it may be accessed only via a narrow, steep and dangerous climb up a rock face on the landward side. While such an access point offers good defensive capability, it would take an inordinate time to man for either defensive or refuge purposes without ladders.

Nearby, in fact almost next door, is the fort of **Dun Teadh** (24), located about 800m along the cliffs to the north-east. Although the two are very close together, this fort is a product of nature rather than of military design. It is less dramatic and more like the seaward end of a downward slope separated from the rest of the hillside by a wall and some evidence of excavated gullies. The third fort in the western part of the island is at **Rubha nic Eamoin** (33), south of Tarbert, and takes advantage of a precipitous pincer-shaped promontory surrounded by sheer cliffs, with any landward access protected by a rampart. The final definite fort is at **Sean Dun** (35) on Sanday, which generally lacks the precipitous coastal profile seen on Canna. This irregular basalt stack is one of the few suitable locations but is very much a poor relation to the others. The sides are sheer and the height on the landward side has been further enhanced by a wall which runs the full length of the stack, punctuated by an entrance in the centre.

Another monument type normally associated with the Iron Age is the souterrain. Situated underground, as the name suggests, these leave virtually no trace on the ground surface other than perhaps a low mound. This goes some way to explaining why many of them are found accidentally through collapse rather than by systematic survey. They usually consist of a low, stone-lined underground passageway roofed with lintels leading into a wider chamber. The traditional interpretation is that the chambers were used for storing food in cool conditions, but this fails to explain why passageways were needed. There is no evidence for any of them being used for burials, and it is conceivable that they were used as temporary concealed refuges or even for some kind of ritual purpose. Their densest distribution is in eastern Scotland, but there are over fifty known examples throughout the

Western Isles and Skye. The Canna example lies on the south-facing slopes of Beinn Tighe on the eastern side of the island. The entrance is now grass-covered but a surveyed plan of it can be found on the trove.scot website (NRHE ID 10726). It shows a passageway cut through the rock running towards a collapsed chamber marked by a low mound to the north. The passageway is about 10m long and barely 1m wide. It was discovered when part of the roof collapsed, giving rise to an original but incorrect interpretation that there were two souterrains, one running in each direction.

One final monument merits mention in the context of the Iron Age, albeit tentatively. Overlooking **Tarbert Bay (40)**, on a south-west-facing ridge of Beinn Tighe, it consists of a large, turf-covered mound some 14m in diameter on which later structures have been built. It would seem to represent a circular building rather than the simpler kerbed mound or cairn typical of a burial. Circular buildings of this size are not uncommon in the Iron Age in the west of Scotland, where there are numerous examples of roundhouses, brochs and wheelhouses, particularly on Skye, grouped under the catch-all term 'Atlantic roundhouses'. T.C. Lethbridge is recorded as having identified this one as 'probably a wheelhouse' on an Ordnance Survey record card in 1953. Pottery has been recovered from the rabbit scrats but has not so far proved diagnostic.

Christian impact

Like Muck, Canna belonged to the Church, possibly as a result of the Christian mission from Iona in the sixth century, and retained links with Iona through much of its history. The earliest indications of this relationship are to be found in Columba's biography, *Life of Columba*, written by Adamnan, a monk on Iona writing at the end of the seventh century, who in recording Columba's activities and travels referred to an island called 'Hinba', where a monastic foundation was established. According to Adamnan, it was to 'Hinba' that Columba frequently paid visits and where miracles were said to have taken place. The whereabouts of 'Hinba' are unspecified in Adamnan's work, but John Lorne Campbell has put forward a strong argument in favour of it being Canna, further contending that the focus of Christianity on the island can be identified by the placename 'Keill'. This is also the location of an important decorated early standing cross and a collection of smaller cross fragments identified as probably belonging to the seventh or eighth century. It was also later to become the township of Keill. The earliest documented reference to Canna's association with Iona, however, is as late as 1203 in a papal document. This places the island under the jurisdiction of the Benedictine Abbey of Iona, and mentions a church dedicated to St Columba. In 1549 Monro wrote that Canna 'pertaines to the Abbot of Colmkill' (Iona), and in 1626 Thomas Knox, Bishop of the Isles, reporting on the state of his diocese, referred to Canna as 'a small Hand belonging to the Abbott of Icolmikill'. Monro additionally commented on the quality of the falcons there, suggesting that it was part of the Church estate earmarked for falconry.

The church mentioned in 1203 is no longer visible, but its existence is fairly well documented. Monro alluded to a 'kirk' on Canna in 1549, and Martin Martin mentions a 'chapel' there in the late seventeenth century. By 1773 it was described as the 'ruins of a chapel' by Thomas Pennant and was still 'ruinous' by 1788, according to a British Fisheries Society report. Whatever might have been left of it was presumably carried away in the mid nineteenth century together with the rest of the Keill township dwellings, in order to build walling for the sheep. This same helpful 1788 Fisheries report, which seems to have been of more use to the historian than to the fishing industry (it resulted in no positive fishing outcomes), also mentions a Mass House (no longer standing), which was presumably where services subsequently took place, as well as containing an enclosed burial area.

The first *Statistical Account*, written in 1794, makes no

mention of any church in Canna, and this was confirmed in the second *Account*, written in 1836. Later still, the ecclesiastical historian T.S. Muir, who visited the islands in 1856, wrote that 'only slight traces' of a church were visible on Canna, and finally the first-edition Ordnance Survey map, surveyed in 1877, uses an antiquities symbol to point out where a church once stood. Today, all that can be seen of where the township and the church used to be is the burial enclosure, some undulations where the Mass House may have been and a lonely cross standing in a field of nettles. That said, there may be a further vestige of the stone church in the nearby form of the so-called **Punishment Stone** (28), also described by Muir and marked on the first-edition Ordnance Survey map. This earth-fast tall stone has a small hole at the top into which offenders allegedly had their thumb wedged as punishment. The purpose was presumably not dissimilar to the stocks, but there is no record as to whether this was just a public shaming or whether the guilty party had material thrown at them as well. The relevant point, however, is that this Punishment Stone has all the appearance of a stone door jamb, one larger than those of domestic dwellings and which may therefore have belonged either to Columba's church or to the Mass House.

The standing cross at **Keill** (27) is of more than a little interest and like the fragmentary cross on Eigg would appear to depict images that are both pagan and Christian. Carved from yellow sandstone, it stands in what is assumed to be much the same place as when originally sited, possibly still in its original socketed base. It has a height of over 2m, but the top part, one arm and the decorated side of one narrow edge are broken off, local tradition ascribing the damage to cannonball practice during the Napoleonic wars. Both front and back faces and the surviving edge are highly decorated, as is the circular centre piece at the junction of the arms. Sadly, weather erosion over the centuries has taken a major toll on the sharpness of the relief carvings.

The two faces show a curious mixture of animals, humans and scenes. One face is split into panels, the top panel containing spiral decoration, below which are four panels containing pairs of beasts or serpents, the lowest one depicting a human figure being attacked by a pair of animals, one either side. The circular centrepiece is decorated with spirals of interlace. Interlace also appears on the jutting flange which runs down the side of the shaft. The other face is more boldly illustrated. At the top are the curved shapes of two animals which appear to be fighting, below which is a rider on horseback. Below that are two figures, one holding a baby in what must be an adoration scene, and below that is a scene in which a stag and a dog appear to be in combat. The flange at the edge contains interlace and a human figure heroically bent in supporting the cross arm. The surviving edge depicts two rather wooden human figures.

The cross is dated to somewhere between the ninth and the tenth century and, like its cousin on Eigg, exemplifies an incongruous relationship between the pagan art of animals and serpents and the Christian iconography of the adoration scene and the holy Cross. Unlike its Eigg cousin, however, it cannot be explained by reuse. This is a monument of single workmanship combining the cultures of both pagan and Christian worlds, erected in a setting argued to be one of the most important in the West. The animal and serpent elements are those of the Norse world, or are at least derived from it, and are thought to be testimony to Norse conversion – symbols familiar to Norse culture but given a Christian interpretation. The cross's setting is far from random, and geophysical survey combined with keyhole excavation carried out by this author in 1994 showed it to stand slightly to the east of the buried foundations of a stone-built structure. These foundations belonged to a rectangular building measuring approximately 20 × 6m and are presumably the only surviving remains of the church dedicated to Columba recorded from the sixteenth century onwards. They provided no clue to its dating, but it was probably built in the Middle Ages, replacing earlier versions on roughly the same footprint and respecting the position of the cross. Any structure dating from Columba's time would almost certainly have been in timber rather than stone and may underlie it. But why was the church sited in that location in the first place? The answer might be provided by the same keyhole excavations, which demonstrated that it was built over earlier disturbed burials which appeared to be from a cairn. In other words, as at Eigg, the Christian focus was centred in a place that was already ceremonial and a long-standing burial ground.

The standing cross is just one of several fragments of sculptured crosses found in the area round Keill. Ian Fisher's corpus of medieval sculpture has identified twelve further simple incised pieces, all of Torridonian Sandstone. Seven of these are now retained for safekeeping in **Canna House** (12) at the east end of the harbour, and the other five were salvaged at the time of the Clearances and re-erected in the 'modern' burial ground at Keill. All twelve have been described in detail and illustrated by Fisher. One at Canna House nevertheless deserves special mention. This is a cross represented by two large shaft fragments found in a field wall around 1895 and two other fragments belonging to it subsequently recovered from different parts of the island. The two shaft fragments are the most interesting. On one face are three panels of interlace and knotwork, each panel becoming progressively more complex towards the top of the shaft. There is also interlace on both edges. On the other face is a figure wearing a coat or tunic with arms folded and a serpent entwined around the leg. Sadly, the head is missing. In common with the standing cross at Keill, it shows a mixture of different cultures deliberately engineered for Christian purpose.

While a degree of conjecture surrounds the existence of Columba's church and mission, there is one site on the island which is tangible testimony to early Christian activity. This is **Sgorr nam Ban-naomha** (36) – literally 'Cliff of the Holy Women' – located on a terrace at the foot of the southern cliffs in the west of Canna. If anyone wants to know what an archetypal early Christian monastic site on the Celtic model looks like, this is it. Thanks to the conservation ethic of John Lorne Campbell and the site's dangerous access, it appears to have remained in a virtually untouched state for over thirteen centuries. It consists of a sub-circular stone wall enclosing an area of around 35m in diameter, in the centre of which is a circular structure some 5m in diameter. Outside the enclosure there are further structures, some rectangular. It also has a natural water supply running through it, along which a simple mill has been constructed. Configurations such as this are known from across Ireland, where the enclosure represents the focal point of a monastery with a central oratory, the enclosure wall itself, or *vallum monasterium*, representing a symbolic division between the outer secular world and inner divine space. The structures on the outside of the enclosure would have been for sleeping, working and food preparation, or temporary huts for pilgrims. With almost sheer cliffs rising to the north and a virtually impossible sea access to the south, it is exactly the kind of remote location favoured by ascetics, possibly a place dependent on a more mission-based establishment further along the coast at Keill.

The name of the site is significant, as it indicates a centre for 'holy women', presumably some form of nunnery. Early nunneries are rare, but there is a reference to this centre in a letter of 1428 sent by the Abbot of Iona to the Pope, complaining about a feud between himself and the convent on Canna. This suggests that there were two active religious establishments at the time and that one was for women. The site appears to have escaped the attentions of seventeenth-century writers and may have fallen out of use or been abandoned after the Reformation, as perhaps confirmed by a mid sixteenth-century source which described 'old Columban cells at the foot of a steep cliff'. The date of foundation, however, is not in much dispute. By analogy with similarly configured sites it probably belongs to the seventh century, supported by the discovery of three early carved cross fragments inside the enclosure. All three are of Torridonian Sandstone, two showing incised or pecked crosses, the other a relief cross. All three are held in Canna House.

It is worth pointing out at this stage that Canna and Sanday remained staunchly Catholic, despite the impact of the Reformation and the efforts of the Protestant Church to convert the population. According to Walker, the island was entirely Catholic in 1758, with the exception of the school teacher and his family. His *Report* of 1764, having commented on the strength of Catholicism on the island, even went as far as recommending that the young people there should be sent by boat to be educated elsewhere, away from the influence of their staunchly Catholic parents. Such was the hatred of Protestantism on the island that naughty children were threatened by their parents with being sent to the devoutly Protestant Rum. Thirty years later the first *Statistical Account* mentions that the Protestant minister who lived on Eigg visited Rum and Muck on a monthly basis to take services, but went to Canna only once a quarter. He doubtless found trying to preach in Canna a waste of time but needed to tick the box to keep his bishop quiet.

Norse impact

It is difficult to get excited about the Norse period on Canna and Sanday because there is so little that is tangible and so much that is confusing. Norse raiding was rife in the late eighth and early ninth centuries, Iona was devastated twice and it would be surprising if Viking raiders had not availed themselves of the easy pickings further north at the monastic centre at Keill and the nearby nunnery. There are no records to show that they did, but the distribution of Scandinavian elements in placenames across Canna and Sanday is sufficient to believe that the Norse became a dominant cultural presence one way or another. One distinguished Scandinavian linguist, Professor Alf Sommerfelt, who visited Canna in 1943, on viewing the landscape and hearing the placenames for the first time, commented that it was 'like coming to the west coast of Norway' (hence the epigraph to this chapter). While there are a number of obvious Norse names and elements, the greater majority would seem to be hybrid or corrupted versions. In his book on Canna, Campbell devoted an appendix to the placenames, systematically working his way round the island identifying those which may have been Norse or contained Norse elements and which had subsequently been 'Gaelicised' during the later Middle Ages. Campbell was a placename purist, even to the extent of producing a list of incorrectly spelled names on Ordnance Survey maps which he sent to their mapping department. He accused the Ordnance Survey of altering some names so that they could be pronounced more easily and lambasted them for not employing 'adequately qualified Gaelic scholars to correct their transcriptions and to avoid pseudo-learned restorations'.

Two factors emerge from Campbell's studies. Firstly, attempting to understand placenames in the Small Isles is a minefield, on account of both the admixture of Norse and Gaelic languages and persistent corruption over time. Secondly, the placenames, or placename elements, especially in coastal areas, make it clear that there was a significant Norse influence on Canna and Sanday. The question remains as to whether this was the result of widespread immigration of Norse families or of the establishment of an elite dominant few. Opinion is inclined towards the latter and the belief that, as elsewhere in the Small Isles, the existing Gaelic-speaking population was still numerically greater throughout. This Norse domination must also have influenced other aspects of administration, such as the land division system of ouncelands and pennylands, which rears its head in later documents and which was of Norse introduction and is well evidenced elsewhere, especially on Eigg.

Campbell's reluctance to allow anything invasive on the islands, including archaeological excavation, means that none of the supposed Norse sites has ever been investigated and hence that the objects of Norse origin that have been discovered are from random activities such as ploughing. Any tangible testimony of Norse Canna and Sanday is consequently rather weak – a glass bead and a Viking-type ring-headed bronze pin recovered during the construction of the Protestant church.

As a result of archaeological surveying undertaken between the two wars, Canna is said to have contained a number of Viking graves. These have been exhaustively looked at, but not excavated, by various scholars including the above-mentioned Scandinavian professor who visited the islands in 1943 and identified a 'whole cluster of Viking graves' at Rubha Langanes on the north coast of Canna above Tarbert. His claims have since been dismissed on the grounds that none of the supposed graves are of the traditional Scandinavian boat-shaped or circular design common in the homeland. Moreover, the Canna 'burials', typically represented by rectangular lines of stones, are unknown in Scandinavia. All are flat landscape features and none have been covered by mounds. Those in coastal locations can be more satisfactorily explained as kelp kilns, with parallels on the other islands, but those in random inland locations are less easy to interpret. They may belong to some aspect of domestic farming, such as storage platforms, but without excavation this is pure conjecture. None of the other three islands has anything like them and they remain a mystery.

One of the stone settings at **Rubha Langanes** (32) has for reasons that are unclear come to be described as the grave of the King of Norway. There is no record as to which king or why he should be buried there. It consists of a loosely laid out boulder setting about 10m in length and 2m wide running downslope, with some of the boulders hard-set into the ground. There are some other earth-fast stones and possible walling seemingly conjoining it at the north. The headland location is appropriate for a burial, but the configuration is more appropriate to a shelter or shieling pen. Why it should be located in that particular place is another question. There are other narrow, rectangular stone settings with similar configurations, including two at **Beul An Iola Sgoir** (8) at the south-west. All seem to be characterised by narrowness and by the single line of stone that defines them.

Medieval and post-medieval landscapes

The history of Canna in medieval times is as bleak as that of the other three islands. John Lorne Campbell's trawl through the relevant documents and subsequent analysis drew a blank. 'We know nothing', he wrote, 'about the history of Canna in the period between the mission of St Columba and the beginning of the thirteenth century.' It was in the papal bull of 1203 that Canna was first mentioned, and the island remained under the wing of the Church through the Bishop of the Isles until the mid sixteenth century. It was then leased to the Clanranalds who, by the beginning of the nineteenth century, owned it together with Eigg and Muck.

This Clanranald connection caused problems for Canna in the sixteenth century, when in 1588, along with Muck, Rum and Eigg, it was recorded as having been attacked by Lachlan MacLean of Duart in retaliation for the alleged desecration of Iona by the Clanranalds. The houses were burned down and the islanders put to the sword. According to an account of a criminal trial that followed in 1590, all four of the Small Isles had the same fate, although it seems unlikely to have involved complete depopulation.

The only other significant recorded event in Canna's history occurred following the unsuccessful clan uprising of 1745, at a time when all four of the Small Isles were regarded as hotbeds of insurrection by the Crown and treated with disdain whenever forces were sent to search for hidden arms and fugitive Jacobites. The information is sparse but has been drawn together by a late eighteenth-century clergyman called Robert Forbes, whose life's work was dedicated to collecting reminiscences of the uprising. One source recounted how in 1746 an English force of sixty men landed on Canna, their lieutenant demanding beef and mutton for them to take away for their troops. The request was reluctantly honoured and the cattle obtained and slaughtered, but bad weather set in and the force was unable to sail out for four days. During that time the meat went off and the lieutenant demanded the same again. On being told that this was unfair and that the islanders had suffered enough already, he rounded up all the remaining cattle on the island and had them shot out of spite. This was one of a string of atrocities to befall the island. Not long afterwards another naval vessel landed for the sole purpose of allowing a crew of frustrated soldiers to rape the women and girls. The ship was under the command of the infamous Captain Ferguson, but the brutality was thwarted by a tip-off that allowed the females to hide in caves around the island. Ferguson was also involved in the abduction of Canna's baillie in order to extract information from him. He was kept in London for a year, eventually being returned to find that all his cattle had been killed.

Walker's *Report* of 1764, which provides an objective account of Canna's population, is complemented well by Thomas Pennant's descriptive account of less than a decade later. Together they offer a vivid snapshot of island life, quite different from the short, bland statements on the quality of the land, the cattle or the excellence (or otherwise) of the fishing typically presented by earlier commentators. Pennant spent time on both Rum and Canna and was a shrewd observer. Like other commentators he was taken by its richness, noting that 'each shore appeared pleasing to humanity; verdant, and covered with hundreds of cattle', but his view of it changed as he began to talk to the islanders. Harvests had been poor, they were living on fish and milk and had 'neither bread nor meal for their poor babes'. Even this diet was vulnerable, as the island had run out of fish hooks. Cattle were plentiful but were exported to pay the rents rather than being consumed domestically. Given these circum-stances Pennant was surprised to find that there were 'horses in abundance' which were used for a ceremonial purpose known as the 'Cavalcade' each year at Michaelmas. On that day each man on the island would ride bareback with a girl or a neighbour's wife behind him, then the females would 'treat' their rider before taking part in a large feast. Pennant is unspecific as to the nature of this 'treat', but the fact that it was eventually banned by the laird's tacksman suggests that it was not entirely appropriate. The horses appear to have been kept and maintained solely for this event.

Pennant also provides information on the persistence of the Norse pennylands land division, the manufacture of clothing from the wool of domestic sheep, the curious phenomenon of Compass Hill, and other features of interest, such as a 'lofty slender rock' on which was perched a small building which could only be accessed by 'a narrow and horrible path'. This is the first recorded mention of the so-called 'Castle' at **Coroghon** (**19**), a structure which sits near the top of a steep basaltic pillar some 25m tall that juts out on the east side of the island near the harbour. By all topographical rights the pillar should have enjoyed the status of an Iron Age fort or dun but was too small. Pennant refers to it as being 'scarce to be able to contain half a dozen people'. In the seventeenth or eighteenth century this small structure, which appears to defy gravity, was built on the side of the pillar, being noted appropriately in the second *Statistical Account* as 'Corra Dhun', meaning 'unstable fort'. Built of rubble walling, it consists of two floors divided into rooms with windows at different heights. There is a possible pit for cellarage. Parts of the rock facings are incorporated as walling and access is through a doorway on the north face.

The structure itself is of unknown origin or even function. For defensive purposes it sits on the wrong side of the rock pillar to be seen from the sea or be used as a lookout. Tradition holds that it was used as a prison by a jealous worthy who locked his wife up on account of her great beauty. Some antiquarian excavations took place there and Campbell records the presence of undecorated handmade pottery. A combination of the story, the hazardous position of the Castle and Victorian gothic romanticism guaranteed nineteenth-century visitor interest, exemplified by an 1875 illustration of the Castle being used by witches, now held in the Victoria and Albert Museum.

DEMOGRAPHICS AND TOWNSHIPS

Neither Walker nor Pennant provided much evidence as to where the island population lived, or more specifically where the townships were located. On the basis of Walker's population figures, those recorded later by formal census and some less reliable ones recorded earlier, a population of around 200 or less would be a reasonable estimate for the seventeenth and possibly sixteenth century, probably amounting to between thirty-five and forty dwellings. These figures are well below the saturation point of 436 souls documented in 1821 but still large enough to absorb the best land and, as in the past, occupy the most appropriate places for dwellings in terms of convenience and shelter. Traditions of farming and agriculture were ingrained, and the descriptions given by Pennant might well have been the same had he visited the island several centuries earlier. The same might be said for the population foci, data for which comes in the unlikely form of reports by the British Fisheries Society in 1787 and 1788, the later one describing a population of 320 souls concentrated in four townships. The largest of these townships was said to contain thirty families, although 'much useful ground is thrown away by the houses being scattered here and there without any regularity'.

By the late eighteenth and early nineteenth centuries population pressures were forcing lairds throughout the Western Isles to review how income might be improved and how the land might better be divided up to remedy some of the ills of growing poverty. The Clanranald cartographers were tasked with providing accurate maps of their islands to see how these aims might be achieved. This was undertaken on Canna by

William Bald in 1805, who subsequently mapped Eigg a year later (see plate section). In many respects it is a remarkable piece of cartography and shows the island in greater (and more useful) detail than the maps of the other islands.

The map shows six population centres which might be equated with townships, together with areas of cultivated land and field divisions. Four of these townships are on Canna itself – the same number of centres as is mentioned in the British Fisheries Society's report – at Garrisdale, Tarbert, Keill and Coroghon. One of those centres the society referred to as being the 'principal town', with ruined chapel and 'a curious shaped cross' and a burial ground in a state of disrepair. This is unquestionably Keill, and Bald's map depicts about thirty individual buildings there, which again equates with the number in the society's report. There is also a symbol for the standing cross. The map shows Sanday as being divided into two parts by a boundary winding from north to south, Lower Island and Upper Island respectively, with a population centre in each. All six centres are depicted by individual dwellings and configurations of dwellings, Keill being by far the largest.

Life in late eighteenth-century Canna and Sanday is best illustrated in the second report of the British Fisheries Society. The first report considered the harbour, local fish stocks and the support of the tacksman, Hector MacNeill, and made several recommendations regarding the need for storage buildings and a pier. The second report seemed more interested in matters such as the quality of the tacksman's house, the building of an inn, harvests and cattle, the absence of sheep, local cottage industries, kelp harvesting, the number of tailors and even religious issues. The society's comments give a much more subjective and enthusiastic description than the first *Statistical Account*, written six years later, acting as a useful precursor to Bald's map, which followed both.

The society's description of the local fishing and fish stocks is telling. The harbour was swarming with small fish the size of haddocks which could easily be caught, but it seems that the islanders used them only for their oily livers, the rest of the flesh being thrown out. Further out at sea there were rich sources of ling, cod, mullet and herring which could be caught, but it would have required more substantial vessels than the domestic boats currently employed if the fishing was to have any effect on the local economy. Pennant had already worked this out over a decade earlier, even to the extent of researching the costs of larger vessels, lines and equipment, which were manifestly beyond the means of the islanders. Fishing on Canna and Sanday existed at an altogether different level. It was constrained by the availability of fish hooks as much as anything, which almost had the status of currency. Pennant rued that he had presented the islanders with irrelevant trifles as gifts when 'a few dozen fish hooks would have made them happy'. The Fisheries Society's recommendation that a fishing station should be built on Canna together with a jetty, huts and equipment stores, all at the society's expense, would have been greeted with a mixture of enthusiasm and considered scepticism, the latter based in part on the amount of salt required to make any increased fishing initiative worthwhile. The issue of salt for preserving the fish was a long-standing complaint. There were heavy duties on salt which had to be bought from an authorised custom house, the nearest of which was at Tobermory on Mull. Land was allocated for a fishing station by tacksman Hector MacNeill, but after two years' bickering between the society and the Clanranalds, in which the tacksman played no small part, the initiative was abandoned. The only positive outcome of the whole debacle was that the society's papers included a sketch illustration and plan of the harbour area by the Society's Lt. Pierce, which depict a number of contemporary buildings located around the harbour.

MacNeill had made a number of significant changes around the island, notably in this harbour area. Principal of these was his residence, Coroghon House, which he built on the harbour shore together with a barn. It had a central core of three floors and a wing at either end. Although viewed as a rather grand edifice from the exterior, the Fisheries Society report referred to the interior as being 'rather miserable'. The associated barn was of the bank barn type, set at some distance away to the east, and was designed to offer a variety of agricultural functions including stabling, winnowing and use as a byre. Lt. Pierce's sketch map also depicts a mill. This was another component of Hector MacNeill's rejuvenation of the island. It was water-powered and involved a dam and a lade, traces of both of which survive although the original mill mechanism does not. Also a product of Hector MacNeill's time but not illustrated by Lt. Pierce is what is probably the oldest inhabited structure on the island. This was known as the Changehouse and sits in the 'square' below Keill. It was constructed as a three-bay single storey cottage and was the building used by MacNeill as an inn. Built of whitewashed rubble, it also had associated steading.

The townships on Canna were divided physically, and lengths of the turf and stone marches still survive. These run the full width of the island, roughly from north to south, dividing it into four township blocks, with a further block of moorland denoted as 'Common' covering most of the land to the west. Some unusual turns in the dykes suggest they may have been following earlier territorial divisions, a hypothesis that may be supported by a number of additional lengths of walling which seem to make no positional sense.

Working from east to west, there are no visible traces of eighteenth-century foundations for the Coroghon township, although the British Fisheries Society's sketch map of Canna harbour depicts nine buildings in a place called Lagg a' Bhaile (Dell of the Town). None are shown on Bald's map seventeen years later. Although some licence by the society's sketcher might be assumed (Lt. Pierce drew it later from memory), the same information appears in the first *Statistical Account*, suggesting that the Rev. Donald McLean who compiled it gave it some credence. The reason for the absence of these buildings on Bald's map may simply have been that they were no longer occupied, the Clanranalds having already moved the population across to Sanday in order to support the fishing initiatives proposed by the society in view of the collapse in the kelp market.

Further west, Keill is fairly well attested as having had around thirty structures, although none of the foundations are visible today. **Tarbert (39)**, probably the most fertile area on either Canna or Sanday, is shown to have had at least nine rectangular buildings, most of which can still be seen as turf-covered foundations associated with a few enclosures and small mounds. Additionally, there are over twenty small mounds that lie to the south. These may be clearance cairns reflecting the expanse of local lazy beds, although there is some suggestion that they may be early pilgrim cairns in view of their regular layout.

The most westerly township is that of **Garrisdale (25)**, which lies beyond the 'Common' on the map and is very much an outlier. By far the smallest of the four it presumably took advantage of the soils on the lower north-west-facing slopes and seems to have been carefully defined by what is now a dilapidated stone wall. The map shows fields and enclosures as well as at least three buildings. Five unroofed buildings are shown on the first-edition Ordnance Survey map of 1877.

One of the curiosities of settlement in the north-west part of Canna is the presence of a series of building foundations at **Conagearaidh (18)** on the north-west terraces just below the township of Garrisdale. They can be traced as a series of stone footings for at least six rectangular structures as well as two enclosures and areas of lazy beds. None of these features appear on Bald's map and they may represent a later extension to Garrisdale to take into account a growing population. Both settlements, however, are shown on the first-edition Ordnance Survey map of 1877, though every building is depicted as uninhabited. Unusually, Conagearaidh also has its own small burial ground. With an expanding population in the two clusters, and with both settlements located a considerable distance from the island burial ground at Keill, the township folk may have found it more practical to bury their dead locally.

On Sanday Bald's map shows the snaking line of the boundary between Lower Island and Upper Island townships running roughly north–south across the neck of land from Tallabric to Cnoc an Tionail, the former township being much the larger in terms of area. There are clusters of structures on each. On Upper Island five buildings are shown lining the harbour shore at **Am Mialagan** (5), two of which can be located from their turf-covered stone footings. On Lower Island there are two clusters of buildings, about twelve in all, set in irregular scatters at **Greod** (26) in the shelter of a knoll. Stone footings of some of these can be made out on the ground. Some may relate to the early clearance of families being moved across from Coroghon on Canna, but the latest string of structures probably reflects the post-1851 influx of émigrés from Canna (see below). None are shown as being inhabited on the 1877 Ordnance Survey map.

SHIELINGS, KELP AND THE 'OLD SYSTEM'

The land of each township included an exclusive area of moorland for summer pasture. In addition, the moorland designated 'Common' on Bald's map appears to have been available for common use and was particularly convenient for the townships of Tarbert and Garrisdale, whose boundaries adjoined it. The transhumance process, which allowed cattle to graze on the higher slopes, left numerous footprints on the landscape, typically in the form of the stone or turf foundations of huts used as temporary accommodation, pens, small enclosures and even lazy beds. Estimates suggest that there are around one hundred of these shieling huts spread across the moorlands of Canna and Sanday, although they can be easily confused with earlier features. In fact, some may have been specifically sited to utilise stone from existing structures. Many of them sit on low mounds, which represent the accumulation of seasonal detritus.

The antiquarian T.C. Lethbridge excavated one on Compass Hill in 1925 and noted the existence of several layers of peat ash flooring. He claimed that the hut dated to the fifteenth or sixteenth century. It might well have done but he gave no evidence for it.

Good examples are not difficult to find. Anyone who cares to stroll up the south-facing slopes of Beinn Tighe in the Keill township will come across small groups of stone foundations or the turf-covered mounds of collapsed huts. There are more tangible clusters in the Coroghon township at **Blar Na Carraigh** (9), at **Bual Thial Sgorr** (10) in an enclosure on Compass Hill, at **Allt Gheodrain** (3) in the Keill township and on Sanday at **Suileabhaig** (38). Some huts made use of existing prehistoric boundary stones, such at **Druim Na Tire** (22) in the Garrisdale township, or natural rock facings and boulders, such as at Tarbert township's **Buidhe Sgorr** (11).

This division of the landscape into bounded townships with associated shielings reflects the evolved population centres and land divisions at the very beginning of the nineteenth century. This was before the population swelled to its maximum a couple of decades later, mostly as a consequence of the money that could be made by harvesting and burning kelp. Because of its low-lying nature, Sanday was especially suited to kelp processing, which became fundamental to the island's economy. It initially provided well-paid work for the islanders, profits for the tacksman and even larger profits for the landowner. When the bubble finally burst around 1820 as a result of the collapse of the kelp market, the population of Canna and Sanday was mostly left out of work, starving and unable to pay any rents. As elsewhere there were also issues of land shortage, caused by the division of family holdings, and low cattle prices were being paid by the greedy mainland dealers who held a monopoly. The demise of the kelp industry was the climax of things going wrong.

Kelp burning was a simple process that involved collecting seaweed, laying it out to dry and then burning it in a crude kiln near the shore, stirring it until a homogeneous mixture was obtained. Once it had solidified it could be collected and sold. It seems to have been a remarkably clean process which left no residual traces. It relied on little in the way of structure or superstructure, typically a rectangular setting of stones around 5 to 7m long and barely 1m wide. Excavation of one of the kilns at Suileabhaig on Sanday showed that the interior contained little more than a thin bed of stones and patches of burnt soil. Other kelp kilns on Sanday are known from **Rubha Camas Stianabhaig (31)** and from **Creag Nam Faoileann (21)**, originally thought to be Viking graves.

THE CLEARANCES

By the early nineteenth century, when poverty and overpopulation were rife, the Clanranalds could be found in the south of England, where the current laird, having been educated at Eton, was the Member of Parliament for Plympton. The Clanranalds were finding themselves obliged to sell much of their holdings in order to maintain their lifestyle, and in 1827 Canna was sold off to its sitting tacksman, Donald MacNeill, but not before the kelp market had been decimated. Before the sale the Clanranald's factor had proposed that 200 folk should be deported from Sanday to Cape Breton, Nova Scotia, at the government's expense. He put the problem down to excessive population and general idleness. 'The people neither fish nor do anything else,' he wrote, 'I cannot imagine how they live. They are most miserably poor.' It appears the islanders were so far in rent arrears that they could not even contribute to their passage. Exactly how many of them were sent to Cape Breton and when they departed is unclear, but the census of 1831 shows that the population had shrunk from 436 to 264 in a decade.

A more significant episode occurred in 1851, one that resulted in further evictions as well as a complete change in land use. After the death of Donald MacNeill in 1848 the new leaseholder,

Donald MacLean, took advantage of inheritance problems among the MacNeills to rent the island on terms extremely favourable to himself. These included an insistence on the complete exodus of small tenants from Canna and all families from Keill. He also required a tall stone wall to be built to separate hill land from arable land. Much of this stone was derived from the houses at Keill and from the graveyard and ruined chapel. He also demanded an upgraded road and a pier. By the time his demands had been met, Keill, populated since Columban times, was little more than a wilderness. Canna's population had more than halved to 127 and the island was full of sheep. More significantly perhaps, Canna was recorded as having only twelve inhabited houses, whereas Sanday had seventeen. Sanday had for a second time become the dumping ground for those who would not, or could not, emigrate from Canna.

Later ownership

On the positive side, MacLean built **Canna House** (13) in 1860 to use as his main residence in place of Coroghon House, which he reduced to a single floor, the shell of which now constitutes the island's bothy, rented for holiday purposes. The new building was a large two-storey villa with a hipped slate roof that sloped to all four walls, later supplemented by a two-storey extension at the rear. The construction was of coursed rubble with two bay windows and a porch. It remains much the same today but with the addition of a conservatory at the east end. In 1881 the island was sold again, this time to the Thoms, a family of shipowners from Glasgow, who paid £23,000 for the island and all its stock. The family did much to improve the planting and upgrade the workers' dwellings. One of Robert Thom's early initiatives was to build an oak pier in Canna in 1892 in order to support the herring industry. This was restructured into its present form in 1971, before the modern ferry terminal was built.

It was during the Thom lairdship that two churches were

built on the island. An impressive **Catholic church** (14) was built on Sanday, commissioned in the late 1880s by the Marchioness of Bute in memory of her father. It has a large rectangular nave with a rose window at the west end and an internal corbel course containing stone heads of knights and priests. The chancel is semicircular and surmounted by a three-storey tower with a belfry and louvres. A combination of its size and construction (a rather depressing coursed dark rubble, broken by thick, lighter-coloured string courses) makes it somewhat anomalous in the landscape. It was closed for safety reasons in 1963 and, despite attempts to convert it into a hostel, remains shut. In the early twentieth century a much smaller but brighter **Presbyterian church** (30) was built on Canna overlooking the harbour. This was in memory of Robert Thom and commissioned by his sons. It is of a characteristic Irish style with a round pointed tower and pointed leaded windows to match. Unusually the pews are arranged longitudinally to the nave, which has a type of pointed barrel-vaulted ceiling. It sits within a stone-walled burial ground with an ornamental gate decorated with birds and fishes.

John Lorne Campbell and his wife purchased the island from the Thoms in 1938 and moved into Canna House. Campbell was a remarkable man who turned his back on the class-based landowning society he was born into in Argyll and strove to balance his hands-on farming management of the island with a strong conservation ethic. He will best be remembered as a scholar whose range of interests across Gaelic culture are reflected in his many books and translations, not to mention the exhaustive collection of Gaelic poetry, music and ballads that he and his wife Margaret Fay Shaw amassed together. She too was no mean academic, as well as a musician and folklorist.

Canna House became not only their residence but also a home for their growing collection of Gaelic literature, music and sculptured stone from around the island, together with Campbell's reference collections of moths and butterflies. It also became a place where the Campbells hosted other scholars and writers. At the time of their purchase of the house the combined population of Canna and Sanday was down to 38. Campbell died in 1996, but not before he had generously donated the island and all its buildings to the National Trust for Scotland. He died in Italy and had wished to be buried where he fell. His body was later repatriated to Canna and buried in one of the woodlands he had planted in **Keill (29)**, the grave being marked by a simple Gaelic inscription on a stone brought from his family estate in Argyll.

Places to Visit: Canna

Allt Bhre-Sgorr

*1. **Hut circle.** NRHE ID 142496. Grid ref: NG 2152 0448.*
This hut circle, which measures about 7.5m in diameter, sits within a framework of land division involving earth-fast stone boundaries with which it appears to be associated.

*2. **Hut circle.** NRHE ID 142489. Grid ref: NG 2158 0464.*
Less definitive than hut circle 1, this has a diameter of about 4.5m and sits within an area of presumably associated stone boundary features. There is some evidence of exterior wall facing.

Allt Gheodrain

*3. **Shieling huts.** NRHE ID 142386. Grid ref: NG 2608 0586.*
This group of at least four shieling huts and mounds is located at the edge of a stream. One of them is of double-celled figure-of-eight construction and measures about 5 × 2.5m. The other four would appear to be single-celled, roughly 2 × 2.5m. Other mounds in the vicinity may represent additional collapsed huts.

An Doirlinn, Sanday

*4. **Bronze Age burial mounds.** NRHE ID 137751 and 137752. Grid ref: NG 2672 0491 (centre).*
These mounds take a prominent position overlooking the crossing to Canna. The largest stands over 1m in height and has a diameter of around 9m, with some kerb stones evident. A

smaller one measures about 6m in diameter. Other mounds in the immediate vicinity may also represent burials.

Am Mialagan, Sanday

5. Township settlement. NRHE ID 137767. Grid ref: NG 2688 0463 (centre).
There is now little left of the small township of Upper Island, located on the west shore of the harbour. The 1805 map shows five structures, of which probably only two can be identified from turf-covered foundations. The more obvious one is rectangular at some 8.5 × 4m.

Beinn Tighe

6. ?Neolithic structure. NRHE ID 10716. Grid ref: NG 2441 0593.
A potentially important Neolithic monument is represented by a low mound of a collapsed structure spread across an area measuring some 20m in diameter together with ard marks. Rabbit scrat has yielded flint flakes and prehistoric pottery including Neolithic Unstan Ware. The remains of a small adjacent structure may be associated.

7. Hut circle. NRHE ID 137806. Grid ref: NG 2349 0601.
This hut circle measures around 11m in diameter and has some stone showing on both the interior and exterior faces. It stands in isolation from boundary or field divisions, which may have been buried in the moorland.

Beul An Iola Sgoir

8. ?Viking graves. NRHE ID 10771. Grid ref: NG 2195 0450.
Originally thought to be Viking graves, these narrow rectangular stone settings are now considered to be the basis of some form of agricultural platform. One measures 7.5 × 1m, the other 6.5 × 1m. They have no parallels elsewhere in Scotland or in Scandinavia

and remain enigmatic.

Blar Na Carraigh

9. Shieling huts. NRHE ID 10695. Grid ref: NG 2711 0604 (centre).
There are the remains of at least twelve huts here, typically 2 × 1.5m, together with a large number of mounds which may represent additional huts. The group is spread across a stream and includes one double-celled example measuring about 6.5 × 2.5m.

Bual Thial Sgorr

10. Shieling huts. NRHE ID 10714. Grid ref: NG 2783 0597(centre).
This group of seven huts on Compass Hill is contained within an oval enclosure, together with mounds which may represent earlier huts. There is also a sub-rectangular structure measuring about 6.5 × 4.5m, which may be later.

Buidhe Sgorr

11. Shieling huts. NRHE ID 142436. Grid ref: NG 2500 0668.
There are the remains of at least four huts of different sizes built within the boulder scree here, their sizes dependent on the natural features available. The smallest is about 1.5 × 1.5m, the largest roughly 3.5 × 3.5m. There are also other features that may lie in association.

Canna House

12. Cross fragments. Grid ref: NG 2749 0551.
There are ten cross fragments made from Torridonian Sandstone housed in Canna House (see Fisher 2001). Seven of these have been collected from various parts of the island, including stone walling, and three from the monastic or convent site of Sgorr nam Ban-naomha on the south coast (site **36**). All but one are

simple incised or pecked Latin crosses. The exception consists of two large fragments of a standing cross, one face of which contains interlace and knotwork, while the other depicts part of a human figure with a serpent entwined around its legs.

13. *Canna House*. *NRHE ID 76045*. *Grid ref: NG 2749 0551*.
Canna House was built in 1860 as the laird's residence in place of Coroghon House and has changed little since. It was designed as a two-storey villa with a hipped slate roof sloping to all four walls and was built of coursed rubble with a porch and bay windows. A two-storey extension was later added to the rear. John Lorne Campbell added a conservatory to the east, having purchased it in 1938. It now houses his music, books and collections.

Catholic church

14. *Church*. *NRHE ID 76049*. *Grid ref: 2754 0479*.
This rather sad-looking building has been closed since 1963. Originally built in the 1880s by the Marchioness of Bute in memory of her father, it has a large rectangular nave with a western rose window and a semicircular chancel with tower above. A construction of heavy, dark coursed rubble and thick string courses belies a brighter interior, the nave decorated with a corbel course containing stone heads of knights and priests.

Ceann Creag Airighe

15. *Hut circle*. *NRHE ID 141568*. *Grid ref: NG 2251 0556*.
There is at least one hut circle in this area on the side of a gully. It has a diameter of over 9m with some outer facing stones visible. Lengths of adjacent boundary walling of earth-fast stones indicate complex field divisions.

Cnoc Loisgte

16. Hut circle. NRHE ID 142479. Grid ref: NG 2269 0486.
This hut circle has a diameter of around 7m within a stony bank. Parts of an earth-fast stone boundary system are visible in the vicinity, although lengths have been robbed out. It appears to belong to a boundary that runs down to the gully Allt na Criche Tuatha, where it joins a major boundary extending across the island.

Cnoc Rugail

17. Hut circle. NRHE ID 141617. Grid ref: NG 2303 0579.
With a diameter of some 8m, this hut circle sits adjacent to an earth-fast stone boundary system that can be traced for about 160m running down to the gully Allt na Criche Tuatha, where it joins a major boundary extending across the island.

Conagearaidh

18. Settlement and burial ground. NRHE ID 141514. Grid ref: NG 2120 0555 (centre).
This settlement is not shown on the 1805 map and is therefore later, possibly an extension of the Garrisdale township or later farm. The buildings are depicted as uninhabited on the 1877 Ordnance Survey map. The site consists of the foundations of probably at least six structures broadly rectangular in shape, together with enclosures and lazy-bed cultivation. Nearby, to the east of the structures, is a small burial ground measuring approximately 13 × 10m enclosed by a collapsed wall.

Coroghon

19. Coroghon Castle. NRHE ID 10709. Grid ref: NG 2796 0552.
This so-called 'Castle' sits on the side of a basalt pillar some 25m tall and consists of a roofless two-storied edifice with a ground area of little more than 3 × 2m, accessed by a dangerous

narrow path. It probably belongs to the seventeenth or eight-eenth century, tradition holding that it was built by a jealous husband to imprison his wife on account of her great beauty. Ascent is not recommended on safety grounds.

Creag A' Chairn

20. Bronze Age burial cairn. NRHE ID 137797. Grid ref: NG 2423 0564.
Probably the only definitely identifiable early burial cairn on Canna, this is located in a prime position overlooking Tarbert. It has a diameter of around 14m and stands well over 1m in height. Some external kerbing is evident, as are some projecting earth-fast stones.

Creag Nam Faoileann, Sanday

21. Kelp kilns. NRHE ID 10763. Grid ref: NG 2875 0394 (centre).
Originally considered to be Viking graves, these two stone settings at the top of an inlet are now thought to be kelp kilns. Both settings are rectangular; one is approximately 7.5 × 2m with an open end, while the other, which lies about 40m to the south-west, is shorter, about 6.5 × 2m, and in poorer condition.

Druim Na Tire

22. Shieling huts. NRHE ID 141565. Grid ref: 2203 0528.
This solitary shieling hut measures approximately 3 × 2m and has been constructed against the boulders of a prehistoric boundary, which may have been used to provide the stones. There are some larger rectangular structures also backing against the boundary in the vicinity.

Dun Channa

23. Fort. NRHE ID 10764. Grid ref: NG 2058 0478.
Sheer on all sides, this is the most dramatic of the promontory

forts on Canna. Its plateau top measures about 35 × 30m and can be accessed only via a steep, narrow climb to an entrance on the landward side. The top of the landward side has been supplemented by a tall wall and there are two enclosures inside flanking the entrance. Access is not recommended on safety grounds.

Dun Teadh

24. Fort. NRHE ID 10738. Grid ref: NG 2090 0537.
This promontory is sheer on three sides but part of a sloping hillside on the landward side. The top of the promontory, which measures about 90 × 35m, has been emphasised by the construction of a wall from cliff to cliff on the landward side. This is about 40m long and collapsed to a width of about 3m. There are remains of possible walling inside.

Garrisdale

25. Township settlement. NRHE ID 141559. Grid ref: NG 2163 0532 (centre).
The most westerly of Canna's four townships, Garrisdale is depicted on the 1805 map as a series of structures together with fields and enclosures. Only the foundation remains of three structures, which may belong to a later farmstead, are visible. The buildings are all enclosed within a now dilapidated stone wall. The 1877 Ordnance Survey map depicts five unroofed buildings.

Greod, Sanday

26. Township settlement. NRHE ID 10756. Grid ref: NG 2741 0454 to NG 2749 0460.
Greod was the building focus for the Lower Island township on Sanday. Twelve buildings are shown on the 1805 map, of which a string of seven can still be located on the ground, each measuring some 10 × 4m. They probably belong to the post-1851 clearance

from Canna, though there is evidence of earlier remains below, possibly from the earlier clearance from Coroghon. All are shown as uninhabited on the 1877 Ordnance Survey map.

Keill (A'Chill)

27. Standing cross. *NRHE ID 10705. Grid ref: NG 2695 0553.*
Standing on the site of the cleared township of Keill, this partly broken ninth- or tenth-century cross still stands to a height of around 2m. The three surviving faces are carved in relief and present a combination of animal, human and decorative images reflecting both Christian and pagan traditions. Geophysical survey and keyhole excavation have shown that the cross stood immediately east of a stone-built structure, probably St Columba's church. A later nineteenth-century burial enclosure lies about 100m to the south-west.

28. Punishment Stone. *NRHE ID 10708. Grid ref: NG 2688 0554.*
This unusual earth-fast stone stands about 60m west of the standing cross (site 27) and is wedge-shaped and roughly 2m tall. Tradition holds it to be a 'punishment stone', whereby a miscreant's thumb would be wedged into a small hole near the top and the owner subjected to ridicule and shame. It is possible that the stone was originally a door jamb, being of a size commensurate with an important building such as a church rather than a domestic dwelling.

29. Grave of John Lorne Campbell. *Grid ref: NG 2698 0540.*
John Lorne Campbell, the last Laird of Canna, died in Italy where he was buried in 1996. His body was later brought back to Canna and reburied in a small wood that he himself had planted not far from the standing cross. His headstone came from his birthplace on the Inverneill estate in Argyll and is inscribed in Gaelic.

Presbyterian church

30. Church. NRHE ID 76044. Grid ref: NG 2766 0538.
This small Church of Scotland building was constructed in 1914 in memory of a former laird, Robert Thom. It was built in an Irish style with pointed tower and windows to match and a small nave with the pews set longitudinally. An ornate wrought-iron gate was added to the enclosure in 1969.

Rubha Camas Stianabhaig, Sanday

31. Kelp kiln. NRHE ID 10744. Grid ref: NG 2884 0424.
This is probably the longest kelp kiln on the island. Rectangular, it measures about 12 × 1.5m and is defined by lines of boulders. It sits at the bottom of a slope but well above the shoreline.

Rubha Langanes

32. ?Viking grave. NRHE ID 10733. Grid ref: NG 2411 0657.
For no known reason this has been described as the grave of the King of Norway. It consists of a narrow setting of single stones measuring some 10 × 2m, with a possible addition at one end lying off centre. The headland location is appropriate for a burial, but it seems more likely to have an (unknown) agricultural function.

Rubha nic Eamoin

33. Fort. NRHE ID 10767. Grid ref: NG 2379 0485.
This pincer-shaped promontory is protected on the landward side by a rampart which encloses an area of approximately 30 × 20m. The rampart is 5m wide and runs from cliff to cliff at the neck of the promontory for about 20m. The cliffs are precipitous on the three seaward sides.

Rubha Nam Feannag, Sanday

34. ?Bronze Age burial mounds. Grid ref: NG 2740 0496.
There are six cairns on this spur of headland overlooking the
harbour entrance. The largest has a diameter of about 8m
but shows no evidence of kerbing. All six sit in a cluster in a
dominant position and are too distant from any agricultural
activity to be related.

Sean Dun, Sanday

35. Fort. NRHE ID 10741. Grid ref: NG 2811 0398.
This is one of the few natural stack locations on Sanday. It lacks
the precipitous nature of the stacks on Canna and is irregular
in shape, housing an area of about 60 × 25m. There are low
cliffs on the seaward sides but the more accessible landward side
has been supplemented by a wall across its full length with an
entrance in the centre.

Sgorr nam Ban-naomha

*36. Early Christian ?nunnery. NRHE ID 10766. Grid ref: NG
2299 0439.*
Viewed best from the top of the cliffs, this remarkable site
represents a barely touched early Christian monastic outpost,
almost certainly a nunnery. Situated on a low terrace, it consists
of a sub-circular stone *vallum monasterium* containing a central
circular cell or possible oratory. Fragments of carved crosses
discovered there are now housed in Canna House (site 12).
Outside the wall are the remains of a series of other cells and
buildings, including a mill for domestic use. The setting is
isolated from the sea by rocky cliffs and from the land by
an almost vertical cliff. Visiting is not recommended on safety
grounds.

Sron Ruail

37. Hut circle. NRHE ID 10769. Grid ref: NG 2101 0471.
This large hut circle has a diameter of over 8m, with stonework evident on one side. It sits within an area of land divisions constructed of earth-fast stones, possibly representing an associated field system set within broader landscape boundaries.

Suileabhaig, Sanday

38. Shieling huts. NRHE ID 10752. Grid ref: NG 2807 0422.
There are at least three huts located here in the shelter of a crag among the boulders. One is large, double-celled in a figure-of-eight configuration and measures about 7 × 4m overall. The other two are single-celled, surviving only as depressed mounds of stones.

Tarbert

39. Township settlement. NRHE ID 10730. Grid ref: NG 2407 0559 (centre).
The 1805 map shows nine buildings in this township, traces of which can still be found on the ground in the form of turf-covered stone footings and eroded enclosures. The buildings were all rectangular but varied in size, the largest measuring about 13 × 5m. Only one of them is shown as being roofed on the 1877 Ordnance Survey map. Some twenty regularly placed small cairns to the south, each 2 to 4m in diameter, may be pilgrim cairns.

Tarbert Bay

40. ?Iron Age building. NRHE ID 10735. Grid ref: NG 2493 0563.
This mound, which has a diameter of around 14m, would appear to disguise a substantial circular structure, possibly of the Atlantic roundhouse variety such as a wheelhouse or broch.

There is evidence for both inner and outer wall facings, although the remains of later structures have confused the overall shape. Rabbit scrats have produced a small number of domestic objects, such as a spindle-whorl and whetstone, as well as undiagnostic pottery fragments.

5 Rum

'The Forbidden Island'

Introduction

A description of Rum written in 1764 by Dr John Walker as part of a government report on the Hebrides pointed out that 'by far the greatest part, may be judged wholly irreclaimable, consisting of steep mountains, deep mosses and tracks of land overspread with rocks'. Less polite was an early nineteenth-century visitor who described it as being 'the wildest and most repulsive of all the islands', although in fairness he had been storm-bound there and was not in a mood to be objective. These are just two descriptions of many, but all such express much the same opinion, and Rum's reputation of being physically unfriendly led to its being considered culturally unfriendly and tagged the 'Forbidden Island', an image that was reinforced by stories, superstitions and anecdotes.

Apart from the fertile area around Loch Scresort at the east and a few green patches of land around river estuaries, this comparatively vast island of over 10,000 hectares consists of barren mountains and cliff faces that exude hostility. It is as though the soil has been stripped off and the island abandoned to time. The open landscape is perhaps reflected in the derivation of the island's name from Norse 'rom-ey' (spacious island) or Gaelic 'rum' (wide space or area).

Rum's unfriendly physical personality has been shaped by

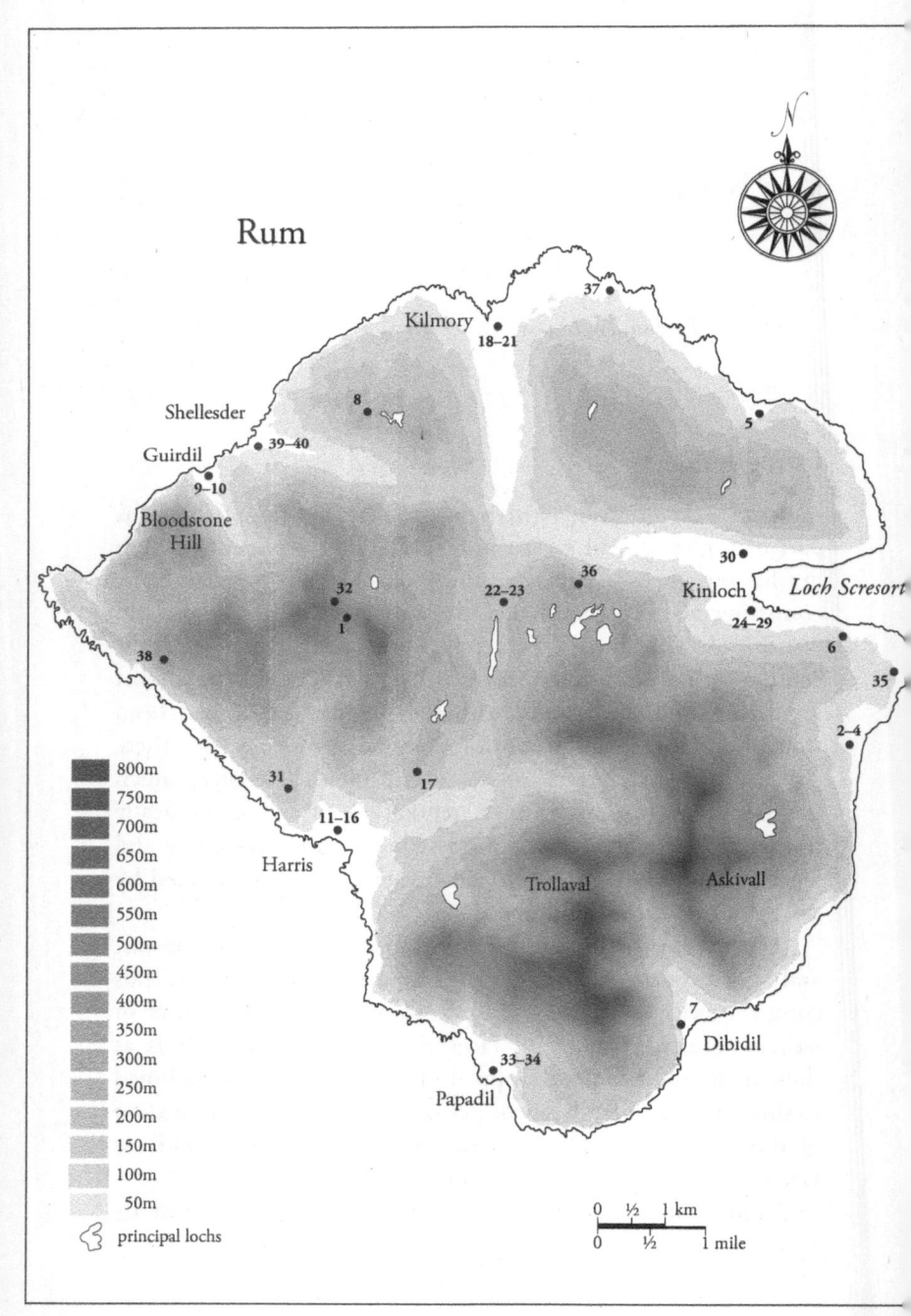

Rum

Kilmory

Shellesder

Guirdil

Bloodstone
Hill

Kinloch

Loch Scresort

Harris

Trollaval

Askivall

Dibidil

Papadil

800m
750m
700m
650m
600m
550m
500m
450m
400m
350m
300m
250m
200m
150m
100m
50m
principal lochs

0   ½   1 km

0   ½   1 mile

a string of volcanic eruptions and collapses, pushed up by the movement of magma from deep in the earth then sculptured by successive glaciers to leave it in its present form of bare rock and wet moorland. Now good only for sporadic upland grazing and running deer, it is hard to believe that it was once wooded, as implied by its early superstitious name 'Riogachd na Forraiste Fiadhaich' (Kingdom of the Wild Forest). It is also hard to believe that it was ever occupied to any great extent given the dearth of useful land. It was valued at only one ounceland in the Middle Ages, the same as Muck despite being over seventeen times larger than Muck in acreage. The amount of cultivatable land was so small that the island was recorded as having only two ploughs at the end of the eighteenth century, whereas there were eight ploughs on Eigg and seven each on Muck and Canna. It was also said that the ploughs were only ever used on two fields.

Walker's *Report on the Hebrides* of 1764, which provides the first reliable set of population figures, recorded 304 souls on the island, divided into fifty-seven families. 'Such a Number of people', he wrote, 'living in the way of Husbandry, upon so small a Property is not perhaps to be found anywhere else in Europe.' A generation later the number had swelled to the island's peak population of 443, which explains why every available patch of soil, no matter how poor, was turned into lazy beds for growing potatoes. This scarcity of land has had archaeological implications, in that it effectively channelled successive generations of islanders into the same places, each eroding or eradicating evidence of those that went before.

What Rum might have lacked in soil, however, was more than compensated for in the wildlife that abounded in its open landscape and in the coastal waters. Writing in 1549 Donald Monro commented that the ground-nesting wildfowl were only ever disturbed by the deer and bred in such number that their eggs could be easily collected. There are also specific references to grouse and puffins, the latter being found in large numbers. Rum's rivers, according to Martin Martin in 1695, were good for salmon, and when visiting the island in 1772 Thomas Pennant wrote of 'small whales, called here Pollacks, that when near land are often chased on shore by boats'. Almost every writer from the eighteenth century onwards comments on the abundance of fish in Loch Scresort and the ease with which they could be caught either with nets or by the use of fish traps. Pride of place in the wildlife stakes, however, was taken by the deer population for which the island was traditionally famed and which to a large extent has underpinned its cultural status from medieval times through to the present day.

As a consequence of its physical character Rum has a very different life story to tell in terms of its place in social history, the nature of its monuments and its role in the evolution of the Small Isles. It was generally considered colder and windier than the other three, less good for crops and a more austere place in which to live. John MacCulloch, a regular traveller in the early nineteenth century, noted that the island was stormbound seven of the eight times he passed by. 'It possesses a private winter of its own,' he wrote, 'even in what is here called summer.' Yet it had its positive side. A distinguished Cambridge professor, the Rev. Edward Daniel Clarke, visited the island in 1797 and took shelter in a shepherd's cottage in Guirdil. Not expecting to receive much in the way of hospitality he found himself being offered a 'fine old Lisbon wine' from a consignment that had been washed up from an unfortunate vessel which had lost its cargo in bad weather.

By all accounts the islanders were a particularly hardy lot, Thomas Pennant referring to them in 1772 as 'a well-made and well-looking race' that scarcely knew sickness. A decade earlier Walker's *Report* remarked on the historical longevity of the Rum population and recounted the story of an islander who had died at the age of 103 and was 50 before he ever tasted bread. Thereafter he ate it only between November and February, living entirely on milk and fish for the rest of the year.

With Walker's *Report* we enter an era of written information about the island, starting with a trickle but developing into a stream of descriptions, comments and observations through the late eighteenth and nineteenth centuries. Before that era there is necessarily a greater reliance on archaeological evidence, which in the case of Rum has thrown up some remarkable findings. Of the four islands Rum has the earliest evidence for human activity in the form of the natural presence of bloodstone, the common name for a hard, coloured cryptocrystalline quartz with similar properties to flint. This occurs among the mountains at the west of the island in a place now called Bloodstone Hill and appears to have been exploited as early as 8000 BC. While bloodstone's flint-like physical properties rendered it suitable for making arrowheads or scrapers, it may also have been believed to possess prized magical properties on account of its colour, its enigmatic island location and the extreme difficulties that must have been experienced in sailing to exploit it. It was quarried and worked on the island on a seasonal basis and is one of Rum's few tangible testimonies to early prehistory.

Rum did not present a landscape conducive to early farming, and apart from a group of hut circles from the Bronze Age and burial cairns on the coastal fringe there is little to see. By the time of the Iron Age the remains are more tangible, with the presence of three promontory forts which at least demonstrate the existence of some form of organised population, although there is no indication as to where that population may have lived. Common sense points to their homes being in the same few places as the townships of the seventeenth to nineteenth centuries, namely on the edges of the green land around the river estuaries or on the shores of Scresort Bay. Successive settlement on the same footprint will have scoured away any evidence.

Later, the Christian missions that established themselves firmly on Canna and Eigg appear not to have had much joy on Rum, possibly because there was little in the way of a population to preach to or convert. It may, however, have been a suitable venue for individual monks. There is a tradition according to which the seventh-century monk Beccan lived there, and the discovery of an early cross indicates some form of early Christian presence. Moreover, one of the placenames, Kilmory, which is the location of one of the townships with a long-standing burial ground, has a Gaelic root ('Cille', meaning chapel) and compares favourably with the similarly named townships of Kiel on Muck, Keill on Canna and Kildonnan on Eigg, all of which appear to have early Christian origins.

If evidence for early Christianity on Rum can be described as thin, then evidence for Norse settlement is even thinner and survives only in a small number of placenames. In all fairness the island offered little to a population with a pedigree of mixed farming. The other three islands were more attractive propositions. Rum was, however, firmly under the control of the Lordship of the Isles in the twelfth century, which nominally owed its allegiance to the Norwegian Crown and which somewhat later became part of the vast estate of the MacDonalds of Clanranald. This estate also included Eigg, which was prized because it was an important Christian centre and because the Clanranalds could achieve considerable prestige and status through their patronage. But why Rum? On the face of it Rum had little in the way of resources other than its wilderness.

Perhaps that was the clue – Rum was an excellent base for hunting. The wildlife was exceptional and the landscape well suited to herds of deer, which had no natural predators other than eagles. In his 2001 book Denis Rixson suggests that it may have been highly valued as a type of hunting reserve within the larger Clanranald estate and used specifically for hunting parties. This makes good sense and is supported by the remains of deer traps which can still be traced for hundreds of metres on the mountainsides. Hunting deer was the type of large-scale activity that required planning, organisation and manpower and thus could only be undertaken by someone of considerable wealth. Although sources indicate that deer hunting on Rum eventually went through a process of decline, it appears to have still been thriving as a pursuit when the island passed to the MacLeans of Coll, probably in the sixteenth century. It remained under MacLean ownership until the early nineteenth century.

Although there are one or two mentions of incidents on Rum in the sixteenth and seventeenth centuries, and again after the 1745 uprising, it is only with Walker's *Report* of 1764 and travellers' accounts from the late eighteenth century that there is a clearer picture of life on the island. By that time (according to Walker) there were seven townships spread unevenly across most parts of the island, reflecting the available land resources; for example, there were seventeen families in Kilmory but only three at Papadil. In many senses Walker's *Report* is a snapshot of the island at the end of the 'old system' of mixed farming, communal activity and local self-sufficiency. It was a domestic economy that consumed what it produced and had in place a well-tried system of land use that optimised the resources available. This included the practice of transhumance, for which there are at least four hundred shieling huts scattered around the higher reaches of the island.

By the end of the eighteenth century a combination of population increase in relation to usable land, the introduction of sheep and the growth of the kelp industry saw much of the mixed farming being abandoned. Kelp harvesting was more profitable, although on Rum there were comparatively few suitable beaches where kelp could be drawn up. Some emigration occurred, but once the kelp bubble burst in the early nineteenth century the income dried up and the population became unsustainable. By that time the deer population had become all but extinct. Laird MacLean of Coll's solution was to evict and, like many lairds elsewhere, introduce sheep on a massive scale to obtain a more reliable income. Rum was partially cleared in 1826 and then again two years later, when in July 1828 all but possibly as few as two families left to be replaced by 8,000 sheep. MacLean's venture into sheep farming on an industrial scale proved to be a hopeless failure, and in 1845 he sold the island to the English politician Lord Salisbury, who attempted to improve the infra-structure and return the island to a hunting estate for the great and the good. He had a modicum of success, although with one particular disastrous building venture. Hunting estates were very much in vogue when the island passed into the hands of the Bullough family at the end of the century, but the ownership of George Bullough brought about the greatest disaster of all in turning Rum into a louche playboy retreat complete with so-called 'Castle'. His widow, Lady Monica Bullough, sold the island in 1957 to the current owner, the Nature Conservancy Council (which subsequently became Scottish Natural Heritage and is now NatureScot).

Rum's reputation as a 'forbidden isle' did much to ensure its place in history, particularly under the Bullough regime. One of the earliest accounts of the island is Thomas Pennant's perceptive *A Tour in Scotland and Voyage to the Hebrides, 1772*, which described his time on both Rum and Canna that year. There is also a good seventeenth-century description of deer hunting by John Taylor in *The Penniless Pilgrim* (edited later in 1876). Subsequent works include *The Cruise of the Betsey* by the Edinburgh geologist Hugh Miller, who ventured widely across Rum and Eigg in 1845 although his book was not published for another seventeen years. One of his chapters is devoted almost exclusively to bloodstone. Rum's bloodstone was also of interest to Edward Daniel Clarke (see Otter 1825). Information about the excavations of the Mesolithic bloodstone working site at Kinloch can be found in Caroline Wickham-Jones' book *Rhum: Mesolithic and Later Sites at Kinloch: Excavations 1984–86* (1990).

Lancastrian writer and poet Edwin Waugh spent several months on Rum in 1882. He was a sick man and ventured only around the Kinloch area, but his book *The Limping Pilgrim* (1883) is rich in detail about people and living conditions. More recently John Love, a conservationist and historian who lived on the island, wrote a detailed book, *Rum: A Landscape without Figures* (2001), which describes the history of the island, particularly the causes and effects of emigration in the early nineteenth century, and quotes numerous letters and documents that colour the last three centuries of life on the island. His knowledge of Rum's landscape and history is second to none and his book is an invaluable compendium of information. He also wrote articles on shielings and deer traps and remains the person most credited with our understanding of Rum's natural and historic environment.

A number of works focus on the Bullough era and its aftermath. One is a fascinating autobiography by Archie Cameron, the son of a gamekeeper, whose *Bare Feet and Tackety Boots* (1988) gives a vivid picture of life and class structure on Rum in the years before the First World War. Alastair Scott's *Eccentric Wealth: The Bulloughs of Rum* (2011) goes part way to dispelling some of the myths that surround the Bullough household, while Karl Sabbagh's *A Rum Affair* (2001) analyses the latest mystery to have arisen on the island, concerning the discovery (fraudulent or otherwise) of a species of plant reputed to have survived the last Ice Age. Full references for all the above works are given in the 'Further Reading' section at the end of the book.

Prehistory

The dearth of archaeological sites on Rum is more than compensated for by the discovery of a Mesolithic bloodstone working site at Farm Fields, **Kinloch** (27), at the head of Scresort Bay. Dated by domestic food waste to as far back as the eighth millennium BC, the site is one of the oldest known places of human activity anywhere in Scotland. It was discovered accidentally in 1983, when flakes of bloodstone were found in plough soil and were recognised as debris similar to that produced by working flint for making items such as arrowheads, blades and scrapers. Unlike flint, bloodstone offered an attractive visual appearance, being coloured dark green, grey or cream with red spatters or veins, but it had similar physical properties to flint for working purposes.

The major excavation that followed yielded tens of thousands of similar flakes that had been abandoned in the manufacturing process (debitage), which appears to have continued for several thousand years. It was a seasonal activity that presumably used natural caves for shelter, and was undertaken in the summer months when the seas were calm and the island could be foraged for whatever food resources were available. Post-holes found in the ground show that working took place behind small screens or windbreaks; there were also a number of pits of unknown purpose.

The raw material could have been quarried from a seam on Bloodstone Hill, on a steep slope called Creag nan Stairdean, and carried down to the bay, where there was a more suitable environment for working. A quarry symbol was shown there on the 1877 Ordnance Survey map but not on later editions, and there is no longer anything to see on the ground. Alternatively, bloodstone could have been sourced more easily among the pebbles down in Guirdil Bay, a short distance to the north-east of Bloodstone Hill, presumably washed out from a different seam nearby. Guirdil Bay was visited in 1797 by a distinguished Cambridge mineralogist, Edward Daniel Clarke, who reported finding 'immense fragments of a beautiful dark green stone, which the lapidaries of Edinburgh term green jasper, and estimate at a very high price. Some of it was marked with bright red spots, others with white; and in some we observed broad stripes of blue, red, or yellow.' Secondary deposits such as these may also have been a more easily accessible source of prehistoric supply and one approachable by boat as opposed to an inland route requiring an unenviable trudge through the mountains.

The activity site in Scresort Bay remains one of the few sheltered areas on the island and was well positioned for small boat access as well as for export of the finished products to other parts of Scotland. Bloodstone objects have been found within a radius of 80km across Lewis, Skye and parts of the mainland, providing an interesting insight into exchange networks in prehistory. Flint was probably a better commodity for manufacturing tools, but bloodstone clearly had a property that was in some sense regarded as special, possibly related to its colour, or to the belief that it empowered the user. Perhaps it was believed that bloodstone tools were somehow better empowered for killing or for giving their user strength. The perceived special nature of the material also begs the question of whether this prized commodity was in any way owned, its exploitation controlled, or whether it was simply a free-for-all. It would almost certainly have been surrounded by superstition, which may have given rise to the long-standing tradition whereby the island was seen as somehow 'forbidden'.

Apart from some residual working of bloodstone through into the Neolithic there is little else to show of Rum's earlier prehistory, much having been removed by the more intensive cultivation that began during Neolithic times some 4,500 years ago. Only three hut circles have been identified, all from **Shellesder** (39) at the north-west of the island, adjacent to a promontory fort. There are also three likely burial cairns, located at **Harris** (11), **Kilmory** (18) and **Guirdil** (9), which may be contemporary or earlier. All three take prominent positions and all three have been heavily disturbed.

Whatever the nature and size of the population in the Iron Age, Rum was sufficiently well organised to have modified three promontories for ostensible defence or refuge, although they are rather poor examples. Kilmory and Shellesder are both at the north, with Papadil in the remoter part of the island at the south. It is probably coincidental that all were located on the edge of fertile estuaries, which were themselves proven population centres in later centuries. They were probably constructed in the last half of the first millennium BC, at **Kilmory** (20) and **Shellesder** (40), both based on precipitous rocks protected by landward walls, and at **Papadil** (34), protected by less regular walling but where nearby caves have produced Iron Age pottery and midden material.

Christian impact

There is no evidence for there having been a monastic settlement on Rum, apart from the intriguing name 'Papadil' on the south-west of the island. This remote location on the coast contains a small freshwater loch fed from mountain streams and a patch of greenery which later became the site of a small township. Similar 'Papa' placenames are known from a small number of other places in Scotland and are widely recognised as indicating the location of a monastic community, 'papa' being the Norse word for priests. In many respects the place is ideally situated for housing a small group of monks dedicated to a life of piety, seclusion and prayer. Sadly, there is no evidence for their presence other than the name itself, although traces may lie beneath the later buildings.

A more substantial Christian centre, though unlikely to be a monastic one, was probably represented by the burial ground at **Kilmory** (19) at the north, also the location of a township and the only known burial ground on the island. The origin of the name (Gaelic 'Cille', meaning chapel) would seem to indicate a Christian centre, which, according to a stone bearing an incised cross from among the burials, may be from as early as the seventh or eighth century. There is no sign of a church that might be associated with the burials, although there are written references to one, the earliest being by Martin Martin, who in 1685 noted, rather unhelpfully, 'There is a chapel in this isle; the natives are protestants.' In 1772 Pennant described 'the ruins of a church' but failed to say where the ruins were, although he did add that services were currently held in the open air as there was no church anywhere else. Maps add some further interest. Blaeu's *Atlas of Scotland*, published in 1654 but based on Timothy Pont's drawings of half a century earlier, gives a very schematic view of the island at a small scale and depicts a church and burial ground very clearly at Kilmory and another church at the other end of the island, presumably Harris but described as 'Kaming'.

There is no doubt over an 1801 map by George Langlands, which includes a church symbol with the word 'Kirk' in bold letters in the general Kilmory vicinity (see plate section). The first edition of the Ordnance Survey map (1877) depicts only the burial ground there. There is evidence of a later church being built, but this was in Kinloch, after the Clearances, and was constructed of wood. Edwin Waugh rather unkindly described it as being 'like a haystack with two windows'.

The absence of any substantial population on Rum probably obviated the need for any focused early Christian mission for conversion purposes, as happened, for example, on Eigg, but it did provide an appropriate wilderness setting for ascetics. It is reasonable to assume that it was a place of interest for monks seeking solitude within the Christian mission flowing from Ireland and Iona up into western Scotland. Evidence for this can only be documentary, as the surviving archaeological evidence is likely to be nil. It has long been claimed that Rum was once home to the monk Beccan, who was known as a scholar and poet on Iona in the mid seventh century and has a historically recorded death around 677. His time on Rum is well supported by both tradition and anecdote, and by an amalgam of Irish sources which refer to him variously as 'Beccan of Rum' or 'Baccanus solitarius' (Beccan the hermit). There is, for example, a large rock on the side of Loch Scresort known locally as the 'Priest's Stone', located by the modern pier where Beccan reputedly tied up his boat when he first landed on Rum. There is also a cave at **Bagh na h-Uamha** (2 and 3) on the east coast, which is where he is said to have lived. Conveniently close by on the shore, a cross-marked pillar stone some 1.5m long was found partly embedded in the sand in 1977, incised with an equal-armed cross on a pedestal. Dated to the seventh century, it has since been re-erected at the beach head, thus strengthening the Beccan tradition in that area.

Norse impact

Together with the other three islands, Rum technically came under the sovereignty of Norway during the Lordship of the Isles in the twelfth century. By that time Viking raiding had long ceased, settlement had been consolidated and populations integrated, but placenames are sadly all that is left of several centuries of Norse heritage. The Norse may have controlled the island from an administrative point of view, but it seems unlikely that they settled there in any number. Although the island had a similar mountainous environment to their homeland, it lacked the extent of fertile lower slopes that might have made farming worthwhile. The fact that only one farm has a Norse element in its name ('Raonapoll', Norse 'poll' meaning farm) and is located adjacent to the main fertile area around Kinloch makes the point. Norse topographical elements are also present in suffixes such as '-dil' (Norse 'dale', valley), as well as in the names of mountains such as 'Askival' (Spear-like Mountain) and 'Trollaval' (Mountain of the Trolls), but these are just as likely to have been used as navigation markers from the sea as from the land. Overall, like the three other islands, Rum appears to have been controlled and influenced by a minority ruling elite but in a manner that was enduring. Thomas Pennant, writing in 1772, was critical of the way farmers on Rum were permitted only a certain number of cattle according to their 'pennyland' divisions – the name of a land value division that had been imposed centuries earlier in Norse times and that still persisted.

Medieval and post-medieval landscapes

Whereas most of the Clanranald estate, which eventually included all four of the Small Isles, survived right the way through into the nineteenth century, Rum, exceptionally, was sold off to the MacLeans of Coll, probably in the sixteenth century. Until then Rum may well have been used as a deer park, or at least as some form of hunting estate, to satisfy the recreational interests of its owners. High in the mountains are a series of stone features which can be interpreted as deer traps. In some cases these are hundreds of metres long and the product of laborious human activity. The way they worked was relatively simple. The deer were driven up into the mountains by dogs and then chased down between two lines of scree gathered from the slopes. The gap between the two lines was wide at the top but narrowed into a funnel shape at the bottom. The deer, reluctant to tread on the scree, became progressively enclosed as they descended until, at the bottom, they found themselves caught in stone pens where they were slaughtered.

The lines of scree and enclosure walling are impossible to date. But if they are argued to represent a designated playground of the Clanranald elite within their vast estates, then the traps' origins are to be placed firmly in the medieval period. There are references to similar traps, or 'tynchells', elsewhere in Scotland in the Middle Ages, providing a context for those on Rum. According to reliable early sources, operating a deer hunt of this kind required a few hundred men to drive the deer and to control their movement with dogs. There has never been a recorded population of that magnitude on Rum and the exercise could only be achieved if the hunt was a communal activity under the leadership of a chieftain who was able to arrange it and provide the resources. It would have been a major undertaking, not something that could be carried out on a whim. It needed transport, food and accommodation and would have had to be set up well in advance. There is a good early description by Taylor of a similar hunt which took place on the Earl of Mar's estate on the mainland in 1618, in which 'five or six hundred men' were needed together with dogs to round up the deer and drive them down into the pen for slaughter. An exercise of that nature chimes well with the idea of Rum being a kind of game park within a much larger estate.

The way the traps worked has been described in several early texts, including the first *Statistical Account*, written in 1794:

> Before the use of firearms, their method of killing deer was as follows: on each side of a glen, formed by two mountains, stone dykes were begun pretty high in the mountains, and carried to the lower part of the valley, always drawing nearer, till within 3 or 4 feet of each other. From this narrow pass, a circular space was enclosed by a stone wall, of a height sufficient to confine the deer; to this place they were pursued and destroyed.

If the second *Account* is to be believed the island held several deer traps, referred to as 'Tigh'n Sealg' (hunting houses), where 'at the termination of the dikes, houses were erected, into which the deer were constrained to enter'. The writers of both *Accounts* seem to have been very familiar with the mechanics of the process, but the implication was that this form of hunting no longer took place. The earliest reference which might be construed as being contemporary with the 'tynchell' belongs to Dean Monro, who in 1549, in addition to commenting on the abundance of deer on Rum, described the process with some familiarity. He describes the similar method of deer hunting on Jura in much the same way and in the present tense, giving the impression that it was a well-honed activity and a long-standing tradition. It is a fair assumption that deer hunting was actively pursued on Rum in the Middle Ages but ceased to be viable as a result of deforestation and the loss of woodland habitats. It is conceivable that the Clanranalds sold out to the MacLeans of Coll sometime in the sixteenth century partly for this very reason.

There are at least two deer traps still clearly visible on the island. The most obvious and better preserved is that at **Orval** (32) in the mountains at the west, where the pair of funnelled scree sides drop down several hundred metres into a tall stone enclosure. The sides are part scree and part broad low walling.

The funnel narrows down to little more than a metre at the bottom where the deer are channelled individually into a pair of enclosures where they could be held and then killed in a confined space. The first enclosure measured about 8 × 5m, while the second was slightly larger. Both had tall stone walls which in places still survive to some 2m, to prevent the deer from leaping out. The rather unsporting nature of this method of hunting might perhaps be balanced by the need to provide venison for food. Another trap, in a poorer state of preservation, can be seen at **Ard Nev** (1) slightly to the south-east. Less evident, the two main 'funnel' elements are more sporadic and appear to have been rebuilt at the bottom, the original enclosure being replaced.

On a wider front, apart from an alleged assault on the island in 1588, Rum appears to have maintained an uneventful existence through into the eighteenth century. The assault, which was also suffered by Canna, Eigg and Muck, was at the hands of Lachlan MacLean of Duart, who decided to take revenge on all of the Small Isles for some desecration that the Clanranalds had wreaked on Iona. From Rum's point of view this was rather unfair, in that the island may no longer have been Clanranald property. Nevertheless, sources claim that houses were burnt to the ground and most of the population killed. While there may be some truth in this, a complete decimation of the population seems unlikely, especially given the difficulty of pursuing small populations in Rum's remoter locations in order to put them to the sword.

DEMOGRAPHICS AND TOWNSHIPS

It is difficult to ascertain what the population of Rum would have been at the end of the sixteenth century, but estimates suggest that it would not have been more than about 200 folk. There is a brief reference to the island dating from shortly after Duart's assault, which mentions two centres named 'Kilmoir' (Kilmory) at the north-west and 'Glenhairie' (Harris) at the south-west. Walker's *Report* of 1764 records townships not only at Kilmory (84 persons in seventeen families) and Harris (74 persons in fifteen families) but also in five other places: 'Sandyess' (Samhnan Insir, located east of Kilmory, 43 persons in seven families), Kinloch (46 persons in eight families), Papadil (12 persons in three families), Guirdil (22 persons in five families) and Bagh na h-Uamha (20 persons in three families). Langlands' map of 1801 depicts all seven of these (with varying spellings) and adds two more, at 'Cammasplasaig' (Camas Pliasgaig) at the north-east of the island and at 'Glendibble' (Dibidil) at the south-east. Habitation is crudely depicted by house symbols. All are given two house symbols to show a place of multiple occupation with the exception of Harris which has three, presumably in recognition of a relatively greater density. In Walker's time the population stood at over 300 and far below its recorded maximum of 443 thirty years later, roughly when Langlands' map was drawn up.

In his account of his tour of 1772 Pennant commented specifically on the paucity of arable land and referred to 'nine little hamlets that the natives have grouped in different places; near which the corn is sown in diminutive patches'. One of these was at **Kinloch** (29), where Pennant recorded 'about a dozen houses', giving some idea of density. He described them as having thick, low walls with thatched roofs, only one having a chimney and windows, cooking being carried out by a pot suspended over the fire by a rope from the roof. Some of the turf-grown foundations of these buildings can still be seen on the shore around the bay in the camping area. There are more visible remains at Kilmory and Harris, which also appear to have been substantial townships. With only the shells of empty homes left behind from the Clearances of 1826 and 1828, these are sad places to visit. Waugh wrote in 1882 that he could only trace 'the faint outlines of these ruined habitations, here and there, overgrown with grass and moss, and wild lichens'. At **Kilmory** (21) there are the remains of at least sixteen rectangular buildings north of the burial ground by the Kilmory river, representing a range of building sizes and functions together with associated lazy beds. None appear to have been inhabited by the time of the 1877 Ordnance Survey map.

Harris (15 and 16) was probably the most populous site and is visible in two discrete parts separated by the river valley. As at Kilmory the buildings are in a range of sizes and represent functions ancillary to homesteads, such as byres and outhouses, together with enclosures and cultivation strips. One part, known rather clinically as 'Harris 1', lies on the lower terrace to the south of the river and contains the footings of as many as thirty structures. A small group set at a slight distance may be later. The other part of the township, 'Harris 2', lies on a higher terrace to the north of the river, where the remains of about ten buildings have been more severely damaged by cultivation. Some appear to have a fill of earth or turf in the wall cores, which might indicate a slightly earlier date than those in Harris 1. Despite the size of the settlements the Ordnance Survey map shows only two being roofed in 1877.

The remaining townships are all much smaller, possibly reflecting the paucity of land in the remoter parts of the island. There are probably eight sets of rectangular foundations at Camas Pliasgaig (5), six at Bagh na h-Uamha (4) ('Cove' on Langlands' map) and four at Samhnan Insir (37). There are at least five structures at Guirdil (10), where in 1797 Edward Daniel Clarke recorded 'a few huts with a small boat or two, drawn up on the beach'. Several of them have associated patches of cultivation. There are also remains of two buildings at Dibidil (7), although these may be contemporary with later individual farmsteads, such as at Papadil, which now shows no evidence of its original small township. There is also a later shepherd's hut at Guirdil which is now a bothy. Both the Papadil and Guirdil shepherd huts were shown as still being roofed on the 1877 Ordnance Survey map.

Life in late eighteenth-century Rum is best illustrated by Pennant's account of his 1772 tour, which took place when the kelp industry was beginning to gather steam. He describes the island as being rich in resources of corn and potatoes, but 'so small is the quantity of bere and oats that there is not a fourth part produced to supply their annual wants: all the subsistence the poor people have besides, is curds, milk and fish'. The milling process, which took place using imported and costly hand querns, he describes as being 'very tedious', and he makes a general point about the fishing potential being limited by a lack of suitable equipment, notably fish hooks. Twenty years later the same complaint was still being voiced in the first *Statistical Account*, despite the fact that fish continued to be an essential part of the islanders' staple diet.

A number of shore-based fish traps around Loch Scresort are recorded by Edwin Waugh in the 1880s. These would involve the construction of a low dam of loosely built stones across the head of the bay, over which the fish would swim at high tide, becoming trapped inside the wall as the tide ebbed, at which point they could be caught with nets. Although difficult to discern, the remains of a fish trap at Kinloch are still visible at low tide in the form of an incomplete arc at the north-west of the bay. Waugh also heard of an earlier technique involving a dam of bundled heather, which expanded in the water and entrapped the fish like a net as they tried to escape. It is easy to underestimate the importance of inshore marine resources, which were an essential subsistence requirement. Even in the hardest of times, scouring the shore for shellfish could keep body and soul together, but it was the bottom line. When the British Fisheries Society visited Rum in the 1780s it found the inhabitants busily packing herrings for their winter provision. The amount they could cure was limited by the amount of salt they could afford, salt being a highly taxed commodity that had to be brought from the nearest custom house at Tobermory on Mull. The issue of the salt tax was a continual grouse. The Fisheries Society suggested that the laird (MacLean of Coll) should build a quay and supply salt and casks to facilitate fishing, but the proposal came to nothing. It was another half century before a pier was finally completed at **Kinloch (28)**, not so much to boost commerce as to support the growth of a shooting estate under the later ownership of Lord Salisbury.

In contrast to this growing hardship Pennant makes special mention of the high-quality black cattle and the prices they fetched and the fine-tasting local mutton, not to mention the excellence of horses bred on the island, also noted by others. According to the first *Statistical Account*, the wool from native sheep was of exceptional quality and worth up to twice as much as wool from other sources at mainland markets. The overall picture of life on Rum in this period is one of both poverty and wealth that is difficult to interpret. Further contact outside the island took place with the sale of fish in the Clyde markets, which for some reason was preferred to internal consumption. Pennant also encountered islanders who were concerned with the production and export of goat hair for making wigs. He related that people collected the hair, sorted it according to levels of fineness and sold it in Glasgow for making wigs that were then sent to America.

SHIELINGS, KELP AND THE 'OLD SYSTEM'

Before the kelp bonanza black cattle and sheep were among the mainstays of the domestic economy and required the use of summer pastures and therefore of shieling huts. Rum is second to none in its provision of these, not least thanks to the tireless research of John Love in identifying, recording and sketching plans of them to produce an astonishing estimate of almost four hundred individual huts, often in clusters, scattered across the island. His is the most detailed study ever undertaken and shows a range of configurations, cellular, chambered and rectangular, mostly lying above the 100m contour. The earlier ones sit on mounds, reflecting the accumulated debris of many seasons of occupation; some are sited in areas of scree or rock face to facilitate construction, others where the stone from earlier monuments provides suitable material. This itself might go some way to explaining the paucity of prehistoric monuments, particularly hut circles, on the island. The large number of huts on Rum is a response to the landscape, which, as well as being more extensive than that of the other three islands, is better suited to sheep and reflects a type of domestic grazing that was almost entirely obliterated by the Clearances.

Few huts stand in complete isolation and they are usually to be found with small pens and enclosures in association. John Love found it possible to group them on geographical grounds to individual townships: Guirdil (114 huts), Harris (124 huts), Kilmory (103 huts) and Papadil (35 huts), all lining the higher ground along their respective river valleys in ones and twos or in clusters. Anyone trekking through the mountains would be hard pushed not to fall over the remains of one. There are good examples of clusters with single- and double-celled huts at **Loch Monica** (31), at **Hugh's Brae** (17), along **Kilmory Glen** (23) and in **Glen Shellesder** (8) next to a trackway that runs along the glen, enabling easier transport of produce back to the township. A recorded group of twenty-five at **Kinloch Glen** (30) in 1972 has now been reduced to about twelve as a result of afforestation.

An unusual landscape feature that may have some connection with transhumance practices is to be found on the coastal cliffs at **Sgorr Reidh** (38), on the western tip of the island. A stone dyke runs along the edge of the cliff for around 300m, interspersed with at least a dozen huts or cells. All are corbelled and have sunken floors. They were certainly not part of a deer trap and make little sense for transhumance purposes. The least unconvincing solution is that the shieling grounds were on the landward side and the huts were positioned at the very edge of the pasture, with the stone walling offering the cattle a modicum of shelter against the prevailing westerlies. The huts are in a generally good condition and none of them sit on accumulated mounds, both facts pointing towards a relatively recent date.

By the turn of the century the 'old system' characterised by the shielings and the infield/outfield method of farming was still in use but far from flourishing. The financial benefits of kelp harvesting were taking over, and kelp was no longer being spread on the fields as a fertiliser. Kelp was the new gold. It could be dragged ashore, burnt in pits and the hardened alkali residue sold to England at a good price. It was harder to harvest on Rum on account of the rugged coastline, but the island nevertheless saw a population increase from around 300 in 1764, according to Walker's *Report*, to around 400 in 1821, having declined a little from a recorded maximum of 443 a few years earlier. This growth was little different from that experienced on the other three islands, except that when the kelp bubble finally burst with the import of cheaper alkali from Spain there was little in the way of cultivatable land to fall back on, too many mouths to feed and too little rental income for the laird. Like many other lairds, MacLean of Coll, who owned Rum, saw a brighter financial future for himself in farming sheep on an industrial scale. The old clan system of unity was breaking down and the lairds were turning away from leadership and duty towards capitalism.

THE CLEARANCES

By 1830 no fewer than 8,000 sheep had been introduced on Rum, but this could only be done by evicting the islanders. By all accounts MacLean was a benevolent laird and was prepared to provide assisted passages across the Atlantic. Limited emigration had already taken place in the late 1700s, but the first formal eviction took place in 1826 at some cost to himself, and the second in 1828, when the ss *Lawrence* called in at Kilmory and took all but a few families away to Nova Scotia along with many from Muck. The townships were abandoned and stripped of anything worth having, to prevent them being reoccupied, and the majority of the shielings were never used again. The number of families left behind is debatable. It could have been as few as two.

The anger of the islanders must have been compounded when, at the time of the first emigration in 1826, factor Lechlan MacLean built himself a fine new house at **Kinloch (25)** at the head of the bay. Appropriately named 'Kinloch House', it was still standing when Edwin Waugh wandered around the bay in 1882 and noted 'a plain, strongly built stone house, with a steep roof and with a porch, and with a small wing at each end, one of which is used as a gun room and the other as a kitchen'. It was set in its own grounds and planted with woodland, and was, as it later transpired, ideal for accommodating guests who were interested in hunting.

It was during those wanderings that Waugh met an old shepherd who had been an eyewitness to the 1828 emigration, later relating his memory of events:

> On that day, when the people of the island were carried off in one mass, for ever, from the sea-girt spot where they had been born and bred, and where the bones of their forefathers were laid in the ancient graveyard of Kilmory ... the wild outcries of the men, and the heart-breaking wails of the women and their children filled all the air between the mountainous shores of the bay; and that the whole scene was of such a distressful description that he should never be able to forget it to his dying day. But they went away wailing across the stormy sea; and the wild hills of their native isle will see them no more for ever.

This emotionally charged description has much truth to it. At least one family was allowed to remain, the family of Allan MacLean, who lived at a farm called Carn nan Dobhran Bhig (Cairn of the Little Otter) on the south side of Scresort Bay with his wife and two children, Kenneth and Catherine. The MacLean family could not be evicted because they had been granted the *duthchas* for an area of land there many generations ago. This was an ancient clan-based privilege that had no legal standing but was seen as an inalienable right of tenure. The MacLeans did not own the land as such but they had similar rights to that of ownership stretching far back into history. Even the laird with all his wealth and power was not inclined to overrule on such a sensitive issue that might have repercussions among his peers. The MacLeans were allowed to stay on their land and a family of shepherds was retained at Papadil to help with the sheep. By all accounts this was the Chisholm family, who lived in the newly abandoned small township, their main access being by sea.

It is hard to believe that an island that had been populated for around 8,500 years and had seen countless generations of families work the land should suddenly be emptied and reduced to two households set miles apart. Before the exodus the islanders made a bold statement of their discontent and their anger against the laird by rolling a huge round boulder into a prominent position on a flat rock roughly halfway along the track from Kinloch to Kilmory. Known as the **Protest Rock** (36) it can still be seen. From it is a view across to Kilmory Bay where the ss *Lawrence* lay at anchor to take on board the émigrés. Wedged firmly in place with chocking stones, the rock is a memorial to the traditions, learning and experiences of all those who departed, effectively leaving behind an island without a memory. In the middle of the nineteenth century the geologist Hugh Miller lamented that Rum was 'a landscape without figures', a phrase which John Love later used as the subtitle of his 2001 book.

All that remains of the Chisholms' dwelling at Papadil are some stone footings and enclosure walling lying on the edge of the loch facing the sea. By 1877 the Ordnance Survey map shows two roofless buildings there. **At Carn nan Dobhran Bhig** (6) Allan MacLean's farmhouse and associated structures are more substantial and represent some of the few groups of walled remains still to be seen on the island. They can be approached by a trackway and the ruins can be found hidden in a later plantation. The initials of his eldest grandson, Hector, can be seen on the gable wall crudely incised as 'HMcL'. Several smaller outbuildings sit in the immediate vicinity, one at some distance. All the structures are still shown as being roofed on the first- and second-edition Ordnance Survey maps. Allan MacLean's land is marked by an earthen dyke up to 3m wide in places that encloses a wide area leading down to the shore, presumably the original extent of the *duthchas*. Lying a short distance from the dwelling but inside the dyked area is a simple grave with an unmarked headstone which is thought to belong to Catharin MacLean, a relative and a pauper who died of tuberculosis in 1863. As a pauper she would have been denied a resting place in a formal cemetery.

MacLean of Coll's venture into sheep farming was an unhappy one. The island was empty and the shepherding of 8,000 sheep was far beyond the powers of the single shepherd's family at Papadil. More shepherds were brought in from Skye and the island's population slowly began to increase, provision being made for some form of service industry and infrastructure for those who were beginning to settle. On the coast, east of Allan MacLean's dwelling, **Port na Caranean** (35) was resettled in order to provide accommodation for more incomers from Skye. There is a group of nine buildings that can still be seen there, many with walls standing to wall-head height. Solitary farmsteads emerged at the former townships of Dibidil and Guirdil and by 1831 the census shows the population back in three figures, but it slowly declined thereafter. By 1839 the sheep venture had failed, MacLean became bankrupt and in 1845 the island was sold to Lord Salisbury. By that time the population was recorded as consisting of only seven families.

Sporting estates and later ownership

Lord Salisbury was a London politician who had no interest whatsoever in sheep. His motive for the purchase was purely that of seeing the island as a potential sporting estate, ideal for fishing, shooting and stalking. Hugh Miller, the geologist, who visited Rum in the same year as the sale, was quick to notice the irony of the situation, namely that the island, once a natural wilderness for wild animals, which had been settled and cultivated by generations of islanders, had now been returned to its original wilderness state in what he saw as a 'strange and most melancholy cycle'.

Salisbury's lairdship lasted for twenty-five years but was less than satisfactory. He maintained seasonal visits to Kinloch House for sport, although his wife, Lady Salisbury, seemed to relish the rural isolation and spent time there outside the hunting season without him. Salisbury would seem to have been well-intentioned but ill-advised. On the plus side he restocked the island's deer population, improved the salmon fishing with fish ladders, carried out a great deal of maintenance and investment in building and repairs, and improved the infrastructure. He is also recorded as having made some attempt to revive the exploitation of bloodstone. Yet while substantial improvements were certainly made (and at great cost), his ownership is more likely to be remembered for his disastrous attempt to divert the Kilmory river to improve the fishing. To this end labourers from Eigg were brought in to construct a dam in **Kilmory Glen (22)**, which consisted of a double-faced, battered drystone wall, over 10m thick at the base, arcing for 60m across the river higher up in the hills. Associated with it was a lade cut through the rock and running for around 300m. It was a monumental piece of engineering which took months of construction but which, embarrassingly, was breached within three days of completion as a result of flash flooding. Attempts to rectify the problem proved ineffective and the project was abandoned. It was never rebuilt and the broken remains are still visible. Salisbury also commissioned a large circular lime kiln at **Kinloch (26)** to facilitate additional building work on the island. On completion it was discovered that the stones used to build it were unable to stand the heat of the fire. The structure was worthless and was also abandoned. He had better luck with his pier and was able to consolidate the jetty that was being constructed at the time of the first *Statistical Account*.

After Salisbury's death in 1868 his widow remained at Kinloch House, eventually selling the island in 1870 and returning to London, where one of her sons had become prime minister. Little is known of the new owners, part of the Campbell family, whose lairdship coincided with Edwin Waugh's visit in 1882. Although Waugh says little about them, it seems clear that their ownership was also focused on hunting. He estimated that the population was still small, around eighty, but more than double the number Salisbury had inherited. He refers to 'one or two wild-eyed Celtic herdsmen' whose dwellings were either 'in the solitary nooks of the isle' or scattered around the shore of Scresort Bay, describing the dwellings in some detail:

> They are all strongly built of fragments of basaltic rock; and they look as if they had been built a long time, for they all are more or less moss-grown, especially near the ground, where grass as well as moss has crept up the walls. They are little and low, although they look strong; and their thatched roofs are crossed and re-crossed with ropes, from the ends of which heavy stones are slung, to keep the thatch on in stormy weather. Only two of them have each a little rude chimney, which have evidently been added a long time after the cottages were first built; from the rest, the smoke escapes by a hole in the roof, or by the doorway.

Waugh was also interested in people and personalities and had plenty of time to stop and talk. He had several conversations with Kenneth, son of Allan MacLean himself, who still lived in the family home at Carn nan Dobhran Bhig towards the end of road on the south side of the bay. Kenneth, who had been thirteen years old at the time of the great exodus of 1828, argued that seven generations of MacLeans had lived there before him. His work ethic was less than impressive, according to Waugh, who noticed that he took 'a long time to do very little', which appeared to be an island characteristic. That said, Kenneth was comparatively well-read. Waugh was happy to be regaled with the history of the island and subsequently referred to him as 'a man of mark among the simple herdsmen and fishers who dwell in the straggling line of huts upon the shore of Scresort Bay'. Kenneth was also a charitable man who had taken pity on a young lad called Kenneth Chisholm whose father was a shepherd out at Papadil. Early every Monday the lad, described as being 'as hardy and as shaggy as a highland colt', would walk the five miles over the mountains from Papadil to the school in Kinloch, walking back again the following Saturday. During the week he was accommodated at Kenneth's dwelling and fed with Kenneth's own children. Kenneth was not married until his early fifties, hardly surprising given that much of his early life had been spent on an empty island, deprived of the company of other children. He started his family late with a young wife from Soay who was only nineteen when they married, the age difference no doubt giving rise to a few comments.

In the later years of the Campbell ownership the island was leased out to John Bullough, a Lancastrian industrialist of considerable wealth who enjoyed not only hunting but also hobnobbing with his social superiors. His was 'new money', and although he already owned a Scottish estate in Perthshire, where he could quench his thirst for hunting, perhaps a sense of needing to improve his social standing induced him to buy the island outright in 1888. There were a number of other interested purchasers, one of whom was dissuaded by his agent, whose advice was reported in Love's book:

I have read with much interest your memo as to Rum and I cannot find in it one redeeming feature. Roads bad.

Peats ditto. Lochs inaccessible. Rivers spoilt by artificial endeavour to improve on nature. No salmon. Difficulty of access. Climate abominable and generally everything uncomfortable. Ugh, ugh. I wouldn't live on the place tho' you gave it me for nothing.

Unsurprisingly, the sales pamphlet and the notice of sale in *The Times* provided a different, more glowing picture, together with some useful information. They outlined Salisbury's not inconsiderable achievements, the size and viability of the estate farm at Kinloch, the population of between 60 and 70 and the extent of the deer fencing. Bullough knew the island well enough to be aware of the pros and the cons. Like Salisbury and Campbell before him, he was content to allow the MacLeans to retain the *duthchas*, even though none of them is likely to have known what it meant. John Bullough lived only a few more years, dying in 1891, but not before he had built a series of hunting lodges and shepherds' houses around the island at Papadil, Kilmory and Harris and planted thousands of trees. He was remembered as a benevolent proprietor who did much to improve the island but never lived to fully enjoy his investment.

The lodge he built at **Papadil** (33) now exists only as the shell of a four-roomed building set within a plantation on the landward side of the loch, away from the sea. In original form it was similar to the lodge at **Harris** (12), which is still intact and used as a research station. It has a slate roof and an outshot at the back. The Kilmory lodge survives only as lengths of foundations. Together with Guirdil all three have some evidence for isolated post-clearance farmsteads or lodges.

After John Bullough's death in 1891 the island passed to his son George, a gallant, six-foot-seven army officer who had already blotted his copybook over an alleged relationship with his father's second and much younger wife. As a result he seems to have been packed off on a world cruise on his father's yacht, during which he developed hobbies in collecting weapons and photographing executions. On Rum one of his first ventures was to have a mausoleum built for his late father at **Harris** (13). It consisted of a neoclassical entrance leading into a tiled chamber of dubious artistic merit. A journalist later likened it to a London public lavatory, upon which an irate George Bullough removed his father's remains and had it blown up. The replacement mausoleum, also at **Harris** (14), may again have lacked taste but was much bigger and could be seen for miles around. It was constructed in sandstone in the style of a classical Doric temple, with a pitched roof supported by stone columns. It was, and remains, a striking cultural anomaly within the Hebridean landscape and offers remarkable visual testimony to social attitudes of the time. John Bullough lies behind the columns in a granite table tomb.

A similar criticism might be made of George Bullough's 'Castle', which was built at **Kinloch** (24) as a replacement for Kinloch House, formerly the prime residence on the island. Kinloch House, which had served its purpose well in housing previous lairds and their guests, was razed to the ground: it was simply not grand enough for George Bullough's pretensions. Little can be seen of it today apart from the gates, some hefty garden furniture and the vestiges of landscaped grounds now heavily overgrown. It was replaced by a massive structure which was little more than a glorified country house but to which George Bullough gave the grand title of 'Kinloch Castle'. No expense was spared in its construction. The renowned architects Leeming and Leeming were commissioned for the design, which seems to have been heavily influenced by George Bullough himself. It stands today, largely as it was built, as a 'holiday home' in the form of a vast country house in baronial style with turrets and crenelations, fronted by a covered walkway which one critic described as being reminiscent of a railway platform.

The location of the house among earlier plantations at the head of the bay, in its own grounds and gardens, was something in its favour, but its construction in a special red sandstone brought in from Arran gave it an appearance that many felt to be unnecessarily austere and incongruous with the landscape. Masons were imported from Lancashire and, unusually, were instructed to wear kilts during construction. To enhance its setting in the bay it was given a low, crenelated curtain wall along the beach head into which was built an octagonal crenelated gazebo. The grounds were landscaped using top-quality soil imported from Ayrshire; formal gardens were later designed across the site of the former Kinloch House as well as to the south, with a Japanese water garden complete with a bridge over one of the burns. Much of the imported soil was used in a walled garden behind the building to facilitate self-sufficiency, together with glasshouses for growing exotic fruits and (extraordinarily) tanks with heated water to maintain turtles for turning into soup, as well as alligators for no apparent reason other than for effect. Any functioning estate needed a service infrastructure and this was provided by extensive steading and stabling, an icehouse, dog kennels, a dairy, a laundry located out at Kilmory well away from guests, and housing for staff. Archie Cameron, whose father was one of the Bulloughs' gamekeepers, recounted that the estate required forty to fifty full-time staff including gamekeepers and ghillies, the number increasing significantly during the hunting season. In fairness Bullough did much to improve the deer population, introducing stock from other parts of Britain for breeding.

The house interior was constructed around a central courtyard and designed with bachelor living in mind, with a galleried hall for partying, a dining room, a smoking room, a billiard room and a ballroom with minstrel's gallery. It boasted cutting-edge technology in its flushing toilets, central heating, dental surgery, turbine-driven electricity, a type of rare electric organ, showers and an internal telephone system. Bullough purchased a refitted yacht, a 210-foot steam schooner called *Rhouma*, which he used to ferry guests to the island, including any ladies required for the entertainment. To all intents and purposes it was a retreat for a rich playboy and his friends. Islanders and even staff were not allowed to converse with guests, and rumours as to goings-on there were rife. Kenneth MacLean's centuries-old right of *duthchas* was overridden and the family was evicted to the Bullough Perthshire estate at Glen Lyon on the mainland. No heed was given to the fact that they had lived at Carn nan Dobhran Bhig for several generations. The MacLean land was taken over and planted, the house being left to fall into its present state. Kenneth's eldest son Hector, who had painstakingly incised his initials on the gable wall, was unable to claim his inheritance. Access to the island by outsiders was not allowed, doing much to cement Rum's reputation as the 'Forbidden Island'. Alastair Scott's *Eccentric Wealth*, which explores the Bullough dynasty, goes some way to investigating and demystifying the rumours.

In 1901 Bullough was knighted for supplying the *Rhouma*, suitably kitted out, as a hospital ship for the Boer War, and two years later he married into society, although in a rather clumsy way. His bride was a femme fatale, Monique de la Pasture, better known as Mrs Monica Charrington, wife of a brewing magnate, with whom Bullough had been having a liaison. Gossip related that she had also featured in the private life of Edward VII, but the divorce cited George Bullough as co-respondent, presumably to avoid a royal scandal. It may have been a marriage of convenience rather than of affection, each having their own quarters at Kinloch and their own companions.

Lady Monica's presence inevitably required partial redesign and redecoration of the interior of the building. This included creating new bedroom suites, painting over some of the dark wood panelling and introducing French neoclassical furniture as well as ornaments. The landscaping of the gardens was carried out under her influence, her initials being placed on the gate. More than thirty years of partying ended with the death of Sir George on a golf course in France in 1939, after which Lady Monica's visits to Kinloch became less frequent. Sir George was buried next to his father in a granite tomb in the mausoleum at Harris. On his death many of his possessions were recorded as being disposed of in the sea, including one of his cars, a Glasgow-built Albion Shooting Brake, the chassis of which can still be seen at low tide on the north side of Scresort Bay.

It was only some years later that Lady Monica encountered Professor John Heslop Harrison, a renowned botanist from Newcastle University who was highly respected among academic peers and a Fellow of the Royal Society. He believed that because of Rum's unique topography and microclimate, certain species of grass in the mountains might have survived the last Ice Age. With Lady Monica's approval he set about proving his theory by undertaking seasonal survey with students from Newcastle University, and in due course claimed to have discovered new species in the samples found by students. The veracity of his claim was doubted in some circles, however, notably by Cambridge academic John Raven, who raised suspicions that Heslop Harrison had been cultivating the plants at home in his garden then replanting them on Rum for the students to find later in the year. The argument for both sides is carefully explored in Karl Sabbagh's book *A Rum Affair*.

In 1957 Lady Monica sold the island to the Nature Conservancy Council (now NatureScot) at a bargain price to ensure its future well-being, and the Castle and its contents were thrown in for good measure. She returned to England where she died in 1967 at the age of ninety-eight, her body later being taken back to Rum to be buried next to those of her husband and father-in-law in the mausoleum at Harris. The Castle itself, still furnished as it was left by the Bulloughs, was open to the public until relatively recently, but is currently considered dangerous and access is prohibited. The area immediately around Kinloch is now owned by the community itself, the Isle of Rum Community Trust, and houses the majority of the modern population. The rest of the island remains a natural wilderness, particularly for the study of deer, under the care of NatureScot. The gardens and many of the outbuildings of the Castle are derelict and overgrown and are simply a reminder of a particular stratum of society in a particular era. With all its ornamentation inside and out, Kinloch Castle is very much a 'marmite' creation, loved or hated, the majority leaning towards the latter. John Love picked out some choice comments for his book, including one by Sir John Betjeman, a well-known supporter of tradition and the 'old school', who described it as 'an undisturbed example of pre-1914 opulence ... Good money was paid for good workmanship.' He tactfully avoided the question of taste, unlike Scottish writer and photographer Alasdair Macgregor, who referred to it as 'a nightmare of an edifice. Into it Sir George and Lady Bullough crammed the most ponderous and pompous articles of furniture they could find.'

Like the Mesolithic, the Age of Saints and the Clearances, the Bullough era constitutes an archaeological and historical layer, albeit a narrow chronological one. Like it or loathe it, it is part of the past to be reflected upon. What is sad is that this era, a mere blip in the ten millennia of human life on Rum, should have come to so dominate a landscape as to cast into near oblivion all that went before it.

Places to Visit: Rum

Ard Nev

1. Medieval deer trap. NRHE ID 21939. Grid ref: from NM 3404 9926 to NM 3424 9928.
Sporadic lengths of this trap survive at the top of Glen Duian on the north side. The two small enclosures into which the deer were funnelled lie further down to the north-east and show indications of replacement or rebuilding. There are no tracks and access is not recommended without local advice.

Bagh na h-Uamha

2. Cave. NRHE ID 22197. Grid ref: NM 4228 9741.
This cave is reputedly the one used by the eremitic monk Beccan in the seventh century. Although quite shallow it has been used as a shelter and contained midden material, mostly of animal bones and shells but also a worked bone playing piece. A pillar stone with a pecked cross (site 3) was found nearby. If visiting, local advice should be taken regarding tides.

3. Pillar stone with cross. NRHE ID 22201. Grid ref: NM 4216 9731.
This stone is almost 1.5m in length and triangular in section and was found partly buried in sand in the bay not far from the cave (site 2). At the top of one face there is a pecked equal-armed cross with small terminals. The stone was re-erected at the head of the bay at this grid reference but may since have been partly

buried by sand.

4. Township settlement. NRHE ID 22203. Grid ref: NM 4208 9736 (centre).
Marked 'Cove' on Langlands' map, this small township consists of the remains of six rectangular buildings surrounded by cultivation, probably one of the 'little hamlets' noted by Pennant in 1772. The buildings vary in size, the largest being about 8 × 3m.

Camas Pliasgaig

5. Township settlement. NRHE ID 11220. Grid ref: NG 4023 0236.
There are probably at least seven sets of rectangular foundations located between two streams here, representing the township cleared in 1828. The remains of an eighth building lie nearer the shore. The township is not mentioned in Walker's 1764 *Report* but appears on Langlands' map of 1801 and is probably a later development.

Carn nan Dobhran Bhig

6. Dwelling. Grid ref: NM 4120 9900.
This is the dwelling and small farming unit of Allan MacLean's family, who were allowed to stay on their land throughout the emigrations until they were evicted by George Bullough. Later taken over by his son Kenneth, the ruined farmstead is now hidden in a later plantation. The main dwelling, about 10 × 4m, still stands to wall-head height and is fronted by a stone-lined lade that carries water across to the house from a nearby spring.

Dibidil

7. ?Township settlement and later buildings. NRHE ID 21958. Grid ref: NM 3930 9274.
Very little evidence of this former township survives in this deep valley, apart from the footings of two small buildings lying to

the north-west of the nineteenth-century farmhouse. Some of the shieling huts higher up the valley may be associated. The farmhouse is now used as a bothy and has been covered in the HES mountain bothies survey.

Glen Shellesder

8. Shieling huts. *NRHE ID 11001. Grid ref: NG 3398 0180.*
There are probably more than fifteen shieling huts located here on the north side of the glen, spread across an area some 150 × 100m and including both single- and double-celled examples. A detailed survey has been carried out by HES (see NRHE ID 11001).

Guirdil

9. Bronze Age burial cairn. *NRHE ID 11015. Grid ref: NG 3227 0143.*
This burial cairn measures about 10m in diameter and 0.7m in height and is the only one of the three on the island with a few remaining kerb stones. Later structures have been built on top of it.

10. Township settlement. *NRHE ID 11018. Grid ref: NG 3188 0117.*
On this south-west side of the glen are the remains of five rectangular structures, the largest, measuring about 8 × 3m, located a short distance from the shore. According to Walker's 1764 *Report*, Guirdil housed 22 people in five families. After the Clearances the shepherd's cottage and farm buildings were located by the shore on the opposite bank of the river.

Harris

11. Bronze Age burial cairn. *NRHE ID 21911. Grid ref: NM 3420 9552.*
The largest of the three burial cairns on the island, this has

a diameter of around 12m and survives to a height of over 1m. Another cairn has been built on top of it and is probably modern, as are two other cairns in the immediate vicinity.

12. Hunting lodge. NRHE ID 200219. Grid ref: NM 3367 9573.
Built by John Bullough around 1889, this unassuming building stands above the shore at the end of the bay. It consists of four rooms and has a slate roof, rendered walls and an outshot at the rear. The building is still used by the deer research teams.

13. Mausoleum 1. NRHE ID 200220. Grid ref: NM 3356 9571.
This was built by George Bullough for his father, who died in 1891. It had a neoclassical entrance and was decorated internally with mosaics and tiles. Bullough had it blown up after it was criticised as looking like a public lavatory, upon which his father's body was moved to a new resting place (site 14). Fragments of tile can still be found scattered across the ground.

14. Mausoleum 2. NRHE ID 21945. Grid ref: NM 3363 9565.
Built around 1900, this second mausoleum built by George Bullough for his father was even more bizarre than the first (site 13). It takes the form of a Doric-style temple built in sandstone with a pitched roof supported by columns, and is a complete Hebridean anomaly. It also provides the resting place for George Bullough himself and his wife Monica.

15. Township settlement (Harris 1). NRHE ID 21948. Grid ref: NM 3393 9586.
Harris was one of the larger townships, with a population of 74 in fifteen families at the time of the 1764 *Report*. This part of the township is probably the later part and sits on the southern side of the river. There are footings of as many as thirty structures, most of which are built of drystone walling with a rubble fill. They are not all of one period and some are set a short distance from the main concentration. There are enclosures and field systems lying in association. The settlement was cleared in 1828.

16. Township settlement (Harris 2). NRHE ID 21949. Grid ref: NM 3349 9598.
This part of the Harris township was probably earlier than Harris
1 (site 15), several of the surviving foundations indicating earth
or turf filling between the stone faces. At least ten buildings are
represented, set on the higher terrace to the north of the river.
The largest building has three compartments and measures some
16 × 6m. There are lazy beds and cultivation throughout. As at
Harris 1, the settlement was cleared in 1828.

Hugh's Brae

17. Shieling huts. NRHE ID 21931. Grid ref: NM 3458 9653
This group of nine huts is located on the road to Harris. Several
of them sit on mounds, suggesting they may have a long pedigree.
Single-celled, double-celled and sub-rectangular configurations
are all represented.

Kilmory

18. Bronze Age burial cairn. NRHE ID 10979. Grid ref: NG 3578 0416.
This is the smallest of the three burial cairns on the island.
Positioned in a prominent position on the cliff to the north of
the bay, it has a diameter of about 6.5m and a surviving height
of about 0.7m. It shows obvious signs of having been disturbed.

19. Burial ground. NRHE ID 10946. Grid ref: NG 3613 0366.
This burial ground has a raised interior and despite its small size
of approximately 15 × 12m appears to have been the only burial
place on the island. The enclosure is of stone and the interior
contains a number of unmarked memorials but also a pillar
stone, two faces of which are decorated with crosses datable
to the seventh or eighth century. There is no evidence for an
associated church.

20. Fort. *NRHE ID 10990. Grid ref: NG 3509 0425.*
This precipitous promontory sits about 1km north of the bay and is cut off on the landward side by a thick stone wall which runs for about 10m across the neck, giving it a fortified appearance. The area enclosed is little more than 25 × 12m. There are no obvious internal features.

21. Township settlement. *NRHE ID 10993. Grid ref: NG 3613 0359.*
This may have been the largest township on the island. Walker's *Report* of 1764 records it as being home to 84 people in seventeen families. It survives as the remains of a line of dwellings and associated buildings, probably about sixteen in all, running from the coast at the north inland to the burial ground (site **19**) adjacent to a trackway. The dwellings are rectangular and measure typically 10 × 3m.

Kilmory Glen

22. Dam. *NRHE ID 21880. Grid ref: NM 3642 9989.*
This ill-fated venture undertaken by Lord Salisbury in the late 1840s was an attempt to divert the Kilmory river by using a dam and a rock-cut lade, in order to improve the fishing. The dam was about 60m long and 10m wide at the base, and was constructed using two battered drystone walls with an earthen core to a height of about 6m. It was breached almost immediately on completion.

23. Shieling huts. *NRHE ID 21871. Grid ref: NM 3642 9979.*
Not far from Salisbury's failed dam (site **22**) there is a group of seven shieling huts high up above the banks of the Kilmory river. They include a mixture of single- and double-celled types, only one of which sits on a mound.

Kinloch

24. Kinloch Castle. NRHE ID 22200. Grid ref: NM 4016 9954.

No expense was spared in the construction of this 'Castle' at the beginning of the twentieth century as a sporting retreat for George Bullough and his later wife Monica. This vast edifice, built of red sandstone imported from Arran, was designed with crenelated roof and turrets and set in landscaped gardens using soil imported from Ayrshire. In association were hothouses, heated tanks, a dairy, kennels, stabling and steading. The interior was packed with acquisitions from overseas. Not everyone found the external design or internal decor and furniture to their taste. The building is now unsafe and closed to the public.

25. Kinloch House. Grid ref: NM 4027 9959.

This former laird's residence was built by Lechlan MacLean in 1826 in its own woodland and grounds. In 1882 Edwin Waugh described it as 'a plain, strongly built stone house, with a steep roof and with a porch, and with a small wing at each end'. It was demolished by George Bullough and turned into formal gardens for his 'Castle' (site 24). The gates and items of garden furniture are still visible in what later became known as 'Lady Monica's Garden' (NRHE ID 200218).

26. Lime kiln. NRHE ID 108863. Grid ref: NM 4059 9913.

Lord Salisbury's ill-fated lime kiln stands near the pier. Circular in form with a diameter of almost 4m and a height of 3m, it was constructed to facilitate building work on the island. It seems the stones used to build it were unable to withstand the heat of the fire and the kiln was abandoned.

27. Mesolithic activity site. NRHE ID 22202. Grid ref: NM 4038 9986 (centre).

Arguably the most important of all the sites in the Small Isles, although there is now nothing to see. Bloodstone was quarried in the mountains or collected from Guirdil beach and brought here for working into blades, scrapers and arrowheads for export from the bay. Excavation here recovered tens of thousands of waste pieces left by workers as far back as 8,500 years ago.

28. Pier. *NRHE ID 107923. Grid ref: NM 4068 9915.*
The life story of this structure is not well recorded. The first *Statistical Account*, written in 1794, records the construction work for a rubble pier as having started, but it appears not to have been completed in broadly its current form until 1847. It has since been modified and strengthened. The so-called 'Priest's Stone' stands nearby.

29. Township settlement. *NRHE ID 118018. Grid ref: NM 4040 9925.*
There is little to see of this township, which appears to have been based in the same area as the Norse-named farm at Raonapoll located on the south shore of Scresort Bay. In 1764 Walker recorded the township as having 46 people in eight families. The general area is within the current campsite, where turf-covered foundations of these or later buildings can still be found.

Kinloch Glen

30. Shieling huts. *NRHE ID 11217. Grid ref: NG 4064 0034.*
An early record shows some twenty-five huts here spread over a wide area, but the number has since been reduced by about half as a result of afforestation. One of them, with a typical internal measurement of about 2 × 2m, still has part of its corbelled roof intact.

Loch Monica

31. Shieling huts. *NRHE ID 21927. Grid ref: NM 3329 9657.*
There are probably six huts here, all of corbelled construction but of various configurations and shapes. One is double-celled and 7m in length, the single-celled ones being smaller and typically 2.5 × 2.5m or 3.5 × 3.5m. They probably belong to the Harris township.

Orval

32. Medieval deer trap. NRHE ID 21940. Grid ref: from NM 3283 9871 to NM 3289 9886.

This is represented by two lines of walling or gathered scree forming a funnel shape several hundred metres long which pinches together at the bottom and narrows into a pair of stone-built enclosures. Deer would have been chased down into the funnel by dogs and caught in the enclosures for slaughter. There are no tracks and access is not recommended without local advice.

Papadil

33. Hunting lodge. NRHE ID 349964. Grid ref: NM 3657 9222.

One of John Bullough's lodges, built around 1888, this now stands as an overgrown shell. Located in a plantation behind the loch it was built as a four-roomed structure with mortared rubble walls.

34. Fort. NRHE ID 21950. Grid ref: NM 3614 9188.

The largest of the three promontory forts on the island, this encloses a substantial but irregular area of about 85 × 45m. The fortification is provided by natural cliffs on all but the steep landward side, on which an irregular line of walling about 2m wide has been constructed from cliff to cliff. There is no evidence of any internal features.

Port na Caranean

35. Settlement. NRHE ID 22207. Grid ref: NM 4234 9879.

This settlement comprises at least nine buildings of which four are probably dwellings, with some evidence of earlier structures. They probably represent the post-clearance settlement of shepherds brought in from Skye. Mostly in good condition, many of the walls still stand to wall-head height. While there is no recorded evidence of an earlier township here, these do not appear to be the first structures on the site.

Protest Rock

36. Monument. Grid ref: NG 3786 9988.
This broadly circular glacial erratic, over 1m in diameter, sits on a wide platform slab in the heather, chocked up with stones to prevent it moving. It is said to have been rolled there by the emigrants in 1828 as a gesture of defiance and anger against the laird who was evicting them.

Samhnan Insir

37. Township settlement. NRHE ID 10955. Grid ref: NG 3788 0435.
This township is recorded by Walker in 1764 as having 43 occupants in seven families. All that survives today are the partially sand-buried footing of four structures lying to the east of the later shepherd's cottage. The largest is about 11 × 4.5m and has a fireplace surviving. The settlement was cleared in 1828.

Sgorr Reidh

38. ?Shieling huts. NRHE ID 21944. Grid ref: from NM 3120 9833 to NM 3126 9818.
This unusual and enigmatic site consists of a stone wall running for about 300m along the cliff edge interspersed with at least a dozen small huts. The huts have slightly sunken floors and are corbel-built, typically measuring 2.5 × 2m. It may have some connection with shielings, but exactly what this might be remains a mystery.

Shellesder

39. Hut circles. NRHE ID 10995. Grid ref: NG 3270 0205.
There are probably three hut circles here. The largest measures

some 11m across with traces of both inner and outer faces. The other two are smaller and lie approximately 30m and 60m to the west respectively. Both are broadly 7m in diameter.

40. Fort. NRHE ID 10995. Grid ref: NG 3270 0205.
This promontory on precipitous rocks has an added deterrent of a thick wall built across its neck on the landward side. The area enclosed is about 45 × 30m. Internally there is a group of three stone-built huts, which are probably later and which may be associated with lazy beds nearby.

Further Reading

Anderson, A.O. (1922). *Early Sources of Scottish History, A.D. 500 to 1286* (1990 edition), vol. 1. Stamford: Paul Watkins.

Cameron, A. (1988). *Bare Feet and Tackety Boots*. Edinburgh: Luath Press.

Campbell, J.L. (2002). *Canna: The Story of a Hebridean Island* (4th edition). Edinburgh: National Trust for Scotland.

Dressler, C. (1998). *Eigg: The Story of an Island*. Edinburgh: Polygon.

Fisher, I. (2001). *Early Medieval Sculpture in the West Highlands and Islands*. Royal Commission on the Ancient and Historical Monuments of Scotland and the Society of Antiquaries of Scotland Monograph Series 1. Edinburgh: RCAHMS.

Hill, P. (2003). *Stargazing: Memoirs of a Young Lighthouse Keeper*. Edinburgh: Canongate.

Hunter, J.R. (2016). *The Small Isles*. Edinburgh: Historic Environment Scotland.

Lethbridge, T.C. (1925). 'Exploration of a cairn on Canna', *Proceedings of the Society of Antiquaries of Scotland* 59, 238–9 (notes).

Levi, P., ed. (1984). *Samuel Johnson and James Boswell: A Journey to the Western Isles of Scotland and The Journal of a Tour to the Hebrides*. London: Penguin.

Love, J.A. (1980). 'Deer traps on the Isle of Rum', *Deer* 5(3), 131–2.

Love, J.A. (1981). 'Shielings of the Isle of Rum', *Scottish Studies* 25, 39–63.

Love, J.A. (2001). *Rum: A Landscape without Figures*. Edinburgh: Birlinn.

MacCulloch, J. (1824). *The Highlands and Western Isles of Scotland*, vol 4. London: Longman.

MacEwen, L. (2002). *The Isle of Muck – a Short Guide*. Privately printed.

MacPherson, N. (1878). 'Notes on antiquities from the island of Eigg', *Proceedings of the Society of Antiquaries of Scotland* 12, 577–97.

McKay, M.M., ed. (1980). *The Rev. Dr. John Walker's Report on the Hebrides of 1764 and 1771*. Edinburgh: John Donald.

Miers, M. (2008). *The Western Seaboard*. Edinburgh: Rutland Press.

Miller, H. (1862). *The Cruise of the Betsey*. Boston, MA: Gould and Lincoln.

Munby, J. (2007). *Lost Ancestors: Island Families in 1765 on Eigg, Muck, Rum and Canna* (an edition of Neill McNeill's Census of Small Isles Parish, Inner Hebrides, in 1764/5). Oxford: privately printed.

NSA (New Statistical Account) (1845). *The New Statistical Account of Scotland*, vol. 14. Edinburgh: W. Blackwood.

OSA (Old Statistical Account) (1796). *The Statistical Account of Scotland*, vol. 17. Edinburgh: William Creech.

Otter, W. (1825). *The Life and Remains of Rev. Edward Daniel Clarke*, vol. 1. London: Cowie & Co.

Pennant, T. (1776). *A Tour in Scotland and Voyage to the Hebrides, 1772* (2nd edition). London: Benjamin White.

Perman, R. (2011). *The Man Who Gave Away His Island: A Life of John Lorne Campbell of Canna*. Edinburgh: Birlinn.

Pullar, P. (2019). *A Drop in the Ocean: Lawrence MacEwen and the Isle of Muck*. Edinburgh: Birlinn.

RCAHMS (Royal Commission on the Ancient and Historical Monuments of Scotland) (1928). *Inventory of the Outer Hebrides, Skye and the Small Isles*. Edinburgh: RCAHMS.

RCAHMS (Royal Commission on the Ancient and Historical Monuments of Scotland) (1999). *Canna: The Archaeology of a Hebridean Landscape* (broadsheet). Edinburgh: RCAHMS.

RCAHMS (Royal Commission on the Ancient and Historical Monuments of Scotland) (2003). *Eigg: The Archaeology of a Hebridean Landscape* (broadsheet). Edinburgh: RCAHMS.

Rixson, D. (2001). *The Small Isles: Canna, Rum, Eigg and Muck*. Edinburgh: Birlinn.

Rixson, D. (2004). *The Hebridean Traveller*. Edinburgh: Birlinn.

Sabbagh, K. (2001). *A Rum Affair: A True Story of Botanical Fraud*. Boston, MA: Da Capo Press.

Scott, A. (2011). *Eccentric Wealth: The Bulloughs of Rum*. Edinburgh: Birlinn.

Taylor, J. (1618). *The Penniless Pilgrim* (1876 edition). London: Reeves and Turner.

Wade Martins, S. (2004). *Eigg – an Island Landscape* (3rd edition). Hunstanton: PWM Heritage Management.

Waugh, E. (1883). *The Limping Pilgrim*. Manchester: John Heywood.

Wickham-Jones, C.R. (1990). *Rhum: Mesolithic and Later Sites at Kinloch: Excavations 1984–86*. Society of Antiquaries of Scotland Monograph Series 7. Edinburgh: Society of Antiquaries of Scotland.

Withers, C. and Munro, R.W., eds (1999). *A Description of the Western Islands of Scotland circa 1695 and A Description of the Occidental i.e. Western Islands of Scotland*. Edinburgh: Birlinn.

Index

Page numbers in bold indicate detailed
description of sites listed in 'Places to Visit'